IMPROVING GOVERNANCE:
A New Logic for Empirical Research

Laurence E. Lynn, Jr.
Carolyn J. Heinrich
Carolyn J. Hill

Georgetown University Press / Washington, D.C.

Learning Resources
Centre

13237896

Georgetown University Press, Washington, D.C.
© 2001 by Georgetown University Press. All rights reserved.
Printed in the United States of America

10 9 8 7 6 5 4 3 2 1   2001

This volume is printed on acid-free offset book paper.

Library of Congress Cataloging-in-Publication Data

Lynn, Laurence E., Jr., 1937-
  Improving governance : a new logic for empirical research / Laurence E.
Lynn, Jr., Carolyn J. Heinrich, Carolyn J. Hill.
    p. cm. - - (American governance and public policy)
  Includes bibliographical references and index.
  ISBN 0-87840-852-5 (cloth : alk. paper)
    Public administration—Research. 2. Human services—Management—Research.
      I. Heinrich, Carolyn J. II. Hill, Carolyn J. III. Title.

JF1338.A2 L85 2001
351'.072—dc21

Contents

American Governance and Public Policy series
Series Editor: Barry Rabe, University of Michigan

Preface

This book is a companion volume to *Governance and Performance: New Perspectives*, edited by Carolyn Heinrich and Laurence Lynn (Georgetown University Press, 2000). That volume comprised papers presented at a workshop titled "Models, Methods, and Data for the Empirical Study of Governance and Public Management," held at the School of Public Administration and Policy, University of Arizona, and funded by the Pew Charitable Trusts. The present volume is an expanded version of the "framing paper" for that conference, which was circulated as "The Empirical Study of Governance: Theories, Models, and Methods."

The goal of this book is to propose a logic for the systematic, empirical study of governance and public management, utilizing quantitative and qualitative methods. The conviction inspiring this effort is that the rigorous theories, models, and methods of the social sciences, in the hands of investigators dedicated to understanding governance and public management in practice, can yield findings and insights of considerable value to practitioners as well as scholars. This conviction is based in part on the impact on policy and practice that research reflecting the spirit of this volume has had already, especially in the areas of school reform, welfare reform, and human capital development. Examples of this research are included in the earlier volume of conference papers. More advanced research based on these papers was presented at the 21st annual research conference of the Association for Public Policy Analysis and Management (APPAM), held in November 2000, at a panel convened under the title "New Approaches to Governance and Public Management Research."

As with the previous volume, we wish to acknowledge the support of Paul C. Light—who, as Director of the Public Policy Program at the Pew Charitable Trusts, sponsored the grant that supported this work. We also acknowledge the participants in the University of Arizona workshop, who provided valuable criticism, commentary, and advice on the paper from which the present volume evolved. Finally, we wish to acknowledge the continued support of Georgetown University Press.

Laurence E. Lynn, Jr.
Carolyn J. Heinrich
Carolyn J. Hill

About the Authors

Laurence E. Lynn, Jr., is Sydney Stein, Jr. Professor of Public Management at the University of Chicago.

Carolyn J. Heinrich is Assistant Professor of Public Policy Analysis at the University of North Carolina at Chapel Hill.

Carolyn J. Hill is a doctoral candidate at the Irving B. Harris Graduate School of Public Policy Studies, University of Chicago.

Tables and Figures

1

Governance in a Democracy

We can safely pronounce that the true test of a good government is its aptitude and tendency to produce a good administration.
Alexander Hamilton

Public policies and programs in the United States and elsewhere are being administered to an increasing extent through complicated webs of states, regions, special districts, service delivery areas, local offices, nonprofit organizations, collaborations, networks, partnerships, and other means for the control and coordination of dispersed activities. These complex forms of public administration represent a decisive move away from direct provision of services by government agencies and their employees—the standard "bureau model" in favor until the 1960s and early 1970s. Evaluating performance has always been difficult in government; the newer forms of administration make it seem harder than ever.

Some of the reasons for the transformation from direct service provision to third-party (Salamon 1981) or hollow (Milward 1994; Milward and Provan 1993) government are specific. For example, the availability of stabilizing medications has enabled persons who are chronically mentally ill to be released from public institutions to be served as outpatients in their communities. A more general explanation is the combined influence on policymakers, beginning in the 1970s, of intensifying resource constraints on governments at all levels and voters' growing mistrust of government and resistance to taxation. Elected and appointed officials came under increasing pressure to cut back and economize on budgetary resources by contracting with third parties in the nonprofit and for-profit sectors to manage and deliver publicly financed services and by taking into account the actual performance of programs in allocating budgetary resources.

Evaluating program performance under these new administrative arrangements has been difficult (Kramer 1994). For example, the performance of dispersed administrative entities such as states or regions, local offices, and individual contractors varies significantly. In view of this fact, policymakers, public managers, stakeholders, and program evaluators generally want to know, first, what accounts for these differences in performance and, second, how underperforming administrative agencies can be induced to perform like the best. Answering such questions is essential to creating good administration of public programs. Unfortunately, there are no straightforward answers to these questions—and no well-established methods to obtain them.

Cross-site variation in performance, for example, has many possible sources: the characteristics and needs of the people served; the skills or motivations of service workers; the quality of local site management; the clarity of policy direction; factors in the local environment; the extent of system-wide coordination; the strength and enforcement of performance incentives; or other structural characteristics of the system. Some of these factors are likely to be much more influential, or much more susceptible to control by managers, than others. Thus, knowing which factors matter most, and how much, is important if better overall system performance is to be attained. To manage decentralized program operations successfully, policymakers and public administrators must be able to demonstrate accountability, good practice, and high average performance across diverse and dispersed service units.

Designing and managing decentralized operations is just one example of the general problem of governance: How can public-sector regimes, agencies, programs, and activities be authorized, organized, and managed to perform at high levels in achieving public purposes? Problems of governance engage officials in all branches and at all levels of the public sector: legislators, elected and appointed executives, judges, and staffs in federal, state, and local agencies. When these officials craft and interpret statutes, appropriations, administrative guidelines, standard operating procedures, and directives of all kinds, they are creating and maintaining governance regimes. Even casual additions to the language of statutes or guidelines may turn out to have significant effects on how and for whose benefit government agencies and programs operate.

Underlying the general problem of governance is an even broader issue: Can government improve its performance continuously so that citizens—who pay for and are affected by public policies and programs—and their elected representatives once again view their governments in a positive light? In recent decades, declining public confidence in government, combined with the popularity of maintaining at least the appearance of controlling government spending and cutting taxes, has prompted a surge of professional and official interest in government effectiveness and performance-based public management. A plethora of new and revamped tools and techniques for measuring performance and creating incentives for its attainment dominates the literature and discussion of public management. At the same time, observers generally recognize that creating governments that fulfill democratic aspirations is far more than a technical matter. At issue are government's purposes, as well as strategies and techniques for achieving them.

The importance of democratic accountability to the fields of politics, policy implementation, public administration, administrative law, and public management motivates the systematic study of governance—that is, research whose objective is to determine how, why, and with what consequences public-sector activity is, or could be, structured and managed and how, depending on public preferences for the means and ends of public policy, public-sector performance can be improved. This book sets forth ideas for increasing the quantity, quality, and usefulness of governance and public management research. Our belief is that the theoretical and empirical quality of such research goes hand-in-hand with its usefulness to practitioners; research of high quality is more likely to provide useful guidance for practice.

To ensure a thorough exploration of the issues raised by this argument, this book focuses primarily on policies, programs, and agencies that are concerned with providing human services to vulnerable people. The transformation in governance arrangements and a concern for performance have been most conspicuous in this domain of public administration. Human services—which include, for example, public assistance, child protection, job training, drug abuse treatment, public education, and personal social services—

have distinctive attributes that greatly complicate policymaking, public management, and empirical research.

The most salient of these attributes is that human beings constitute the "raw material" of human services; that is, "The core activities of the organization are structured to process, sustain, or change people who come under its jurisdiction" (Hasenfeld 1992, 4–5). Several conclusions follow from the fact that human services are intended to change people (Hasenfeld 1983, 1992; D'Aunno 1992):

- Clients can react to and thus affect—even participate in—the service that is performed. Therefore, human service provision is moral work that requires moral judgments about the worth of clients and the social value of the service or treatment—judgments that are inherently controversial.
- Human service organizations require the support of and necessarily seek to influence the institutional environment, especially the political environment that authorizes policies and appropriates resources; that is, human service organizations "adopt and uphold moral systems that are supported by significant interest groups and organizations" (Hasenfeld 1992, 10).
- The technologies these agencies employ "must be consonant with dominant cultural beliefs about what is desirable and acceptable to do to people" (Hasenfeld 1992, 12).
- There is an inherent indeterminacy to the means employed to reach service goals having to do with "the ability of clients to react and participate in the service technology. The reactivity of clients and their potential capacity to neutralize the effects of the service technology means that the organization cannot take for granted the processes and outcomes of its service technology even if it is assumed to be highly determinate" (Hasenfeld 1992, 15).

Owing to these characteristics of service delivery, human service agencies pose two generic problems for policymakers, public managers, and researchers: The work of these agencies (the "treatment" they provide) and the outcomes of their activities are costly and difficult, if not impossible, to observe and evaluate with any precision. Wilson (1989) characterizes such nontransparent agencies as "coping organizations." Such organizations are likely to experience substantial conflict between workers in the field and the field workers' managers regarding what ought to be done and why. Moreover, effective managerial direction may be impossible with standard administrative tools such as rules and contracts (see Ouchi 1979; Hargrove and Glidewell 1990).

We have chosen to focus on human service organizations not only because of their intrinsic importance to social well-being but precisely because understanding their governance and performance poses a full range of intellectual and methodological challenges to persons engaged in empirical research. These challenges involve theory, modeling, statistical methods, and data. We believe that by exploring these challenges, we are more likely to identify the state of the art in governance and public management research than if our focus were on more tractable governance problems.

What Is Governance?

The term *governance* is widely used in the public and private sectors. It includes global and local arrangements, formal structures and informal norms and practices, spontaneous and intentional systems of control (Williamson 1996). The Institute on Governance defines governance as "the traditions, institutions and processes that determine how power is exercised, how citizens are given a voice, and how decisions are made on issues of public concern."[1] In private-sector applications, the concept of governance usually refers either to the organization and direction of the individual firm or to institutions that maintain the stability of markets. Thus, in the former case, governance may mean controlling and directing multi-product, multinational operations. In the latter case, governance may refer to a regime of rules "which ensures freedom of entry into the market, access to information, and the sanctity of contracts" (Dhonte and Kapur 1996)—that is, rules for ensuring the credibility of commitments and the protection and enforcement of property rights (Demirag 1998; Keasey, Thompson, and Wright 1997; Williamson 1998).

The concept of governance in public-sector applications, especially in human service administration, typically is a good deal more complex than that in the private-sector, for several reasons: The objectives and outcomes of transactions are less transparent in the public sector than in the private sector; the power of direction and control is widely dispersed; and the goals of actors are multifarious and often in conflict. Because the term *governance* has strong intuitive appeal, however, precise definitions are often considered unnecessary by those who use it in public-sector applications. As a result, when authors identify governance as important to achieving policy or organizational objectives (e.g., with respect to achieving reforms in public schooling, health care provision, or child welfare), a reader may be unclear about whether the reference is to statutes, organizational structures and rules, administrative processes, managerial competence and judgment, systems of incentives, administrative missions and philosophies, or combinations of these elements. Governance often seems to mean little more than "whatever must be done to implement change successfully." Imprecise thinking about governance often leads to vague and ineffective strategies for the design and management of change.

The definitions of governance in public-sector literature reflect institutional and network concepts.[2] Uses consistent with institutional concepts include, for example, those that examine linkages between governance and economic development, as constrained by the constitution of the World Bank (Von Benda-Beckmann 1994), and relationships between how organizations are structured and their hierarchical relationships with government agencies (Hult and Walcott 1989). Even more numerous are uses that refer to multi-agency partnerships, self-governing networks, and the blurring of responsibilities between the public and private sectors (Stoker 1998); shifting power from the state to civil society in developing democracies and encouraging public-sector reform (Hewitt de Alcantara 1998); public conflict resolution in which citizens are actively involved (Dukes 1993); and public health care delivery that most successfully involves the public and private sectors, with emphasis on local leadership and political mobilization (Salmon and Whiteis 1992).

Despite the breadth and ambiguity of definitions and the wide scope of applications, governance generally refers to the means for achieving direction, control, and coordination of wholly or partially autonomous individuals or organizational units on behalf of interests to which they jointly contribute. According to Wamsley (1990), governance connotes "the use of authority in providing systemic steering and direction" (25). Vickers (1983) refers to "governing relations"—that is, patterns of interaction—and to the role of authority in maintaining (or modifying) governing relations to "maximize the values" that can be realized through them. Thus, we speak of the governance (or the governing relations) of global financial markets and of local public schools, of the European Union and of federally administered social programs, of international humanitarian aid distribution and of networks of community-based service providers.

In its broadest sense, then, governance in the public sector concerns relationships between authoritative decisions and government performance. To establish a modicum of precision in our discussion, we define the term *governance* as regimes of laws, rules, judicial decisions, and administrative practices that constrain, prescribe, and enable the provision of publicly supported goods and services.[3]

Governance defined in this way subsumes the subject of public management: the behavior and contributions to governmental performance of actors performing managerial roles. Two distinct, paradigmatic approaches to public management appear in the research literature:

- Public managers are regarded as goal-seeking actors who optimize their achievements within a given governance regime or arrangement. Many approaches to public-sector leadership, entrepreneurship, political management, best practices, and innovation explicitly or implicitly take the regime of authority as given—and therefore as defining and restricting a manager's maneuvering room.[4] This essentially short-run view of public management—which is consistent with the typically short tenures in office of politically appointed managers—emphasizes the immediate challenges of managerial roles and tends to feature the psychological, tactical, and communications aspects of public management.
- Public managers also are regarded as participants in coalition politics who use the vantage point of their managerial roles to represent well-established group interests or their agency's mission, programs, and stakeholders. This view, which is less well developed in the literature,[5] is implicit in the notion of "iron triangles" and issue networks, whereby managers work with interest groups and legislators to draft mutually acceptable statutes and rules, as well as in the literature on the social control of bureaucracy. It is explicit in some spatial models of

coalition politics (Knott and Hammond 2000). This longer-run view broadens the subject of public management to the wider domain of governance and the administrative control of bureaucracy; it also broadens the content of management to include the design of governance regimes.

A systematic approach to issues of governance and public management defined in this way, especially in a context in which the goal is the reform or strengthening of administration, involves answering the following questions:

- Over what (or whom) do we wish to allocate (or reallocate) control or authority?
- To whom do we wish to allocate this authority?
- What means, mechanisms, or instruments are available to achieve the desired reallocation?
- What are the likely or possible effects of such reallocations on the actual control or authority of governmental operations and service delivery?
- What are the likely or possible consequences for social, community, and individual outcomes or performance of such reallocations?

Several important policy and management questions can be explored within such an analytic framework:

- How much formal control should be retained by authoritative decision makers and how much delegated to subordinates and officers? How do the answers to this question vary across policy, political, and professional contexts?
- How can particular ideas, or the objectives of particular powerful stakeholders, or conceptual goals such as "efficiency" or "high reliability" be incorporated into existing governance regimes to promote their success?
- How can a governance regime be designed to ensure priority in resource allocation and attention to particular goals and objectives?
- How can dispersed governance regimes (across states, across municipalities within a state, or across local offices or net-

works) be induced to converge on the achievement of particular policy objectives?

- To the extent that public program performance depends on competence and reliability at the street levels of government (for example, public school classrooms, local welfare offices, and clinical treatment facilities), how can governance be designed to ensure greater competence or attention to particular priorities?
- Within a set of governing relations, what kinds of strategies will enable public managers to make significant contributions to government performance? To what extent and at what cost in effort, resources, and reputation should managers seek to modify those relations?

A governance research agenda that addresses such questions encompasses empirical testing of propositions derived from theory (i.e., positive analysis) as well as propositions concerning what government *ought* to be doing (i.e., analysis of normative propositions). Both kinds of research are useful in the analysis and design of governance systems in areas such as public education, health care, child welfare, or public assistance, in which agendas for reform inevitably raise questions concerning their feasibility, cost, and consequences for the many values and interests at stake. Moreover, exploration of such questions is necessarily interdisciplinary: It involves a search for useful insights, knowledge, and approaches across a wide range of relevant disciplines, fields, and subfields.

Complications of Governance Research

If the purpose and general orientation of governance research seem reasonably clear, its actual conduct is anything but straightforward. If research on governance is to maintain verisimilitude and relevance to practice as well as have value as scholarship, investigators must deal with three complicating factors: the configurational, nonadditive nature of the systemic elements that comprise governance; the multifarious political interests that shape the objectives and operations of governance regimes; and the fact that governance encompasses formal and informal authority and therefore cannot be wholly directive or instrumental.

- Governance implies a configuration of distinct but interrelated elements—statutes, including policy mandates and assignments of responsibility; organizational, financial, and programmatic structures; resource levels; administrative rules and guidelines; and institutionalized rules and norms—that constrain and enable the tasks, priorities, and values that are incorporated into regulatory, service production, and service delivery processes. Thus, governance involves extensive endogeneity among its constituent features rather than the mere summing of independent influences (Ostrom 1986).
- Governance is inherently political; it involves bargaining and compromise, winners and losers, among actors with different interests and resources. A given governance regime distributes resources and responsibility for functions, operations, and control within and between offices and organizations in the public and private sectors. Because these distributions are intended to link the objectives of stakeholders with governmental operations, disagreements among stakeholders fuel political competition for the control of public administration. Stakeholders may not have as an objective the effective or efficient performance of governmental activities.[6] Even rational actors in legislatures cannot be expected to create rational organizations to execute their mandates; indeed, they may act to preclude effective administration of a controversial program rather than eliminate it outright (Moe 1989). How should researchers evaluate the effectiveness of programs that are not intended by the coalition that sponsors them to be particularly effective?
- Finally, governance comprises formal structures and informal influence and judgment by the numerous actors involved in policy and program implementation. The links between formal authority—statutes, appropriations, administrative guidelines, and judicial decisions—and government operations may be loose and unreliable, especially if policymakers and administrators disagree about the means and ends of governance (Wilson 1989). Because the interests, information, and other resources of actors within the administrative process differ, the effect of employing the formal instruments of governance on actual operations and outcomes may be highly tenuous, and establishing causal relationships may be difficult.

Addressing significant questions of governance requires an intellectual perspective that enables researchers to approach these kinds of complications in a conceptually appropriate, rigorous, and transparent way.

Purposes of the Book

Our primary purpose in writing this book is to put forward what we believe is a promising approach to theory-based empirical research that addresses the "big questions" of governance discussed above. We recognize that quantitative empirical research is far from our only source of useful knowledge about governance and management. Biography and journalistic accounts, oral histories and intensive case studies, and structured qualitative research involving field observation and interviews often provide instructive insights into the workings and results of government and the relative and absolute effectiveness of management. We maintain throughout this book that quantitative research must be supplemented by qualitative studies if formal models and the interpretation of findings based on them are to achieve theoretical and practical credibility. The big questions of governance cannot be answered, however, through simple observation, participant accounts, or the accumulation of cases based on field research alone; the truth may not lie in what meets the eye. An accumulating body of well-designed research that employs theory, quantitative empirical methods, and systematically obtained data and observations—enlightened by qualitative studies—has the potential to be a primary source of fundamental and durable knowledge about governance and public management that transcends the particular contexts from which the data are collected.

This claim is arguable, and we make it with full awareness of the complex issues involved. For example, Mohr (1999) argues that making "stable generalizations" on the basis of results of empirical social science research generally is impossible; the validity of study results is limited strictly to the domain for which the data were collected—and thus is "historical." This statement does not negate the value of quantitative empirical research, however. Historical "accounts and stories," Mohr argues, "help us, as individuals, to regulate our own affairs" (Mohr 1999, 21). Each empirical study should seek to establish "consummate causal understanding" such that it will be "instructive in thinking about the same or a similar situation in new contexts" (22). Mohr goes on: "How nearly this is accomplished will . . . be affected primarily by the set of events or variables we choose to investigate and the creativity and quality of the way in which we conceptualize them, as well as the quality of measurements, analyses, and presentation" (21).

In subsequent chapters, we propose a framework for research that is based on the premise that any particular governance arrangement—within a policy domain, with respect to a type of government activity, within a particular jurisdiction, or within a particular organization or organizational field—is embedded in a wider social, fiscal, and political context. Within that framework, we propose a logic that links the various features of the regime that is based primarily on the literature of political economy. Political economy integrates economic behavior in political processes and political behavior in the marketplace (Alt and Shepsle 1990) and assumes that this behavior is intentionally rational. Our logic of governance is intended to assist in framing research questions and the selection of events, variables, conceptualizations, and measurements that will achieve consummate causal understandings across different levels of governance.

This integrative, multi-level perspective is too rare in the literature. Investigators often model governance as only loosely connected to or even decoupled from the wider context. Too often, then, the possibility that broader patterns of interrelationships affect outcomes is not adequately incorporated into the design of research or the explanation or interpretation of research findings. For example, a study may attribute client outcomes to client characteristics; to worker and treatment characteristics; or to patterns of interaction between clients, treatments, and workers but ignore the potential significance of local or hierarchical organizational and management variables or of systemwide or institutional mandates and incentives. The logic of governance that we describe proposes relationships between structure and action at various levels of the governmental process, on one hand, and the outcomes or performance of governmental activity, on the other.

Implementing such a logic for governance research, we argue, requires that investigators routinely and characteristically draw on theoretical and empirical resources from a wide variety of disciplines and professional fields. This approach is easier said than done. Potentially valuable contributions to understanding governance and public management are widely dispersed among a great many research literatures: disciplines, subdisciplines, professional fields, and subfields. Authors in these literatures often are unintelligible or baffling to each other because of their specialized styles of theorizing, collecting and analyzing data, and reaching conclusions. As a consequence, what we know about governance is a cacophony rather than an oratorio that harmonizes separate contributions. We urge governance researchers to form habits of search and synthesis so their research is precisely conceptualized, correctly specified, and likely to be intelligible and instructive to researchers and practitioners in a wide variety of contexts.

To support this argument, we proceed as follows. First, we propose and explain a logic of governance. Next, we move toward translating this logic into a strategy for empirical research on governance. Then we attempt a first approach—less than Beethoven but more than barbershop—to an orchestrated arrangement of studies that demonstrates the value to governance and public management research of search and synthesis across diverse fields. To identify relevant literature, we have examined sources that illuminate or are consistent with our logic of governance (i.e., are concerned with causal relationships suggested by the logic) and satisfy some or all of the following criteria:

- They frame questions or propositions to advance theoretical and empirical modeling.
- They develop theory-based, multi-component models or frameworks for empirically testing hypotheses.
- They define and operationalize specific concepts or variables.
- They provide guidance for data collection and the determination of appropriate methodologies for empirical research.
- They present convincing and appropriately framed findings.

Insights into governance of the newer administrative arrangements discussed at the beginning of this chapter are most likely to be found in studies of networks or fields of provider organizations or in models that incorporate multiple levels of decision making and performance within a hierarchy. Furthermore, research that derives testable propositions from a clearly developed theoretical framework and submits these propositions to empirical tests builds a durable knowledge base about governance processes.

Limits to Governance

In addition to identifying determinants of governmental performance and suggesting strategies for management improvement, governance research may usefully explore the limits that formal changes in governance may encounter. Attempts to relocate decision-making authority from higher to lower levels of authority, for example, often do little to alter actual decision-making processes. Bimber's (1994) study of several efforts to decentralize public school governance illustrates this point. He found that despite an expressed desire for decentralization and subsequent implementation of site-based management, "years after decentralization was introduced, governance structures . . . either remained centrally controlled or represented a hybrid of centralized and decentralized arrangements" (viii). Bimber attributes this finding to the difficulty of separating decisions about various aspects of school operations that are in fact highly interrelated—that is, to the configurational, or nonadditive, nature of governance. For example, giving one group meaningful authority over personnel is difficult without also giving it a measure of fiscal autonomy. Bimber argues that it is similarly ineffective to give "schools discretion over use of maintenance funds while reserving authority to veto repair decisions and requiring use of overworked district maintenance workers" (3).

Limits on the potential effectiveness of governance reforms suggest the need to explore other theories of determinants of governmental performance, including sociological, social-psychological, and cultural models of organizations and actors that suggest how nonstructural considerations affect organizational behavior. Nonetheless, appropriate governing relations are essential to enabling if not directing particular strategies for reform and improvement and to facilitating and institutionalizing new norms of practice and performance—both of which are key elements in good administration. Moreover, governance also is an end in itself, a means by which competing interests and values are adjusted and balanced and translated into operational guidance for policies and programs and into political property rights that preserve the stability of a legislative deal.

Altering incentives through formal structures will improve performance, however, only if the changes are specifically designed to affect the exercise of informal authority and the behavior of subordinate managers and primary workers. To improve program performance or change core organizational practices, it may be necessary to make changes in governance within a comprehensive framework designed specifically to elicit changes in core values and commitments. As Bimber (1994) and others have shown, simply redistributing formal authority may not have much effect on desired outcomes—despite claims to the contrary by many administrative reformers. Hence, every reform agenda must consider the need for associated governance changes, where formal processes and structures of governance must be viewed as a necessary but not sufficient condition for public-sector improvement.

What changes are appropriate in specific contexts? For answers, practitioners should have access to an instructive and robust body of knowledge that derives from well-designed governance and public management research.

A Caveat

We stress at the outset that what follows is intended to be suggestive, at most advisory, but by no means prescriptive. Research bearing on a subject as complex as governance and public management could not and should not be standardized or organized around a single reductive logic. Our aim is more modest and, we believe, more realistic: to suggest approaches to research design and interpretation that will promote the creation of a body of knowledge whose value equals or exceeds the sum of its numerous parts.

Notes

1. The Canada-based Institute On Governance (IOG) is a nonprofit organization with charitable status that was founded in 1990 to promote effective governance. Its web site is at <http://www.iog.ca/about.html>.
2. Two separate intellectual traditions have contributed to the etymology of the term *governance* in public administration (H.

Brinton Milward, personal communication with Laurence E. Lynn, Jr., 28 January 1999; Laurence O'Toole, Jr., personal communication with Laurence E. Lynn, Jr., 5 February 1999). First, the study of institutions has emphasized the multilayered structural context of rule-governed understandings. Public choice scholars are among the primary contributors to the institutional roots of governance research. Second, the study of networks has emphasized "the role of multiple social actors in networks of negotiation, implementation, and delivery . . . 'governance' requires social partners and the knowledge of how to concert action among them. . . . " (O'Toole, personal communication, 5 February 1999). For a similar but more expansive definition, see Milward and Provan (2000).

3. We use the terms *configuration, governing relations, regime, arrangement*, and *system* interchangeably, even though these terms have somewhat different connotations. They have in common the idea of many interacting elements whose collective effect is nonadditive—and that is our meaning.

4. Assuming a structure of constraints, opportunities, and information distribution as given or exogenous also is incorporated in formal reasoning; see, for example, Simon (1964) and Niskanen (1975).

5. An exception is Kingdon (1984).

6. The Job Training Partnership Act (JTPA) is an example in which measured performance was a legislated goal. The picture is far murkier in the case of, for example, public education and public assistance; in these areas, multiple, often conflicting goals tend to be incorporated in formal mandates.

2

A Logic for Governance Research

Any governance regime, from the local to the international, is embedded in a wider social, fiscal, political, and cultural context. The influence of context on governing relations is the subject of a varied multidisciplinary literature (Aldrich and Pfeffer 1976; Scott 1998). It is virtually a truism that context shapes the structures, practices, and outcomes of regimes and their policies—which creates difficult issues for research on governance. Researchers must attempt to incorporate hard-to-specify contextual considerations into investigations of structures and management to discriminate between structural causes of policy impacts and the effects of underlying political, social, and economic circumstances. The success of an investigation depends on whether difficult theoretical and empirical problems can be addressed in a satisfactory way.

Challenges of Governance Research

The central theoretical problem in governance research is applying theories that impose a causal ordering or *a priori* structure on the logic that links context, governance, and consequences or outcomes. This problem is extraordinarily complex. In welfare research, for example, how does the investigator incorporate in a theoretical model the local political and cultural climate of welfare administration, the specific design features of policies, administrative structures, the decisions and skills of managers, the beliefs and practices of welfare workers, and the characteristics and responses of welfare recipients to assess the relative effects of policy designs, structures, and management on policy outcomes?[1]

In the face of these kinds of challenges, the temptation is strong to move to one of two extremes: to adduce all manner of potential interrelationships—in a process that might be termed "taxonomic theorizing"—to the point at which the theory is vulnerable to the charge that because it explains everything, it explains nothing or to model governance and management problems narrowly, assuming that the governing regime is only loosely coupled to or actually decoupled from its wider context. The latter strategy usually reflects the investigator's use of a theory that ignores context or the investigator's need to restrict the scope of analysis in the light of data limitations. Often, however, the assumptions underlying restricted approaches are unstated. In discussing modeling problems in areas of regulation, Moe (1985) commented that "it is common in a data-poor world for myopic models to take on lives of their own, and thus for capture or congressional dominance or budget-maximization to attract ardent followings for reasons that have little to do with demonstrated empirical validity" (1095).

A central empirical problem in governance research is obtaining data that will enable investigators to explore causal relationships beyond a narrow perimeter of theoretical possibilities that leaves too much out of the picture. Ideally, data might be obtained from an experiment, from a panel or multi-wave survey, or from a large-scale, one-time data collection effort. The requisite data are likely to be costly or impossible to obtain without generous, trusting financial support. Usually the investigator must resort to more limited data collection strategies or to reanalysis of data that have been collected for other purposes and may be inadequate for the investigator's purpose in many respects.

Meeting these theoretical and empirical challenges can be daunting. As a result, the very real possibility that broad patterns of interrelationships affect governmental outcomes often is inadequately incorporated into research designs or even into explanations and interpretations of research findings. For example, a study may attribute client outcomes to client characteristics; to worker and treatment characteristics; or to patterns of interaction between clients, treatments, and workers but ignore the potential significance of local or hierarchical organizational and management variables, systemwide incentives affecting workers and clients, or features in the local political or administrative context that establish expectations or governing values. Thus, findings from specific studies may not meet the Mohr criterion of establishing sufficiently compelling causal understanding so that they are instructive in other contexts (see chapter 1).

We are not suggesting, however, that governance research that is restricted in theoretical and empirical scope is never worth the effort. Such a view flies in the face of the realities affecting research design: small-scale research is more feasible than comprehensive studies, and careful interpretation of findings may attenuate shortcomings in research design. Moreover, well-designed investigations of restricted scope can produce—and have produced—revealing insights (e.g., Mashaw 1983). We do argue, however, that investigators whose inquiries are restricted in scope should nonetheless be mindful of what is (necessarily) omitted from their models so they can at least speculate on the possible implications of these omissions when they interpret their findings.

This habit of intellectual rigor is especially important for research that is intended to inform policy and practice decisions—a point we cannot stress enough. Stating the causal argument correctly is essential to promoting valid and credible applications of research to problems of administration and management. Findings concerning management strategies that mask or ignore the overriding significance of underlying structural and resource constraints will mislead practitioners who hope to apply them. A sense of responsibility for possible misapplications of findings ought to be part of the ethics of governance research.

With the aim of bringing conceptual discipline into the daunting challenges of conducting rigorous governance research that is of significant practical value, we propose a "logic of governance" that enables investigators to relate their specific questions and issues to a bigger picture and reduces the intellectual challenge to manageable proportions. Such a logic might assist investigators to explore a fuller range of strategies for model construction, data collection and analysis, and interpreting findings and their implications for practice.

In this chapter and in chapters 3 and 4, we develop a logic of public-sector governance that can be a useful guide to empirical work.

To begin to understand the value of establishing such a logic to study politics and public administration, we first show how the logic of market governance serves as a useful frame for the study of how private-sector organization and management affect economic performance. The logics of public-sector and private market governance are substantially different in substance, of course. Nevertheless, the logic of market governance—for which economic theory seems an appropriate starting point—can serve as an example of the value of an organizing logic in the conceptualization and design of specific investigations and establishing empirically the relative contributions to performance of structural and managerial factors.

The Logic of Market Governance

As a starting point for a logic of market governance, economic theory is concerned with examining the existence and properties of markets in equilibrium, comparing the equilibrium properties of different specifications of the system, and evaluating the effects on firms of the structures and characteristics of markets. Until recently, most neoclassical economists showed little interest in management strategy and decision making as factors in firm performance.[2] Recently, however, interest in management on the part of economists has grown with the emergence of a "new economics of organization" that has introduced concepts such as information asymmetry, transactions costs, property rights, and commitment into the modeling of economic institutions and the derivation of implications for and of management strategy. Rather than proving unduly restrictive in thinking about management—by making it seem narrowly "economic" rather than creative, "political," or skillful—a rigorous deductive framework integrates many concepts outside the traditional boundaries of economic analysis and sharpens insights into the role of management in firm performance (Arrow 1985, 50).

The Intellectual Problem

Addressing private management issues from an economic perspective requires a theory of the firm that integrates competitive market models with organizational incentive models—that is, a theory that recognizes the potential significance of external and internal incentives on firm performance. In capitalist economies, a firm forms in relationship to market opportunities and evolves into an internal economy of incentives around issues of delegation, coordination, and "make or buy" choices. The primary goal of owners/shareholders is to ensure that firms are organized and managed in accordance with external incentives created by market structures—that is, that internal and external incentives are closely aligned. From this logic, one can derive the proposition that organizational leadership and management strategies are endogenous to a theory of the firm within its industrial/market structure. The executive or manager is "inside the firm looking out" (Spulber 1992, 536).

Suppose we can show, however, that different leader or manager styles can, in a given market context, significantly influence the internal incentives and the performance of the firm—that managerial skill and judgment can cause some firms to do better than others that are facing the same market incentives. Such a possibility can be attributed to the presence of risk, uncertainty, and information asymmetries; to the incompleteness of the employment contracts by which the firm is created; and to conflicts of interest within the firm itself—that is, to the nature of complex organizations (Bolman and Deal 1991). In these circumstances, owners ought to select a chief executive officer (CEO) whose style and approach fit the firm's specific context (Rotenberg and Saloner 1993) and to their (the owners') preferences (e.g., for risk taking and control). Owners may not be so perceptive, of course, and the persistence of inappropriate management may, despite warning signals from product and share markets, damage the firm's profitability and prospects within its industry. Firm executives often are dismissed following belated owner recognition, based on firm performance, that management was ineffective.

Management strategy—a subfield of the much larger study of organizational management—is used to analyze practical problems of business management within a context that integrates market and organization theory.[3] *Management strategy* "refers to the plan of action of whoever is exercising control over some part of the corporation" (Spulber 1994, 356).[4] Spulber (1994) identifies three components of management strategy (363): organizational strategy, market strategy, and public strategy. Drawing on the more complex economics of principal-agent theory, the theory of implicit contracts, and transaction cost theory adds considerable subtlety to the picture of the relationship between managerial strategy and organizational behavior.[5] Thus, managerial skill may be a significant independent contributor to firm performance.

Despite the subtle implications of the new institutional economics, basing an approach to management strategy on economic theory alone will offend many social scientists as unduly narrow. Organizational theory—in particular, "contingency theory" that relates firm structures to organizational environments or contexts—has introduced a great array of explanatory variables into models of firm performance: for example, firm origin and history, forms of ownership and control, firm size, technology, firm and activity location, and extent of dependence on other organizations (Guillén 1994). Behavioral theories of organizations and management introduce additional variables such as employee motivations, leadership styles, firm and interfirm social structures, and the like. It seems clear that "firms are fundamentally heterogeneous" (Peteraf 1993, 179), and relationships among market structure, managerial strategy, and firm performance are far from narrowly economic.

The fact that standard economic theory may be inadequate to explain management strategies and contributions does not, however, invalidate economic theory as a core logic for an integrative theoretical framework that can generate complex propositions about the contributions of management to firm (or even industry) performance. A core logic enables an investigator to place specific issues and propositions in a wider perspective.

Consider as an example of such an integrative framework the "resource-based view of competitive advantage" (Peteraf 1992). What are the conditions that underlie the competitive advantage of a firm within an industry (or the sustained heterogeneity of successful firms)? Peteraf identifies these conditions as ownership of superior productive factors that are in limited supply, *ex post* limits to competition (for the superior productive factors), imperfect mobility (of superior productive factors), and *ex ante* limits to competition (e.g., a superior location). Thus, "the resource-based model is fundamentally concerned with the internal accumulation of assets, with asset specificity, and, less directly, with transactions costs" (Peteraf 1992, 188). Management strategy, therefore, is concerned with identifying and managing the firm in light of these firm-specific factors (in the generic management literature termed "strengths, weaknesses, op-

portunities, and threats" or "SWOT"). Though the conceptual vo-
cabulary remains "economic," inquiry initiated by a search for
sources of competitive superiority can range far into sociological,
psychological, or even anthropological terrain without becoming
disconnected from the basic economics of the situation.[6]

Though we do not explore the point further, the value of an organizing logic to integrating organizational and management analyses
across nations and cultures is worth noting. In addition to firm- and
industry-specific effects on structure and strategy, can we identify
cultural effects that would differentiate management strategies
across countries? Organizational structures and processes, role perceptions, and role behaviors (note the introduction of sociological
concepts into the logic) can be modeled as governed by external resource dependencies and by legitimating values in the cultural environment (Lachman, Nedd, and Hinings 1994). The importance of
culture is in conferring legitimacy on organizational structures and
in "the social controls and social sanctions that values exert on behavior" at organizational and individual levels (Lachman, Nedd, and
Hinings 1994, 52). "Imported practices may fail, or be ineffectively
implemented, if they are inconsistent with the core values of local
settings" (Lachman, Nedd, and Hinings 1994, 53). The extent of cultural influence may depend, however, on the extent to which resource dependencies are governed by material relationships and the
degree of consensus or discord within the culture or environment.
Culture may be influential, but compared to what, and how much?

Also demonstrating the value of an integrated framework of market governance is Powell's (1990) analysis of conditions that give
rise to network forms of organization. Under certain circumstances,
exchange relationships may be governed by reciprocity and collaboration rather than by (complete and incomplete or implicit) contracts or structures of formal authority. In general, Powell says,

> networks appear to involve a distinctive combination of factors—
> skilled labor, some degree of employment security, salaries rather
> than piece rates, some externally-provided mechanisms for job train-
> ing, relative equity among the participants, a legal system with re-
> laxed antitrust standards, and national policies that promote research
> and development . . . —which seldom exist in sufficient measure
> without a political and legal infrastructure to support them (326–27).

Cross-national variation in the frequency of network forms of organization may be explained, Powell suggests, by variations in state policies that support and sustain collaborations.[7]

Another integrative concept originating in sociological theory is that of an "organizational field" and its implications. "Bureaucratization and other forms of organizational change occur," argue DiMaggio and Powell (1983, 147) "as the result of processes that make organizations more similar without necessarily making them more efficient." Why? Suppose we define a *structural field* as "a recognized area of institutional life" (148), such as "regulatory agencies." Once an organizational field can be identified, what forces govern change and, in particular, why does isomorphism (i.e., convergent structural/functional arrangements) apparently occur? Three mechanisms for inducing isomorphism are political influence (operating as an exogenous influence on firms), standardization of responses to uncertainty, and standardization reflecting professional norms (e.g., of accounting, personnel, and marketing functions). The presence of these mechanisms adds to the agenda of possible explanations for firm structure and performance.

Why a Logic of Market Governance?

The point of this excursion into private market governance is this: A core logic of competitive markets *by itself* suggests that management be viewed as fundamentally endogenous to the system of markets, industries, and firms. *Management*—implying an actor—becomes *management strategy*, implying firm or organizational strategy. Managers become the obedient and reflexive agents of owners to ensure the organization's performance within specific markets.

Controlling for contextual factors, however, allows one to better identify exogenous managerial "contributions" to firm performance. Beginning with the parsimonious view of firms implied by economic logic, a theorist of management strategy can introduce elements of complexity—including those suggested by economic theory itself as well as those suggested by sociological and social psychological perspectives on organizational and interorganizational behavior. Models of considerable refinement and subtlety can result from efforts to depict a richly coupled view of organizations. This elementary logic is schematically summarized in Figure 2.1.[8]

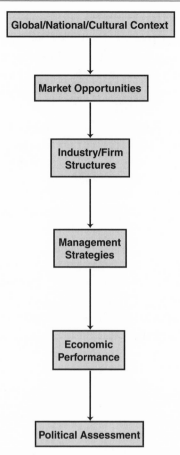

FIGURE 2.1.   *The Elementary Logic of Competitive Markets*

Empirical research suggests, in fact, that the relationship between management strategy and firm success is much less clear than any parsimonious theory would predict. Many empirical management studies are based on behavioral research: descriptions of the behaviors and activities of managers and relationships between what managers do and their effectiveness (as perceived by superiors, subordinates, peers, and other actors). Research has focused on what might be termed correlates of organizational effectiveness or managerial reputation, such as effective internal coordination (Argyres 1995). However, "while the firms perceived to be best managed are more profitable and less risky, and grow faster and reward their stockholders more than less well-managed firms, these variables explain only about 30 percent of the variance in management ratings" (Koch and Cebula 1994).

Thus, private management could not be characterized as self-regulating, nor is it controlled simply by a widely accepted criterion: profitability in particular markets. The conventional view of decisive, bottom line-oriented, self-aware managers may be largely myth (Longenecker and Gioia 1991). Summarizing a symposium on the universality of management science, Aharoni and Burton (1994, 1) conclude, "Unfortunately, there is not a universally accepted theoretical underpinning or even an accepted language and shared definitions that could be a basis of a universal contingent management theory, applicable globally. . . . [L]anguage, culture and fundamental beliefs are important. Good management practices do vary across borders and cultures" (see Smith et al. 1989; Hamilton and Biggart 1988).

Partly in reflection of the indeterminacy of management strategy as either dependent or independent variable, a substantial body of management strategy research tends toward the prescriptive and the normative ("leadership"), on one hand, and the procedural ("management by objectives," "strategic planning"),[9] on the other. Vague, generic (and often circular) prescriptions are prevalent in the private management literature, reflecting the belief that management strategy and managerial behavior are more exogenous than endogenous with respect to competitive conditions and firm performance. Through vision, leadership, and skill, an effective CEO can make or break his or her firm no matter what the limitations of context.

The introduction of institutional and organizational economics into the study of management strategy enables the researcher to impose a useful intellectual coherence on a subject that otherwise exhibits an undisciplined eclecticism, tending toward homiletics. According to the logic of market governance, firms and industries form to pursue profitable opportunities. Firms operate within a legal framework that protects their owners from unconstitutional and unreasonable interference with their property rights and protects society from certain abuses of those rights (e.g., actions in restraint of trade, marketing of unsafe products, unauthorized use of the public domain); such frameworks vary between countries.

Within the prescribed framework of rules, firms are free to pursue their interests in accordance with the preferences of their owners, subject to the vicissitudes flowing from the separation of ownership and control. Though their specific preferences vary, a firm's owners typically seek to earn a positive return on their investments and tend to avoid products and services whose profitability is uncertain or indeterminate. Moreover, though a firm's managers may have specific preferences of their own that relate only in a general way to long-term profitability, their effectiveness from an ownership perspective is based on producing satisfactory returns on their investments, and firm structures and management strategies tend to reflect—although they are not wholly determined by—ownership preferences.

Public-Sector Governance: An Institutional View

The study of public-sector governance and management also exhibits an undisciplined eclecticism and a predilection for impassioned, normatively inspired prescription. We think that one could reasonably suppose that a core logic of public-sector governance might be similarly useful as an organizing and integrating framework for governance and public management research.

As with the logic of market governance, creating a logic of public-sector governance requires a starting point. "The most fundamental distinction between public and private organizations," argue Fesler and Kettl (1991, 9), "is the rule of law. Public organizations exist to administer the law, and every element of their being—their structure, staffing, budget, and purpose—is the product of legal authority." Private-sector governance and management are ultimately responsible to the preferences of firm owners concerning the exercise of their property rights (enabled by the framework of common law governing private conduct). Similarly, public-sector governance and management are ultimately responsible to law and the processes of its creation—that is, to the preferences of various "publics" or citizens and to authoritative decision makers acting in their name. These representatives exercise legitimate authority to enact statutes, appropriate funds, issue administrative guidelines, and monitor and investigate the activities of public agencies and their managers, employees, and contractors, and they sanction those whose performance is unsatisfactory. These publics and the officials acting in their name under constitutional authority create an institutional framework within which public policies are enacted and implemented. Here—within the institutional framework of political economy—is where a logic of governance begins.

A Simple Logic of Governance

The rule of law—conceived broadly to encompass lawmaking, its concrete expressions, and its consequences—can serve as a basis for constructing a simple logic of governance. Any governance regime—within a policy domain (e.g., environmental protection), with respect to a type of government activity (e.g., regulation), within a particular jurisdiction (e.g., a state or a city), or within a particular organization (e.g., a department of human services) or organizational field (e.g., child welfare agencies)—is the result of a dynamic process that can be summarized in terms of a core logic. This process links several discrete aspects of collective action: the values and interests of citizens, expressed politically; choices by legislative bodies, expressed in statutes and appropriations acts; the strategies and actions of executive agents functioning within the constraints of their organizational structures and roles; the production and delivery of collective goods and services by primary workers in the public sector and, as contractors, in the private sector; and *ex post* oversight and assessment by legislatures, courts, elected executives, and publics. The combined influence of these elements has significant consequences for the effectiveness or performance of government as perceived by stakeholders.

With these elements and the dynamics connecting them constituting the big picture (much as a national economy is the big picture for private markets), an important objective of governance research is to identify the influence on governmental performance of these various elements to inform administrative reform, public policy design, and public management practice.

Artifacts of this dynamic process are formal structures—what might be termed the concrete expressions of public policy or of the public "will"—that we usually have in mind when we refer to "the government." These structures include legislated policy mandates; agencies, departments, and offices; policy and program designs; public budgets and associated finance and accounting practices; and personnel—executives, managers, supervisors, workers, and agents operating under grants or contracts. Among the most visible and consequential of these structures are the major organizations or bureaus (the analogue to corporations or firms) designated as agents of the electorate to pursue public purposes. In the modern administrative state, it is difficult to imagine the implementation of the public will without formal organization.[10] Features of these organizations of particular interest to governance and public management are the definition and assignment of responsibilities to executives and others in managerial roles. These definitions and assignments determine the distribution of the power to affect governmental outcomes.

Because governance involves power, it is not neutral. The services and benefits that flow from the structures of public authority have implications of all kinds for those who pay for them, those who provide them, and those who receive them—who usually are not the same people, of course. The ways in which these implications are experienced or perceived by affected stakeholders—including clients, service providers, and public agencies and their employees—produce dissatisfactions and political reactions that often lead to new or modified demands on elected officials. Programs may be considered wasteful, unnecessary, in need of reform, even corrupt. Elected officials, for their part, may alter formal structures of governance to produce outcomes that are more satisfactory: lower costs, greater effectiveness, different goals. Sabel (1993) argues that "governance structures are at bottom strategic responses to competitive environments composed of other governance structures" (70). The result is a continuous process of structural change— "incrementalism," as it is often called (Braybrooke and Lindblom 1970).

The logic of governance thus involves three distinctive aspects:

- The influence of electorally motivated *legislative choice* on the *formal structures* of public agencies
- The consequences for service availability, quality, and cost of these formal structures of authority and how administrative power is used to implement legislation, or *governance* (see definition in chapter 1)
- *assessment* by the public, stakeholders, and governing institutions of the government's *role and performance*, which may lead to political demands for new legislation or administrative reform.

This core logic of public-sector governance is depicted in the simple schematic model shown in Figure 2.2.

A Complex Logic of Governance

The compressed account of governance depicted in Figure 2.2 is merely suggestive of the complex dynamics involved in the rule of law. A framework to guide empirical research on governance must elaborate on and incorporate a causal or relational logic among the central features of the model.

Just as the starting point for the logic of market governance is economic theory, a useful starting point for exploring a more complex logic of governance is theories based in political economy.[11] This approach is concerned with "the consequences of alternative institutional forms on the behavior of individuals and the outcomes of collective decisions, the mechanisms that enable institutions to constrain behavior, and the logic of the processes through which institutions change" (Weimer 1995, 2). A logic of governance based in the concepts of political economy might be sketched as follows.[12]

Responding to citizen and stakeholder interests and concerns (and financial contributions), legislators create coalitions to introduce, support, and enact specific legislation. Coalitions involve both houses of a legislature and the elected executive; they also may

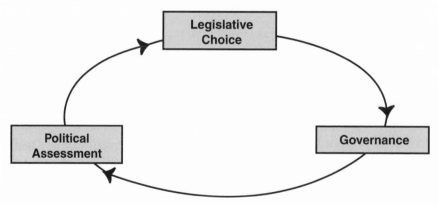

FIGURE 2.2.   *Core Logic of Public-Sector Governance*

include (implicitly) the courts and (explicitly) public managers, who often control valuable resources of information and technical competence.

A legislative coalition reflects mixed motives that are based on members' present and future interests in a variety of issues. Their general intent may be described as "deck-stacking"—that is, crafting durable legislative deals that favor or privilege particular actors and interests over others. More often than not, the coalition's purpose is the distribution of political property rights—access to administrative power and resultant opportunities to influence policy implementation and its consequences—rather than documented accomplishment of specific, outcome-oriented policy objectives (Bird 1999). "Deck-stacking" is accomplished through a variety of mechanisms: administrative decision rules, definitions of decision criteria, apportionment of evidentiary burdens, enfranchisement or empowerment of particular actors, and subsidization of particular interests.

Legislation is one thing; administrative implementation is another. Public managers—especially career civil servants who have tenure in office and thus are beyond the direct control of elected executives—are potential threats to the durability of any deal. Letting their actions go uncontrolled or unmonitored is risky. Consequently, enacting coalitions create governance arrangements specifically to narrow or prescribe the range of executive-administrative discretion and thus ensure compliance with the coalition's multifarious intentions. Controls over administrative discretion are of two types: *ex ante* controls that preclude noncompliant decisions and actions, and *ex post* controls that detect and punish noncompliance. The former give rise to principal-agent problems—that is, controls over bureaucratic activity that are ineffective because formal accountability is problematic. The latter, the legislative version of managing by exception, allow for more flexible *ex post* monitoring, based on the "fire alarms" set off by aggrieved parties, but they may come into play too late to be effective.

Although enacting coalitions seek an adequate measure of control over bureaucracy to secure the deal, implementation of complex legislative mandates necessarily involves administrative discretion and managerial and worker judgment. Discretion, which is implicated in achieving and in thwarting the objectives of the legislative deal, is exercised by actors at various levels of government and within departmental hierarchies, from executives at the federal level to front-line employees in local offices. Within hierarchies, higher-level managers may use (or be directed by legislation to use) their discretion to create additional constraints and controls on lower-level managers and workers. The drift away from legislative intent may originate at subordinate levels of the system, where actors may be relatively immune to the interests of the dealmakers.[13] Governance regimes—even those with substantial *ex ante* controls—create or allow for substantial discretion and influence at the front-line levels of public organizations, where the primary work of service delivery and regulation is performed.

In sum, governance comprises structures and processes guiding administrative activity that create constraints and controls (*ex ante* and *ex post*) and confer or allow autonomy and discretion on the part of administrative actors, all toward fulfilling the purposes of the enacting coalition. To construct an organizing framework for empirical research, this logic of governance may be delineated essentially hierarchically:[14]

- Between (a) citizen preferences and interests expressed politically and (b) legislative choice
- Between (b) legislator preferences expressed in enacted legislation and (c) formally authorized structures and processes of public agencies
- Between (c) the structure of formal authority and (d) the *de facto* organization and management of agencies, programs, and administrative activities
- Between (d) organization, management, and administration and (e) the core technologies and primary work of public agencies
- Between (e) primary work and (f) consequences, outputs, or results (e.g., the availability, quality, and cost of publicly sponsored goods and services)
- Between (f) outputs or results and (g) stakeholder assessments of agency or program performance (i.e., judgments about whether government is "working" that motivate them to political action)
- Between (g) performance assessments expressed politically and (a) public and legislative interests and preferences.

A schematic summary of this more complex, dynamic process is shown in Figure 2.3. The specifications of particular governance models, of course, reflect investigators' research objectives, theories, and data.

Comparison of Figures 2.1 and 2.3 suggests that governance of the private and public sectors is bounded by aggregate and individualistic influences. Each is influenced by the same environment, construed in the widest sense: global, cultural, and socioeconomic. Each is influenced as well by its legitimacy from the perspective of citizens expressing themselves through actions with political significance: voting, contributing resources, initiating litigation, and the like. In other words, the character of the public and private sectors is an endogenous result of society, culture, and economy, collectively and individually expressed. (Each sector also is an exogenous influence on the other—the private sector generating revenues and acting to correct or preclude "government failures," the public sector acting to address "market failures" and employing discretionary authority to regulate and selectively allocate resources.)

Within these bounds, the two sectors exhibit fundamentally different dynamics: The private sector is constituted by economic opportunity, the public sector by constitutionally sanctioned public choice. Management strategies are identified as important in each domain—each being both cause and effect of factors operating at different levels—but the logic in which management is embedded differs fundamentally from the public to the private sector; the former necessarily is governed by politics, the latter necessarily by markets.

That these things are true is only background for our main point, which concerns the framing and content of research agendas. The public and private sectors can be understood as reflecting a core logic that assumes rational behavior by social actors (although we shall discuss the implications of starting with different assumptions in chapter 5). For both sectors, moreover, the core logic is a point of departure for exploring various explanatory theories and models drawn from a wide variety of intellectual sources. In particular investigations, the core logic may recede into the background, but in the ideal situation its potential relevance at least will have been considered. Such consideration is the point—and greater coherence in the body of governance research is the intended result.

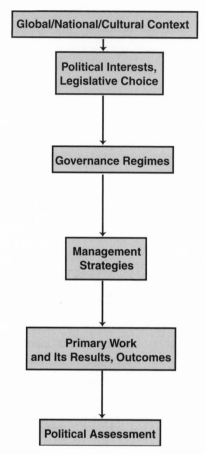

FIGURE 2.3   *A Complex Model of Governance*

The logic of governance summarized in Figure 2.3 becomes, then, a framework for designing and interpreting specific investigations. Reference to this framework can be helpful in addressing questions such as the following:

- How might the causal relationships of primary interest to a specific investigation be located within a broader environmental and governance context?
- From a theoretical perspective, which of the many potentially influential causal relationships (or interactions) seem particu-

larly relevant to the investigation? How might these relationships/interactions be conceptualized or modeled?

- To the extent that potentially relevant causal factors must be omitted from the investigation, how might findings be affected?
- In the light of what was included in and necessarily omitted from the investigation's research, what conclusions can be drawn that might be instructive for other contexts?

Even at a reduced level of complexity, however, the scope of theoretical possibilities is quite large, and modeling problems are potentially unwieldy. To make the task of conceptualizing governance models more tractable, we have simplified the hierarchical logic even further.

Levels of Governance

Our starting point for this simplification is the open-systems model of organizations that was first developed by J. Thompson (1967), which in turn is founded on Talcott Parsons's intuitive distinction between three levels of responsibility and control: institutional, managerial, and technical (T. Parsons 1960).[15] Scholars and practitioners have recognized the existence of "levels" or "layers" in political and organizational life (Lynn 1987). Redford (1965, 1969) draws distinctions between micropolitics, subsystem (or intermediary) politics, and macropolitics. Summer (1980) identifies three separate layers: the level at which "broad strategic alignments" form; the administrative level, which is concerned with the elaboration of strategies into specific details; and the "operating or work" level, where the performance of the actual operations and work necessary to carry out the alignment occurs. In *The Power Elite*, Mills refers to "the top, the middle, and the bottom levels of power" (Mills 1956, 244). Linking this line of intuitive insight with a logic of governance based in political economy, we suggest the following heuristic:

- **The institutional (public choice) level of governance** is concerned with the establishment of governing relations, or broad strategic alignments, at the legislative level—comprising relationships between items (g), (a), (b), (c), and (d) in the fore-

going hierarchy (i.e., between public/stakeholders and legislators, between legislative preferences and the formal authority
governing public agencies, and between formal authority and
the organization and management of public agencies and
programs).

- **The managerial level of governance** is concerned with the
  further shaping of governing relations, or the elaboration of
  strategies, by organizational actors—comprising relationships
  between items (d) and (e) (i.e., interactions between organization, management, and administration and the core technologies and primary work of public agencies).

- **The technical level of governance** is concerned with further
  shaping of governance at the primary work level, where strategic alignments are given their operational expression—comprising relationships between items (e) and (f) (i.e., interactions
  between primary workers and the consequences or outcomes
  for service recipients and other stakeholders).

The value of this aggregated framework (summarized in Figure
2.4) lies in directing attention to the dynamic relations within and
between the institutional, managerial, and operational levels of
governance. Does the process of strategic alignment creation affect
the influence of these alignments on agency management? How
does the distribution of formal power at the managerial level mediate the influence of strategic alignments on primary work? How
does coordination at the primary work level influence the effectiveness of services? These kinds of questions are likely to receive
greater attention in research design—and research design is more
likely to be an interdisciplinary activity—if reference is made to a
framework that recognizes distinctive levels of governance. By recognizing these levels, governance research is more likely to produce usable knowledge about governing instead of ignoring
contexts and processes that are fundamental elements of governance in practice.

This logic of governance is neither a paradigm nor a unified
"theory of governance." It does not depict how governance "works."
Instead, it is a schematic or heuristic framework that suggests how
the elements of governance—the values and interests of citizens,
legislative enactments and oversight, executive and organizational
structures and roles, and performance assessment—might be linked

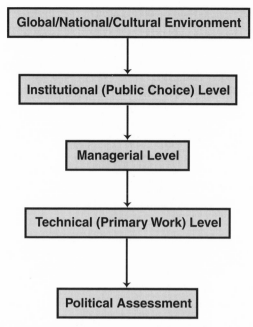

FIGURE 2.4.   *Governance: Levels of the Game*

through a dynamic and interactive process. Within an institutional frame of reference, it is a particular way of identifying relationships that potentially influence policy, program, and organizational performance. Identifying their actual influence requires theory, models, and data.

How might investigators think about the dynamics of governing relations within each level of governance? Chapters 3 through 6 put forward some ideas from the literature that have implications for research design.

Notes

1. See chapter 8 for further discussion of this example.
2. Exceptions can be found among behavioral economists exploring the consequences of departures from strict assumptions of rationality on the part of economic actors (Cyert and March 1963; Simon 1959; Williamson 1981).

3. The field of management strategy originated in the largely atheoretical work of authors such as Peter Drucker; most strategy literature is descriptive and prescriptive, without the intervening stage of theory-based analysis.

4. Thus, "industrial organization" studies firms in relationship to their environment, and the "economics of organization" is concerned with issues internal to firms (Spulber 1994).

5. "The structure of an organization can be defined simply as the sum total of the ways in which it divides its labor into distinct tasks and then achieves coordination among them" (Mintzberg 1979, 2).

6. An exception is Uzzi (1996). In an empirical analysis of apparel firms in New York, he found that standard concepts in political economy such as "self-interest maximization, generalized reputation, and repeated-gaming *fade into the background*, [and] issues of how social relationships promote thick information exchange, rapid and heuristic decision-making, and the search for positive-sum outcomes take the fore. In this logic, the network acts as a social boundary of demarcation around opportunities that are assembled from the embedded ties that define membership and enrich the network" (693, italics added).

7. Japanese *Keiretsu* are examples of a culturally distinct type of network organization with important extramarket functions. *Keiretsu* maximize "the joint welfare (or utility) of the membership by restraining both the bearing of risks and appropriation of returns by individual firms and substituting what appears to be a group-administered allocation plan" (Lincoln, Gerlach, and Ahmadjian 1996, 86)—raising important policy issues for the Japanese government and for Japan's trading partners. More general discussion of interfirm networks appears in Uzzi (1996, 1997).

8. A deeper discussion of this logic would incorporate multidirectional arrows in the scheme (e.g., in developing countries, market opportunities shape and are shaped by cultural norms). It also would incorporate political responses to the aggregate performance of the market economy, which may lead to public policy interventions into the market economy.

9. "Strategic management is the process of making and implementing strategic decisions" (Asch and Bowman 1989, xiii).

10. In the premodern American state, individual public employees often functioned independently with directly appropriated funds, without being bound to any administrative structure and supervised (if one could call it that) primarily by legislative committees.

11. Although this framework is derived from contemporary political economy, the intellectual boundaries of our project overlap substantially with more traditional thinking represented by "The Governing Processes and Their Modes of Operation," Part IV of Friedrich (1963, 387–523).

12. This section is based on the work of Fiorina (1982); Horn and Shepsle (1989); McCubbins, Noll, and Weingast (1987, 1989); McCubbins and Schwartz (1984); Moe (1989, 1995); Noll and Weingast (1991); Shepsle and Weingast (1981); Weingast and Moran (1983); and related work.

13. In the same vein, a drift away from executive, as opposed to legislative, intent may originate at lower levels, where workers are allied with members of legislative coalitions and their constituencies.

14. There is likely to be endogeneity in these interactions, and one should not assume that the causal arrow always points downward (Moe 1985).

15. Lynn (1987) cites other uses of hierarchical "levels" in political and institutional scholarship.

3

Institutional Governance

Institutions may be defined as "fairly stable sets of commonly recognized formal and informal rules that coordinate or constrain the behavior of individuals in social interactions" (Weimer 1995, 2–3), as regimes of rules that affect incentives for a social order and impact behavior (E. Ostrom 1986), or as "the rules of the game in a society or, more formally, . . . the humanly devised constraints that shape human interaction" (North 1990, 3).[1] Two questions arise at the institutional level of analysis. First, how are the formal and informal rules that constitute "institutions" identified, defined, or operationalized? As March (1997) states, institutional approaches to administration and management

> need to identify the rules and institutions that endure; . . . to clarify the ways in which complicated mosaics of rules and identities are converted into actions in particular situations; . . . to understand the detailed micro-processes by which such rules are created, maintained, changed, and eliminated. Most of all, they need some new ideas about the processes they are modeling (694).

Second, why are particular institutions (or governing relations) created, and what are the dynamics of their maintenance and evolution over time? More technically, how and why are structure-induced equilibria sustained or disturbed?

Considerable ambiguity is associated with the term *institution.* For example, Weimer distinguishes between policy design and institutional design. Policies encompass a wide array of "instruments" for achieving policy purposes, whereas institutions are a narrower category: rules or regimes of rules (Weimer 1995, 8). Caiden (1991, 6) distinguishes between "institutional" and "instrumental" bureaucracies—a distinction we explore further below. The focus at the institutional level is primarily on configurations of formal authority that might be operationalized in empirical work.

Governing relations take many forms. Sabel (1993, 69) distinguishes between markets and hierarchies and what he calls "constitutional orders . . . based on trust—the partners' mutual understanding that none will exploit the vulnerabilities that partnership creates—whereas markets and hierarchies presume self-seeking behavior that leads to problems of hold-ups and agency" (*cf.* Williamson 1975; Miller 1992). A constitutional order has constituent units and a superintendent. Jurisdiction and rulemaking authority are limited in two fundamental ways: The superintendent cannot exceed the bounds of its own constitutional order, and all rules must be established in consultation with constituent units. The underlying presumption of the latter requirement is information asymmetry: Constituents know more than the superintendent. Thus, the superintendent is deprived of the freedom to respond with alacrity to changes in the environment (Sabel 1993, 73–75). At the same time, "constitutional orders can solve coordination problems that neither markets nor hierarchies can solve" (75). Designers of constitutional orders set out to create a structure in which "horizontal" relations can be redefined through "vertical" consultation as the context of cooperation shifts (80). There is an

institutionalized presumption that adjustment is risky and precarious because the consequential features of the new context are hard to identify; so hard, indeed, that only the deliberate consultation of constituents and superintendent can achieve a provisional success beyond the reach of the reflexive maximizing adjustments of either alone. What is distinctive about constitutional orders, in short, is that they do not take the success of their powers of self-adjustment for granted (80).

Thus, in Sabel's view, constitutional orders solve the central challenge to markets and hierarchies: opportunism—the inclination of actors to exploit their many different kinds of advantages. The norms of trust that emerge are to be sharply distinguished from a repeated game equilibrium, which is more of a *modus vivendi* rather than trust proper (Sabel 1993, 82).[2]

What sorts of structures do the various political actors—interest groups, elected executives, members of legislatures, administrative officials—find conducive to their own interests, and what kind of administrative state is therefore likely to emerge from their efforts to exercise political authority and influence? Three scholarly traditions are concerned in a fundamental way with producing principled accounts of the purposes and forms of the administrative state: legal idealism (administrative law), political economy (or rational choice theory), and the new institutionalism in organizational analysis (or socialized choice theories).[3]

Legal Idealism

According to Schuck (1994), "Administrative law refers to the legal doctrines—a complex mixture of constitutional, statutory, regulatory, and 'common law' principles—that govern the structure, decision processes, and behavior of administrative agencies" (7). Furthermore, according to Sunstein (1990), these legal doctrines embrace "a constellation of related concerns: to guarantee legality; to promote procedural regularity; and to ensure against irrationality and injustice, defined by reference to common-sense intuitions" (303). Mashaw (1990) has called this approach to administrative law "legal idealism," the quest for a normatively appropriate legal order: "[A]dministrative procedural requirements embedded in law shape administrative decision-making in accordance with our fundamental (but perhaps malleable) images of *the legitimacy of state action*. That is administrative procedure's purpose and its explanation" (268; italics added). In sum, the establishment of governing relations reflects norms of legitimacy that are implicit in our constitutional legal order more than norms of legitimacy that originate in self-interest or socialization.

Modern American administrative law began with the sharp expansion of administrative process during the New Deal, when administrative law was becoming the primary instrument of welfare state expansion: "The solution to the procedure problem was seen to be a legislative code of standards of fair administrative procedure" (Schwartz 1994, 217)—strongly opposed by the agencies of the time but, in 1946, enacted in the form of the Administrative Procedures Act (APA). The continued expansion of administrative authority at all levels of government since that time has been accompanied by concern for the elaboration of appropriate protections of citizens against abuses of administrative discretion. For example, concern began to focus on the legal position of the individual who is dependent upon government largesse. Such largesse initially was held to be a privilege insulated from the requirements of due process. In 1970, the Supreme Court decision in *Goldberg v. Kelly* (397 U.S. 254) introduced the concept of entitlement, which is "more like 'property' than a 'gratuity'"—and, as such, is fully protected by procedural due process.

Further developments occurred in the scope of review in administrative law. In *Chevron U.S.A. v. Natural Resources Defense Council*, 467 U.S. 837 (1984), the Supreme Court held that "courts must give effect to a reasonable agency interpretation of a statute unless that interpretation is inconsistent with a clearly expressed congressional intent" (Schwartz 1994, 214). Schwartz argues that this ruling "upsets the balance in our administrative law" by drastically limiting review and presenting "the danger of undue deference to self-expansion of an agency's jurisdiction" (214, 215). Furthermore, to prevent over-judicializing of the administration of social welfare, the Court has tended to favor cost-benefit analysis, which gives increasing weight to agency autonomy and renews deference toward agencies and the role of experts (219).

The central tension in legal idealism, then, is between the extent to which public officials are granted discretion to perform their duties within a legislated framework, on one hand, and control *by law* of bureaucratic discretion, on the other (Shapiro 1994, 501). The myriad decisions about particular matters of public policy "have so much potential for adversely affecting individual interests that it seems undesirable to leave them entirely to the discretion of a handful of government officials" (507). When, then, is discretion appropriate?

According to Shapiro (1994), "The narrowest view of discretion is sometimes summed up as administrative choice when there is 'no law to apply'" (502). In the broadest sense, discretion exists when a single correct choice is not imposed on administrators, allowing them to base decisions on policy considerations. The law typically enacts mechanisms, however, for supervising and evaluating the exercise of discretion. "[T]here is a general tendency to narrow the boundaries of discretion over time, partly by substituting rules for discretion and partly by introducing various devices that permit at least the post-auditing of the prudence of the decisions reached" (Shapiro 1994, 504). These mechanisms[4] are numerous: establishment of professional qualifications for office holders; requirements for statistical post-audits; the use of budgetary authority; the use of statutes—including statutes that correct judicial discretion; assignment of property rights; procedures to ensure greater public observation of private, informal action by public officials; and discretion to waive rules or make exceptions—a form of discretion that is difficult to protect from abuse. "The attempt to control discretion while purportedly leaving 'political' or 'policy' choice unfettered," according to Shapiro, "has largely taken the form of piling up procedural requirements" (506).

As an analytic framework, legal idealism offers a coherent *normative* rationale for the particular forms that governance can assume: ensuring the legitimacy of official actions through the formal control of bureaucratic discretion, where legitimacy is defined by judicial doctrines and canons. This rationale presumably is the stock in trade of legislators, as well as trial and appellate court judges who have been trained as lawyers. Thus, this perspective contributes insights to legislative choices of statutory controls and administrative arrangements, tensions between the executive and legislative branch over resource allocation control and use, and judicial reactions to alleged violations of constitutional and statutory rights and misuse of administrative discretion.

Political Economy

The study of political economy is concerned with explaining how institutions evolve in response to individual interests, goals, and choices and how, in turn, institutions create incentives that affect the performance of political and economic actors and systems (Alt and Shepsle 1990). The central premise of this approach is the endogeneity of the institutions of governance; formal structures are dependent variables—the products of public choice.[5]

As with legal idealism, the objective of legislators is control, but via a different route: the creation of incentives rather than rules for compliance. The central argument of political economy is summarized by Moe (1995) as follows:

> Public authority . . . defines a crucial set of political actors—politicians—who will participate in political exchange with others, and who have rights to do things that these others cannot do on their own. . . . [P]oliticians have unique and enormously valuable property rights by virtue of their occupation of official positions. . . . [Thus] a theory of political organization must be built around existing public authority. . . . Public bureaucracy . . . is an instance of the exercise of public authority (120–21).

Moe goes on to say that "the political firm, the organization we want to understand in building a theory of public bureaucracy, consists of the entire two-tiered hierarchy linking politicians, interest groups, and bureaucrats. It is not limited to the public agency itself. A theory of public bureaucracy is unavoidably a theory about politics and political organization more generally" (122). Chubb and Moe (1990) state the point as follows: "[P]ublic authority does not belong to any particular individual or group. . . . [P]ublic authority is enormously valuable and widely available[,] . . . a blank check on which everyone wants to write" (29).[6]

The Politics of Bureaucratic Control

In a political economy, legislators are agents for electoral constituencies. A useful starting point is decisions by an interest group (e.g., a political action committee, or PAC) concerning the kinds of structures they want politicians to provide to secure and protect the group's interests.[7] An enacting coalition of legislators must be concerned to create administrative forms that produce positive net present value for their constituencies and can survive active opposition and legislative succession. When will a legislative coalition, in the interest of its constituencies, choose to create an administrative, structural order, and what kind of order will it create in relation to specific circumstances?[8]

Moe (1995) elaborates on the political dynamics of bureau creation as follows. "The more fundamental task for political actors is to find and institute a governance structure that can protect their public organizations from control by opponents" (125). The problem is not one of achieving technical efficiency, as with profit-oriented private firms, but of political control and stability. Continuing in this vein, Moe argues that "[s]tructural choices have all sorts of important consequences for the content and direction of policy, and, because this is so, choices about structure are implicitly choices about policy. . . . " (127). Moreover, "The game of structural politics never ends. . . . [A]ll of the choices that have been made in the formative round of decision making can be reversed or modified later"(146).[9] From this perspective, politics necessarily has familiar characteristics. Opponents try to frustrate agency success; proponents protect and goad; elected executives seek to impose their own will or negotiate deals.

In a similar vein, Calvert, McCubbins, and Weingast (1989) argue that the *ex ante* choices of legislatures and executives are "the primary source of executive and legislative influence over policy outcomes" (605).[10] They develop a parsimonious game-theoretic model of bureaucratic creation. The "appointments stage" of the game includes "any actions that the executive or legislature can take, prior to agency choice, that influence the later goals of the agent or the set of feasible choices available to the agency. Such actions include the structuring of the agency itself, the denomination of its powers and jurisdiction, the specification of administrative procedures to be followed, and the type of personnel with which the agency is to be staffed . . . " (604). The purpose of these governing relations concerns the protection of political property rights as much or more than achieving the substantive goals of public policy.

Heckathorn and Maser (1987) show how transaction cost analysis can explain why citizens rationally resort to public bureaucracies as economical means for conducting planning, enforcing agreements and commitments, and resolving conflicts when strictly private arrangements fail because of "insufficient or excessively costly transaction resources" available for contracting (83).

The Mechanisms of Bureaucratic Control

In the language of principal-agent theory (which we discuss further in chapter 4), legislators in an enacting coalition, as principals, must induce bureaucratic agents to comply with their wishes (as expressed in statutory language, legislative history, and so forth [Horn and Shepsle 1989, 501]) and prevent "bureaucratic drift," as McCubbins, Noll, and Weingast (1987) term it. Opportunistic noncompliance must be detectable and subject to reliable and credible enforcement. "[L]egislators see the choice of administrative structures and processes as important in assuring that agencies produce policy outcomes that legislators deem satisfactory" (McCubbins, Noll, and Weingast 1989, 432). Noll and Weingast (1991) add to the argument that "political actors, in designing the administrative procedures of an agency and in selecting the problems which an agency's employees will be called upon to solve, *create the set of normative values* that the agency will seek to serve" (238; italics added).

The earlier literature on public choice, according to McCubbins, Noll, and Weingast (1987), emphasized reactive monitoring throughout oversight hearings and, if necessary, reprisals. They are critical of this emphasis. "[B]y itself, a system of rewards and punishments is unlikely to be a completely effective solution to the control problem . . . due to the cost of monitoring, limitations in the range of rewards and punishments, and, for the most meaningful forms of rewards and punishments, the cost to the principals of implementing them" (249). Moreover, *ex post* corrections for drift may have limited value; one reason is that the drift will split the enacting coalition. The "McNollgast" contribution is to recognize that *"politicians must foresee potential problems and devise solutions as part of the legislation."* (Horn and Shepsle 1989, 503; italics added).[11]

By creating structure-induced equilibrium, politicians establish significant costs of changing the initial deal. Institutional rules "restrict logrolling behavior and therefore the potential for legislative exchange to upset an equilibrium" (Shepsle and Weingast 1981, 512). Other measures may restrict the power of the executive branch to appropriate the gains. Legislative committee systems institutionalize bias in favor of the status quo, protecting enacting coalitions—as do choices of administrative form (e.g., of forms immune to influence by subsequent enacting coalitions). These systems may attempt to shift monitoring responsibilities to constituents through deck-stacking (i.e., enacting procedures that, for example, facilitate "fire-alarm" oversight)—meaning structural opportunities for stakeholders to observe agency deviations from legislative intent (McCubbins and Schwartz 1984).

Fire-alarm oversight, however, will lower the price legislators can charge for their actions if constituents have intelligent foresight, so they can anticipate monitoring difficulties and the resultant risks they face associated with any administrative form. "In determining a 'political price' or a willingness to pay for a particular statute, private interests take into account the degree of legislative vagueness, the form of the bureaucratic organization charged with implementation and the procedures that organization must adopt" (Shepsle and Weingast 1981, 500). Legislators may want to assign risks associated with bureaucratic drift efficiently, so that they are borne by affected constituencies who can reduce and/or carry them. In turn, affected constituencies will anticipate the ease or difficulty of dealing with implementation costs to them and fight for favorable arrangements—perhaps even in the form of complex procedures—at the time of enactment.

Calvert, McCubbins, and Weingast (1989) place great emphasis on the importance of legislative choice: "[I]f there are any costs to exercising political control . . . then neither latent nor active political control can fully make up for mistakes at the appointment stage" (605). They define bureaucratic discretion as occurring "when the agency succeeds in choosing a policy in line with agency goals, when those goals *differ* from what the executive and legislature expected *at the appointment stage*" (605). Discretion is possible when politicians lack information or the will to monitor agency decision making. *Active* control occurs when agency discretion provokes costly political sanctions. *Latent* control occurs when agency decisions depart from the agency ideal to avoid such sanctions. "The analyst of agency policymaking must ask why the agency has the particular structure, procedures, jurisdiction, and personnel that it does; why particular leaders are in office at any given time; and what unspoken expectations agency personnel might have about the conditions under which their elected overseers might invoke sanctions" (606).[12]

There are various structural means by which an enacting coalition and its supportive constituencies can try to protect and nurture its bureaucratic agents. In Knott and Miller's formulation (1987, 7), "orthodox 'rules' about how to organize a bureaucracy constitute a recognizable 'institution' and . . . this 'institution' [is] chosen at various times and places because a decisive coalition of involved individuals [can] reach agreement on that particular institution."[13] Moe (1989) argues, however, that "legislators tend not to invest in general policy control. Instead, they value 'particularized' control: they want to be able to intervene quickly, inexpensively, and in ad hoc ways to protect or advance the interests of particular clients in particular matters" (278).[14] Moe argues, however,

> The driving force of political uncertainty *causes the winning group to favor structural design it would never favor on technical grounds alone*, designs that place detailed formal restrictions on bureaucratic discretion, impose complex procedures for agency decision making, minimize opportunities for oversight, and otherwise insulate the agency from politics. The group has to protect itself and its agency from the dangers of democracy, and it does so by imposing structures that appear strange and incongruous indeed when judged by almost any reasonable standards of what an effective organization ought to look like (1995, 137; italics added).[15]

Addressing similar issues, Fiorina (1982) and Fiorina and Noll (1978) produced a model of legislative "rent-seeking," in which legislators assign vague administrative responsibilities to agencies and then provide ombudsman services to constituencies, intervening in administrative matters to gain legislative support. Thus, government policies become excessively bureaucratized. (Fiorina provides a variety of models to account for legislative preference for command and control regulation.)[16]

The Consequences of Bureaucratic Control

The success of efforts to control the bureaucracy probably is contingent on a variety of factors. Hammond and Knott (1996, 119) argue that "there are conditions under which an agency will have considerable autonomy and conditions under which it will have virtually none." They review arguments for predominant control of the federal bureaucracy by various actors and conclude that a model that incorporates an explicit theory of how these actors interact to influence bureaucratic behavior is needed. Hammond and Knott construct a model that delineates "the impact that *policy conflict among multiple principals*, just by itself [i.e., ignoring problems of asymmetric information], should be expected to have on political control and agency autonomy" (127). They conclude that, in theory, "autonomy . . . is a contingent matter, and there is no reason to expect all agencies to be constrained to the same degree" (163). Control of the bureaucracy, in other words, is a joint product of collective behavior by a system's actors.

Conflict among actors who attempt to control the bureaucracy can be a gauge or tracking device for authority distribution. "Authority is always redefined by resolution of conflict. . . . Conflict is one response to power allocation, and the cause of reallocation of power" (Rampersad 1978). Through conflict, authority remains in a "continuous process of legitimation" (Rampersad 1978). In combination, such factors may virtually nullify formal authority. Appearance of compliance, not performance, becomes and remains an overriding goal of the organization. Formal authority as a means of governance (i.e., as a solution to problems of coordination and control in achieving the goals of public policy) is notably limited or contingent. When institutional rules are devoid of important resources that the organization (or sector) needs and cannot be easily enforced, they become truly symbolic and have few consequences for the actual delivery of service (Hasenfeld 1992).

The consequences of bureaucratic control as a contingent matter also are reflected in the work of Linder and Peters (1989), who are concerned with "how instruments are viewed by actors inside and outside government who make choices about them and, more specifically, in the criteria used by those actors to judge the suitability of instruments for addressing policy problems" (36). They place particular emphasis on policymakers' perceptions of instrument performance and suitability—an emphasis they call "subjectivist." A central question for them is the extent to which context influences perceptions and choice. Their work attempts to enumerate representative policy instruments and design criteria. "The individuals who comprise an organization are likely to influence the types of instruments that the organization favors" (53). Thus, subjective appraisals of instruments rather than their actual efficacy are important factors in bureaucratic control.

Like legal idealism, under strong assumptions political economy can be used to craft a coherent normative rationale for the particular forms that governance might take in an effort to maintain legitimacy—where legitimacy is based on satisfying interests rather than conforming to abstract principles of legal idealism. In viewing governance as endogenous to processes of public/legislative choice, however, political economy as an analytic framework directs attention to normative issues concerning appropriate means for achieving particular collective purposes and to positive issues relating to explanations for observed relationships between means and ends. As a framework for positive analysis, political economy views legislators, bureaucrats, and judges as actors with interests and goals; their individual pursuit of their goals in the context of the constraints and opportunities they face creates the essential dynamics of politics, policy implementation, and public management. These kinds of models are particularly conducive to prediction and, as such, have been widely used in the study of policymaking and implementation.

The New Institutionalism

Scholars associated with "the new institutionalism" in organizational analysis have tended to focus attention on processes whereby governing relations are socially constructed and sustained. Stone (1980), for example, argues that "the economizing approach may increase our concerns with what is most manipulable—the bureaucratic mechanism; but it may also cause us to ignore *what is more determining—the nature of the larger sociopolitical order*" (32; italics added). Jepperson and Meyer (1991) observe, "[I]nstitutionalism suggests that the interpenetration of environments with organizing (and its actors and technical functions) is especially great with those features of social environments that are themselves highly rationalized, that is, with elements of what was traditionally called 'civil society'" (205). A particular governing order or strategic alignment becomes institutionalized insofar as it conforms to wider societal expectations, even if the transactions environment would justify a different arrangement. In a more instrumental sense, scholars working with socialized-choice paradigms emphasize the relational—as opposed to the goal-seeking or formally legal—elements of governance.

In a classic formulation of the new institutionalism, Meyer and Rowan (1977) argue that "the formal structures of many organizations in post-industrial society dramatically reflect the myths of their institutional environments instead of the demands of their work activities" (341). *Myths* are "rationalized and impersonal prescriptions that identify various social purposes as technical ones and specify in a rule-like way the appropriate means to pursue these technical purposes rationally" (343). Furthermore, myths are "beyond the discretion of any individual participant or organization" and must therefore "be taken for granted as legitimate, apart from evaluations of their impact on work outcomes" (344). Thus, like Moe—but for very different reasons—Meyer and Rowan would predict that bureaucratic structures may bear little relationship to the technical requirements of primary work or to putative substantive outcomes of public policies. Unlike Moe, Meyer and Rowan and other socialized-choice approaches emphasize the "taken for granted" foundations of governing relations.

Of particular interest is Meyer and Rowan's argument that professions represent myths in the sense that "the delegation of activities to the appropriate occupations is socially expected and often legally obligatory over and above any calculations of its efficiency" (Meyer and Rowan 1977, 344). The classification of organizational functions and, presumably, of primary work "are prefabricated formulae available for use by any given organization" (344).[17] Myths become the building blocks for organizational structures; "it takes only a little entrepreneurial energy to assemble them. . . . " (345)—and doing so is essential to ensure legitimacy in the eyes of various constituencies.

As with legalism and political economy, the emergent structures and activities of an organization have legitimizing significance to stakeholders. Structures and processes maintain appearances and validate an organization to the extent that they are viewed as appropriate. In so doing, however, they may create problems for efficient and reliable coordination and control of an organization's tasks. "Categorical rules conflict with the logic of efficiency," Meyer and Rowan argue (1977, 355). Rules may be set at a level of abstraction that make them inappropriate for resolving day-to-day problems, in which case they may come to bear little relationship to the actual work of an organization. What legitimates institutionalized organizations is not the ability to demonstrate efficiency but "the confidence and good faith of their internal participants and their external constituents. . . . Delegation, professionalization, goal ambiguity, elimination of output data, and maintenance of face are all mechanisms for absorbing uncertainty while preserving the formal structure of the organization" (358, citing March and Simon [1958]).

One implication of this argument is that organizations—especially those engaged in similar activities or that compete with one another—tend to become more structurally similar without necessarily becoming more efficient (DiMaggio and Powell 1983, 147). Legitimacy is conferred by the imitation of widely approved forms of organization; appearance may count more than performance (or, rather, appearance and performance are never linked).

By this reasoning, we may observe that organizations are influenced by a process of isomorphism (see chapter 2)—becoming more structurally alike—propelled by three forces: political coercion, self-initiated imitation as a means of reducing uncertainty, and professional domination. DiMaggio and Powell (1983, 157) criticize Meyer and Rowan for failing to ask "how [myths and ceremonies] arise and whose interest they initially serve." The former argue that "policymakers concerned with pluralism [e.g., diversity associated with innovation, creativity, or entrepreneurial leadership] should consider the impact of their programs on the structure of organizational fields as a whole, and not simply on the programs of individual organizations" (158).

A particular way of modeling the social environment in which governing relations are embedded is as a network or an aggregation of networks. In a network analysis, the units of analysis are "the varying interactions that link each pair . . . of social actors in the system" (Knoke 1994, 235). Relationships between each pair of actors have both form and content, whose variations "are expected to explain observed behaviors of individual actors and entire social systems" (235). Subgroups of actors with different relational characteristics might be identified. However, "identifying appropriate relational forms and contents, measuring them properly, determining empirical equivalences, and eliminating redundant and ambiguous relations . . . " (236).

A network analysis might be conducted to discover, for example, "what really goes on inside an organization" (Knoke 1994, 92). The goal might be to identify the prevailing balance between decentralization and integration within an organization (or across organizations) and its implications for organizational performance (Milward and Provan, 1993). Network analysis might be particularly appropriate for analyzing organizations that comprise a network or field of provider organizations (where *network* may be broadly defined to include many different types of coalitions or collaborations with differing structures and/or levels of integration or independence). The study of networks has emphasized that "the role of multiple social actors in networks of negotiation, implementation, and delivery . . . 'governance' requires social partners and the knowledge of how to concert action among them . . . " (O'Toole, personal communication, 5 February 1999).

Theoretical and empirical complications result from the fact that the organizational actors in governance research, which can be modeled as a network, are themselves networks (Stinchcombe 1989, 119). Furthermore, Benz (1993) argues that

> the informal, emerging patterns of interaction which create intraorganizational networks cannot be completely separated from formal structures or decision making and governance. . . . Actors who are not able to coordinate informally can . . . switch to formal mechanisms in order to reach a solution. The availability of this opportunity is often a necessary prerequisite for the working of informal mechanisms (171).

Yet formal and informal coordination mechanisms may be incompatible, each inhibiting the effective operation of the other. "[T]he researcher must look carefully at the dynamics of networks and view them as constantly changing structural patterns" (Benz 1993, 172).

In general, Knoke (1994) observes, "most network theorists and researchers still confine their efforts to the characteristic nodes and ties within one level of analysis. Yet the central challenge for the coming years will be to extend the structural approach to networks crossing multiple levels, showing how they simultaneously condition and constrain one another" (203). Thus, the full potential of network analysis as a method for conducting research on governance involving multiple levels of interaction has yet to be realized.

As an analytic framework, institutional/socialized-choice theories provide richly descriptive interpretations of governance and its consequences that can fill explanatory gaps left by the more parsimonious rational-choice models and yield more insightful explanations of complex interrelationships (e.g., the performance of interorganizational networks and the control of primary work). Despite the rich data that inform institutional analysis, however, ruling out alternative explanations for observed relationships often is difficult. In principle, for example, it may be difficult to distinguish a system in efficient equilibrium from an inefficient one that is institutionalized or rationalized to maintain legitimacy. As Benz (1993) suggests, a solution might be to model socialized and hierarchical relationships as potentially complementary or competitive and test for their relative influence.

Notes

1. For a survey of definitions of "institutions," see Williamson (1995), 211. By the definition above, institutions are synonymous with "structures"; see Scott (1998), 17.
2. On repeated game equilibria, see note 13. Empirical support for such notions is provided by Ostrom et al. (1994).
3. The new institutionalism in organizational analysis—a product, by and large, of sociological scholarship—attempts to interpret the emergence and persistence of formal organizations such as those associated with the administrative state, though without offering an explicit, actor-based theory of governmental organizations (an observation that also is true for older sociological accounts of bureaucracy). See Jepperson and Meyer (1991).
4. Economists also use the term *mechanism* to characterize specific techniques—such as contract design when adverse selection is the issue, procedures for disclosure of information, rules governing decision making, and the like—that are intended to achieve particular results or results that have desirable properties (Kreps 1990; Moe 1995). Thus, *mechanism* is synonymous with the term *instrument*.
5. Institutions may be interpreted more formally as "equilibria in repeated games"—that is, as "regularities in recurrent social situations such that the regularities are common knowledge among the participants, each participant expects that everyone else will conform to the regularities, and it is in everyone's interest to conform to the regularities if everyone else conforms to them" (Weimer 1995, 5, citing Schotter 1981).
6. The "tremendous value, wide availability, and coercive power of public authority . . . are essentially absent from the marketplace" (Chubb and Moe 1990, 30).

7. Per E. E. Schattschneider's (1975) classic dictum: Politics is the mobilization of bias.

8. Fiorina (1982) distinguishes between command and control regulation—which requires a bureau empowered to issue administrative directives—and regulation through statute and the legal process, which requires no bureau but resorts to the legal process for enforcement. Choice is of form (legal versus administrative), and instruments (command and control versus incentive-based mechanisms). Compare Ingram's (1990) typology of statutory structures and Heckathorn and Maser's (1987) application of transactions cost economics.

9. Why, then, do institutions change? Knight (1992) offers a political theory: Institutions reflect the bargaining power of relevant interests. One prediction is that the bargaining process will lead to growing asymmetries in bargaining power over time unless exogenous changes in bargaining power occur.

10. Hill (1985) shows that two conditions that permit stable coalitions to be built in legislatures do not, in and of themselves, ensure stable policy outcomes: The legislature may choose not to legislate on a particular dimension—possibly because it lacks jurisdiction—or "Responsibility for determining the ultimate policy point, that is, for choosing a point on the legislatively ignored dimension, is deliberately transferred to the implementing agency" (277).

11. F. Thompson (1993, 313) cites literature proposing that there are *ex post* tendencies toward the elaboration of rules: threatening situations, abuse, failure-induced standardization, rulemaking, and centralization of authority. Downs (1967) makes the same point in his laws of control duplication and ever-expanding control.

12. A shared authority arrangement can be one response to an organization's or system's plurality of interests; such an arrangement results in certain interdependencies. For example, interdependencies may involve many decisions divided into several parts, with each part having a different locus of authority, or one decision comprising several smaller decisions. We discuss J. Thompson's (1967) typologies of interdependence in chapter 4.

13. One formal approach to this question is derived from political economy. Institutional choice can be modeled as the equilibrium of a repeated game. Because such games have multiple equilibria, players "may solve the coordination problem that players face in reaching an equilibrium by focusing their attention on a particular one" (Weimer 1995, 6, paraphrasing Miller 1992).

14. Compare Mayhew (1974). Related to this argument is a political theory of property rights: According to Riker and Sened (1991), in addition to scarcity, potential rightsholders desire the rights, rulemakers desire to recognize the rights, and those constrained by the rights respect them (Weimer 1995, 7).

15. Compare Moe's (1995) discussion of explicit techniques on pp. 137–38.

16. See Sunstein's (1990) critique of rent-seeking explanations: "[T]o collapse all political behavior into the category of 'rent-seeking' is grotesquely to devalue the activities of citizenship" (305).

17. These myths typically are reified by lobbying and profession-based interest groups.

4

Organizational and Technical Governance

Governing relations created at the institutional level emerge in the form of the executive structures of governments—a collection of hierarchical but interrelated organizational units and subunits (bureaus, departments, commissions, agencies, local offices, and the like)—together with the rules and resources that enable and create interdependence and constrain their actions. Diver (1981) characterizes the policymaking process as "the reconciliation and elaboration of lofty values into operational guidelines for the daily conduct of society's business" (393). The greater the extent of conflict within an enacting coalition, the less the chance that the technical rationality of and effectiveness of agency operations will have been the objectives of legislative choice.

One implication of such a process is that any given public bureau is mandated to pursue multiple goals within complex structures that may not be well suited to achieving public policy mandates. Such administrative organizations cannot be regarded, to use Diver's expression, as "realizations of a single abstraction" or logic, such as providing a social safety net for vulnerable people or balancing benefits and costs in improving air and water quality (Diver 1981, 394). The problem thus created, as Tirole (1994) points out, is twofold. First, "several dimensions of performance are, unlike profit or cost, hard to measure" (3). Second, "the multiplicity of goals raises the issue of their weights" (4). The result, "a noisy observation of managerial performance[,] reduces the efficacy of formal incentive schemes" (4). For these reasons, public bureaucracies as the resultants of legislative choice typically are what Tirole terms *low-powered incentive systems* that are not governed exclusively or even primarily by a core substantive or economic logic.

How do administrative agencies or programs so constructed affect the ways in which the primary work of government is performed? Are problems of policy direction and control and of organizational performance ameliorated or exacerbated at the managerial and technical levels of government? What does the functioning of low-powered incentive systems contribute to policy and program implementation?

The Organizational (Managerial) Level

A logic of governance that is based in political economy features formal and informal structures that predispose action. Within this logic, the study of public management is concerned with action itself: the discretionary behavior of actors in managerial roles subject to the constraints of formal authority.[1] The need for management arises under three conditions: when an enacting coalition has explicitly delegated the "figuring out" of appropriate action to executive agencies; when there is ambiguity in the mandate, providing opportunity (intended or unintended) for managers to figure things out; and when fulfilling legislative or administrative objectives requires judgment in applying rules and standards in particular cases. Because explicit or implicit delegations are the rule, there is almost always a role for management; therefore, managerial behavior is almost always a factor in government performance. How much of a factor, however, and compared to what? An integrating logic that takes into account the wider view of governance regimes in which management is embedded is imperative to the viability of research on the contributions of public management to good government.

Two distinct or paradigmatic approaches to public management may be identified within this logic of governance. First, public managers may optimize outcomes within a given system of formal mandates and constraints. This essentially short-term view of public management emphasizes the quotidian, repetitive aspects of managerial roles and is apt to feature the psychology, strategies, and political tactics of management. A second approach regards public managers as shaping formal mandates—as proactive participants in coalition politics who represent elected executives or agency constituencies. This view is implicit in the notion of "iron triangles" and issue networks.[2] In the literature on social control, this paradigm is implicit in the notion of bureaucracy as active in creating or distorting governing relations. This longer-term view broadens the subject of public management to the wider domain of governance and administrative control of bureaucracy and broadens the content of public management research to include the design of governance arrangements.

For public management research in the context of a logic of governance, the challenge is to explain government results, outcomes, impacts, or performance in ways that allow for the separate identification of governance arrangements and of public management. That is, the problem is separating how the deck is stacked from how managers figure things out and exercise discretion within a governance arrangement.[3]

The Economics of Public Management

Although public bureaucracies may be low-powered incentive systems, a central question is whether incentives are operative in regulating action and judgment at the managerial level. Public-choice scholars generally are inclined to believe that legislative resort to *ex ante* and *ex post* controls constrains agency action formally and informally (Noll and Weingast 1991). More institutionally inclined scholars tend to locate considerable autonomy at the managerial level, to the point where bureaucracy is seriously beyond control (e.g., Gruber 1987).

A related question concerns the extent to which incentives can be employed at the managerial level to control and direct activities at the primary work level. Here, too, opinion is divided. Some scholars regard "street-level bureaucrats" as virtually beyond the control of public managers; others see public managers as stifling creativity, imagination, and competence at the primary work level. Principal-agent theory, transaction cost analysis, and collective action theory can elucidate alternative perspectives on this issue.

Principal-agent theory regards organizations as bundles of explicit and implicit contracts that define the relationship between principals and the agents who take actions on their behalf. These relationships may be multi-tiered. For example, principals may be legislators or executives (elected or appointed), and agents may be executives, public employees, grantees, or vendors. Agents in one setting may be principals in other relationships. Problems arise when principals and agents have different information and when their respective interests conflict.

In some cases, the problem is that the principal cannot observe (or accurately interpret) the agent's action but observes some consequence or outcome that may depend as well on factors other than the agent's action. This problem—known as moral hazard or hidden action—may be especially troublesome in the public sector because not only is inferring effort on the basis of outcomes more difficult; observing or evaluating outcomes also is difficult. Incentives (contractual or other) that are designed to align an agent's action with a principal's goals will be more potent if an observed outcome is a relatively accurate indicator of the agent's action.

Another form of information asymmetry arises when an agent has some private information of value to the principal, and the principal must design some mechanism to induce the agent to reveal the information. Dixit (1999) describes government procurement contracting as an important practical example of this problem. A firm knows its own costs, and the government could secure a better price for the goods or services produced by the firm if it also had this information. The government can induce the firm to reveal its costs by offering alternative contract choices. If truthful revelation is in the best interest of the agent, or if the principal can induce the agent to voluntarily act in the principal's interest, the agent will directly divulge the information to the principal—a situation known in the literature as "incentive compatibility" (e.g., see Laffont and Tirole 1993).

A third problem that is particularly prominent in public-sector principal-agent relationships is the need for costly verification when an agent can observe some outcome more efficiently than the principal and may benefit from misrepresenting the outcome. Adverse selection is distinguished from costly verification in that the agent has the pertinent private information before entering into a contract with the principal, whereas the information advantage in the costly verification case occurs after a contract is negotiated. The principal's problem is determining the frequency or level of auditing necessary to achieve truthful revelation at the lowest possible cost.

An important question for the study of governance is whether managers or other organizational actors possess effective tools to address these problems and whether—in line with our discussion of legislative choice—public authority assists or inhibits their efforts. Multiple principals, multiple tasks with unclear outcomes, minimal competition, and agents whose primary loyalty is to a union or professional group characterize public-sector bureaucracies and confound principal-agent relationships. These problems make the design of efficient, incentive-compatible, and enforceable contracts considerably more challenging, if not infeasible.

Principal-agent models rely on monetary incentives to overcome problems of information asymmetry and incentive incompatibility. In multi-task environments such as public bureaucracies, however, attempts to employ formal monetary incentives run afoul of the tension between measurable and unmeasurable goals (Holmstrom and Milgrom 1991). For example, the concept of "service" involves measurable and unmeasurable elements: Services for deinstitutionalized mentally ill individuals involve medication prescription, which is measurable, and medication management subtleties, which are not. Contractual arrangements that focus on the measurable elements of service will lead to neglect of unmeasurable elements, possibly jeopardizing the overall quality of agency performance. Furthermore, because observing outcomes in a multi-task environment and accurately appraising agents' contributions to them is difficult, incentives that are designed to influence bureaucrats' actions are expected to have negligible effects. Principals may find it more efficient to rely on traditional supervision, employer-employee understandings, and trust—in effect, to rely on incomplete contracts—to ensure incentive compatibility between principals and agents.

One promising application of principal-agent logic involves establishing incentives that are based on the relative performance of or managed competition among multiple providers, who compete to achieve state-defined performance goals (Mookherjee 1984).[4] The "tournament-style" performance incentive system utilized by some states in Job Training Partnership Act programs (Courty and Marschke, forthcoming) is a clear example of this approach. Dixit

(1999) argues that competition can provide sharper incentives for public agencies, although the problem that multiple dimensions of services or outcomes typically are not all observable may again distort these incentives. Thus, the use of managed competition requires solutions to multi-task performance measurement problems.[5]

Other approaches to coordination may take the form of mandated planning and other mechanisms, such as network participation, that may seem inexpensive because of reliance on peer monitoring rather than state surveillance (Lynn 1996b). Such arrangements—termed induced or delegated cooperation (Itoh 1991, 1992, 1993)—are attempts to solve the team production problem: the temptation to "free ride" by members of a team who are rewarded on the basis of joint performance (Holmstrom 1982). Agents often can be induced to behave as a group, engaging in side contracting with each other. This process need not turn into collusion against the principal; the free rider problem can be resolved via mutual monitoring and peer pressure. Principals may benefit by delegating to agents the arrangement of cooperation among them. The principal must make the agents responsible for each other's outcomes—ruling out relative performance contracting. The agents engage in the kind of contracting on the side that the principal cannot incorporate into a contract (Tirole 1988).

Regarding the potential for bilateral principal-agent contracts to solve incentive incompatibility problems, Arrow (1985) calls attention to "the cost of specifying complex relationships," the variety and ambiguity of mechanisms for monitoring contractual relations, and the fact that monetary incentives must compete with "a whole world of rewards and penalties that take social rather than monetary forms" (49, 50). Actual contractual relations appear to deviate sharply from those predicted by principal-agent theory, Arrow notes—affirming the limited power of the theory in practical applications.[6]

The career concerns of public employees generally are not a strong incentive, either, because the market for their services does not give full credit for good performance or penalize poor performance, measured across multiple goals. Dewatripont, Jewitt, and Tirole (1999) show through formal modeling that career concerns typically are most effective in eliciting good performance when an agency has a mission that focuses on a narrow and unambiguous set of tasks. Professionals can be accorded more autonomy, improving their motivation and sense of control and encouraging them to give their best effort. The more commonly observed multiplicity and vagueness of tasks and outcomes, and the consequent need of multiple principals to impose constraints on the actions of professionals, suggest the likely failure of a career-concerns strategy for influencing performance in public bureaucracies. Thus, bureaucratic agents are more apt to rely on "everyday" or "folk" methods to create perceptions of effectiveness among clients, families, and other stakeholders (Anspach 1991). Bureaucratic agents also have incentives to manipulate the information they distribute to clients, families, and other stakeholders to disguise weaknesses in their operations or induce support from strong, sympathetic members of enacting coalitions.

The national campaign to "reinvent government" requires government agencies to measure outcomes, while pledging to reward "results, not rules" (Gore 1995). Principal-agent theory and its extensions, as well as recent research on the implementation of the Government Performance and Results Act (Radin 2000), suggest that the probability of this initiative's success is low in many agencies. Theory predicts that performance-based incentives are most likely to work well where agent performance is easily measured. Yet many government agencies more closely resemble Wilson's (1989) coping organizations, in which neither actions nor outcomes are clearly observed and performance measures are more likely to promote conflict than coherence about agency goals.

The concept of *transaction costs* also focuses on contracts. Unlike agency theory, a transaction costs approach assumes that contracts are incomplete because not all contingencies can be anticipated (i.e., bounded rationality) and enforcement is imperfect (i.e., detecting and punishing noncompliance is costly). The sources of transaction costs include investments in preparations for contracting, the costs of bargaining, and the risks of noncompliance and forced renegotiation (Heckathorn and Maser 1987).

In Williamson's formulation (1975, 1995), incorporating transaction costs into calculations of the putative net benefits of exchange affects the choice of organizational forms that govern the exchange. In particular, it leads to the rational creation of hierarchical organizations (and incomplete contracts) in lieu of markets (and complete contracts) (Heckathorn and Maser 1987).

In their version of transaction cost economics, Milgrom and Roberts (1990) emphasize the short-term bargaining costs associated with using markets to carry out transactions among independent agents. Within private firms, "influence costs" arise when individuals seek to influence firm decisions for their private benefit. These costs, which comprise the opportunity costs of the effort to influence decisions and the inefficiency that results, are an important drawback of centralized control and help to explain why "integrated internal organization does not always supplant market relations between independent entities" (58) and "bureaucratic politics" seems to be prevalent in public agencies, where control of exceedingly valuable property rights is at stake.

The concept of *collective action* can be used to show how incentive and compliance problems arise within organizations. For organizational improvements that are indivisible and nonexcludable (i.e., organizational collective goods), any employee has an incentive to free ride on the contributions of others. To individual employees of a public agency, for example, an expansion of the agency's budget or an improvement in its reputation for efficiency may constitute collective goods rather than personally appropriable benefits. Dunleavey (1991) argues that an agency's employees will contribute greater effort toward improvements in their "private" well-being (e.g., improved career prospects or working conditions) than toward collective benefits such as improved efficiency of service delivery or a favorable reputation for reliability among agency contractors.

The existence of organizational collective goods leads to distinctive "bureau-shaping strategies" on the part of employees at various levels: internal reorganizations, transformation of internal work practices, redefinitions of relationships with external "partners" to reduce uncertainty, competition with other bureaus, load-shedding, and contracting out. Indeed, "there are strong internal pressures for facilitating changes which are popularly interpreted as externally imposed. . . . " (Dunleavey 1991, 236), such as contracting out or privatization. For senior officials of public agencies, activities such as managing contracts that shift risks and liabilities to external agents and increasing the professionalization of a small core staff may be more rewarding than assuming responsibility for lower-level employees. Thus, officials may advocate privatization despite the opposition of lower-level employees, who fear loss of control and perquisites and can be expected to be reluctant implementers.

Collective action problems inside organizations, which often tend to become concentrated at middle management levels, therefore may be an important source of goal displacement and incentive incompatibility that adversely affect organizational performance. They weaken the power of legislated incentives.

Within the theoretical framework of political economy, public organizations are embedded in an economy of incentives. The units of analysis are individual actors, who are assumed to be rational. Organizational power is largely endogenous, derived from explicit, implicit, and unintended delegations of authority by political actors to administrative actors, who are subject to political sanction.

Socialized Choice at the Managerial Level

Arrow's (1985) reference to social rewards and penalties evokes the wide-ranging organization literature that regards managerial and organizational behavior in essentially noneconomic terms, offering possibilities for extending the scope of explanatory models. In socialized-choice frameworks, public organizations are regarded as enmeshed in—in fact, as constituting—networks of communications and resource exchange relationships that rely on cooperation and trust. The units of analysis are organizations, organizational units, social categories of actors, or the networks linking them. Socialized-choice approaches emphasize the cooperative, voluntary, and value-based origins of behavior as more influential—and a more normatively appropriate source of explanations for organizational impact and performance—than the interest-based behavior featured in economic models (Perrow 1986; Sunstein 1990; Ghoshal and Moran 1996).

Socialized-choice approaches have generated a variety of seemingly interrelated concepts and approaches that can extend the reach of empirical governance research. These concepts include embeddedness, power, organizational culture, leadership, and managerial capacity.

The *embeddedness* of organizations in relational networks may contribute significantly to governing relations and have a decisive effect on performance. Achieving the goals of human services policies, for example, typically requires lateral cooperation among numerous, diverse organizational actors. Particular actors or coalitions may favor cooperation to ensure *conceptual control* of policy implementation. That is, the goal is to achieve a style of service delivery that exhibits certain abstract properties such as "comprehensiveness," "continuity of care," "integration," or "community involvement."

Alternatively, the impetus for horizontal cooperation may arise from the technical requirements of service delivery, which requires contributions from a variety of autonomous actors. Technical interdependence may be classified as one or more of three distinct types: pooled (in which each actor "renders a discrete contribution to the whole and . . . is supported by the whole"), sequential (in which actors depend on each other in identifiable sequences), and reciprocal (in which actors produce inputs for each other) (Thompson 1967, 53–54). Reciprocity may pose the most difficult challenges, in part because it depends most on establishing trust.

Agency and group position and influence within the relevant communications and exchange networks form the basis for *power*. Power, which derives from social embeddedness, affects an organization's or a social group's responsiveness to governing relations and to specific mechanisms, mandates, or inducements that originate at the public choice level (Scott 1998). Lack of responsiveness by bureaucracy to its political and social environment underlies stereotypical complaints about bureaucratic turf protection, rigidity, "red tape," and resistance to change. Weber, a sociologist, regarded the power of bureaucratic organizations as flowing from their expertise. "More and more the specialized knowledge of the expert became the foundation for the power position of the officeholder" (Weber 1946, 235; quoted in Scott 1998, 334), and power shifts from the people to administrative elites (Michels 1949; cited in Scott 1998). This shift of power may lead to significant goal displacement as public officials reshape governing relations to their liking.

Furthermore, public organizations may use their power to exert substantial influence on policy making. Skocpol (1985) emphasizes the power of public organizations and their officers to initiate proposals and action. The state, she says, is "a set of organizations through which collectivities of officials may be able to formulate and implement distinctive strategies and policies" (20–21). Public organizations and their leaders "affect political culture, encourage some kinds of group formation and collective political actions (but not others), and make possible the raising of certain political issues (but not others)" (21).[7] Moreover, the serendipitous convergence of separable streams of activity—problem identification, policy advocacy, and political opportunism—can enhance an administrator's power to initiate action (Kingdon 1984). The processes by which these convergences occur are highly complex and have few predictable or controllable factors (Lynn 1987).

Informal social systems within organizations may influence power or control relationships—and consequently governance. For example, Ouchi (1979) has characterized certain organizations as "clans," in which control is exercised through informal social systems. "The functions of socialization," he argues, "are similar in professions, cultures, and clans. . . . Clearly a clan is more demanding than either a market or a bureaucracy in terms of the social agreements which are prerequisite to its successful operation" (837, 838).

Of particular interest to governance research are specific aspects of the internal environment—the *organizational culture* or climate—that managers or leaders of an organization may influence, as well as the relationships between culture and performance.[8] Culture may be considered a "system of shared values (that define what is important) and norms that define appropriate attitudes and behaviors for organizational members (how to feel and behave)" (O'Reilly and Chatman 1996, 160). Definitions of climate have included organizational participants' *perceptions* about the work situation as well as *sets of conditions* such as coordination or involvement in decision making.[9] Empirical research on organizational culture and its relationship to performance often focuses on for-profit organizations. Wilson (1989), however, discusses organizational culture in public organizations, where "an agency's culture is produced in part by . . . the predispositions of members, the technology of the organization, and the situational imperatives with which the agency must cope" (93).

A common hypothesis is that a "strong" culture is positively related to organizational effectiveness; Saffold (1988) challenges this approach, however—concluding that "first, culture can shape organizational processes, but processes also act to create and modify culture. Culture's contribution to performance is a consequence of this ever-evolving interaction. Second, it is likely that culture's link to performance is considerably less straightforward than many studies imply" (553). Other studies have attempted to investigate the relationship between culture and performance, using "strong culture" models (Kotter and Heskett 1992) and structural models that disaggregate and specify components of culture (Denison 1990; Marcoulides and Heck 1993; Denison and Mishra 1995). The empirical results of Marcoulides and Heck (1993) suggest a view of organizational management that is oriented toward employees and is evaluation-based to promote organizational performance—a perspective that is consistent with human resource views of management.

The popular literature and some academic literature often posit a link between organizational culture and *leadership* (e.g., Schein 1992). The potential contributions of leadership to governing relations and organizational performance encompass a lengthy and diverse literature.[10] Yet leadership remains an elusive notion—more an explanation for success *after the fact* than a quality or skill that can be identified *before the fact* and used in planning. For example, Meyer (1979) showed, according to Rainey (1997), that "those in stronger positions politically—those who are elected or are career civil servants, rather than political appointees—show more ability to defend their agency against pressures for change in structure and against the loss of units to other agencies, apparently because of their greater ability to draw on support from political networks" (Rainey 1997, 180).

In contrast to such views, skeptics of the contributions of leadership assert that public officials "make their mark in inches, not miles" (Kaufman 1981, 135). A more optimistic—yet still qualified—notion is that leadership is a result of the right fit between the individual in a potential leadership role and the demands of the particular circumstances of that role: "[A]chievement is favored by a good match of individual skill and the organizational task attempted," and "the favorable match of skill to task must be reinforced by favorable historical conditions if there is to be a significant historical achievement" (Doig and Hargrove 1987, 13, 14). Distinguishing between transformational and transactional leadership also may be important (Burns 1978) for understanding the contributions of leadership to governance.

The idea that leadership is best understood as a configuration of distinct elements also suggests a more socialized view of governance. In a study that sought to identify factors that account for variations in the effectiveness of individual agency managers, Lynn

(1981, 1987) identifies four independent variables that contribute to managerial accomplishment: three individual-level variables— skill, personality, and design (i.e., a manager's goals and the means chosen to achieve them)—and one institutional-level variable—opportunity (e.g., organizational structures and processes and authorizing statutes). Lynn concludes that these variables interact in complex ways but that the choice of a design or model that fits the opportunity seems to be more important than the singular influence of general managerial skill and personality. That is, even mediocre managers might "pick the right model" and be regarded as successes in their particular circumstances. Thus, leadership is contextual, not absolute: the right person in the right place at the right time. Even though leadership may matter to organizational success, many other things matter too, including appropriate governance structures and adequate managerial capacity. Leaders create and benefit from supportive structures and administrative technologies.

Management capacity arguably might be a "platform" for leadership, management, and organizational performance. There has been little intellectual development of—but substantial disagreement about—the concept of management capacity, however. Public management research tends to focus on individual managers, whose activities are investigated primarily in case studies. Occasionally, reference is made to management teams or to "managerial culture." The concept of capacity goes well beyond that limited conception to encompass, for example, information, planning, systems, evaluation, and coordination and integration (i.e., the means whereby managers do their work). We tend to think that managerial capacity exists when structures, information, and internal processes enable managers to pursue their objectives successfully.

Because managerial capacity is a multi-dimensional concept, it is hard to define—and even harder to measure. Traditional approaches to public administration emphasize appropriate and competent functional specialization, on the assumption that a good organization will exhibit good management. To be effective, however, the contemporary public manager must be proactive and adaptable to new and rapidly changing circumstances while ensuring reliability of service and satisfaction of stakeholder expectations. A more advanced concept of management capacity is needed to accommodate this more complex managerial role (Ingraham and Donahue 2000).

Finally, the *nature of primary work* affects strategies at a public manager's disposal: Different types of organizations are likely to require different types of public management (Wilson 1989). *Production* organizations, in which both work and outcomes are observable, give managers "an opportunity to design . . . a compliance system to produce an efficient outcome" (159–60). *Procedural* organizations, in which work is observable but outcomes are not, make granting discretion problematic. *Craft* organizations, in which activities are difficult to observe but outcomes are easy to evaluate (e.g., the U.S. Forest Service), enable managers to be "goal-oriented" and grant employees discretion in day-to-day activities. *Coping* organizations, in which neither work nor outcomes can be observed or evaluated (e.g., public schools), render "effective management . . . almost impossible" (175). In coping organizations, there will be a strong temptation for managers to focus on what is most easily measured and little incentive for them to delegate to subordinates.

The Technical (Primary Work) Level

Numerous veins of organizational theory have emphasized the importance of a construct that scholars have called the technical core, the task environment, core competencies, or—the term we employ—*primary work*. With respect to research on governance, the issue at this level concerns the effects on outcomes or performance that originate in (can be ascribed causally to) the actions and judgments of first-level workers and their supervisors rather than in governing relations established at higher levels.

Many scholars have noted the significance of this level of governance. Thompson (1967) calls attention to the importance of "effective performance of the technical function—the conduct of classes by teachers, the processing of income tax returns and the handling of recalcitrants by the bureau, the processing of material and supervision of these operations in the case of physical production" (10). A. K. Rice argues that every system has a primary task it must perform in order to survive. Primary tasks are the basis of primary work systems, the source of legitimacy and meaning for the organization's employees (Lynn 1987, 245). Wilson (1989) refers to primary workers as "operators": the people who do the work "that justifies the existence of the organization—teachers in a school, doctors and nurses in a hospital, patrol officers and detectives in a police department, . . . grant-givers in a funding agency. . . . " (34). Scott (1998) refers to an organization's "core technology" or "technical core"—the arrangements associated with performing "one or more central sets of tasks around which an organization is constructed" (196). In a study of the administrative behavior of five bureau chiefs, Kaufman (1981) observes that "each of the bureaus was in charge of a distinctive core program defining its identity and character. . . . The core program was the hallmark, the *sine qua non*. . . . [It] was not significantly manipulable by the chiefs. . . . The core programs were highly stable" (159). Glisson (1992) defines the "core technology" of a human services organization as including "the problem or need addressed by the service, the clients who receive the service, the interventions that are applied, and the skills and equipment used in these interventions" (186).

In Thompson's (1967) model, "The primary exigencies to which the technical suborganization is oriented are those imposed by the nature of the technical task, such as the materials which must be processed and the kinds of cooperation of different people required to get the job done effectively" (10). An organization will seek to remove as much uncertainty as possible from its technical core (Thompson 1967, 11), thereby minimizing the disruptive consequences of these exigencies.[11] Thus, one would expect the character of an organization's primary work to have a determining influence on the organization's structures—its arrangements for coordinating (and shielding from uncertainty) the various participants involved in primary work. That is, agency structures should facilitate the effective performance of primary work and induce stability. Scott (1998) argues that "what is the best or most appropriate structure depends—is contingent—on what type of work is being performed and on what environmental demands or conditions confront the organization" (228) Following Thompson, Scott embraces the view that organizations seek to protect or buffer their technical core.

Critics of contingency theory—the argument that the task environment of an organization shapes its internal structure—make a variety of arguments that question the deterministic influence of technology on structure. Identical technologies (e.g., the introduction of tranquilizing drugs into hospital treatment, interactive computer technologies into schools, or computerized databases into child protection services) may lead to different structural outcomes, depending on specific contextual factors—including the strength of myths and ceremonies, the varying expertise of personnel, the path-dependent nature of interactions, influences originating in the organizational field, and the like. Thus, although there may be a general relationship between primary work and organizational form, one should expect to find considerable variation across organizations and contexts.

One source of variation may be the *buffering* or insulating tendency across organizations (Moe 1989). To reduce political uncertainty, bureaucrats employ various means: promoting professionalization; formalizing and judicializing their decision procedures; basing decisions on technical expertise, operational experience, and precedent; monopolizing information. Moe argues, however, that "it would be a mistake to regard the agency as a truly independent force" (284) because various groups and political executives at institutional and managerial levels compete to control the incremental process of structural change and the allocation of scarce resources among tasks and priorities.

How much *power* over organizational performance, then, do front-line workers actually have? Mechanic (1962) argues that personal power, as opposed to formal authority, may be considerable at the lower levels of an organization—particularly for lower-level employees with longevity, expertise, energy and purpose, and centrality to the operation. They derive their power from control over access to persons, information, and instrumentalities of administration. Furthermore, Mechanic argues, lower-level participants achieve power by circumventing structure.

Primary workers also have considerable influence over public policy implementation when their jobs involve substantial discretion, when there are multiple objectives, and when changes in established practices are sought (Lipsky 1980). Building on this insight, Brodkin's (1986) case study of public welfare administration articulates the concept of "policy politics." Political conflict is transferred, or migrates from, legislative and electoral institutions to administrative agencies; the former thereby conceding at least partial control over policy definition as well as implementation to bureaucratic agents. As a result, the consequences might well depart from the objectives of enacting coalitions.[12]

The Dunleavey (1991) model of bureau-shaping behavior calls attention to the importance of preferences prevailing at the technical levels of organizational activity. Dunleavey (202) identifies aspects of work that personnel in an agency value positively and negatively. The potential for conflicts of interest and agency problems is clear from the different valuations made by personnel with different roles and at different levels in the organization. At the primary work level in particular, we encounter special issues associated with the control of professional work.

For example, the generic functions associated with primary work in human services agencies—based on the stage of client involvement with the service—include selection, classification, transformation, and certification (Hasenfeld 1983). "Practice ideologies have self-confirming features [and are] resistant to change or objective assessment"; they are "abstract," yet they "reduce uncertainty" (Rapoport 1960, cited in Hasenfeld 1983, 119). Scott (1998) calls attention to Ouchi's concept of the clan (i.e., substitution of informal, interpersonal controls for formal authority) as a solution to hierarchical failure when complexity and uncertainty are extreme. Peer expectations and pressures affect not only worker effort but worker perceptions of what the job is; such expectations are resistant to change (Wilson 1989, 48).

In a related vein, Scott (1998) argues that "technical complexity does not invariably give rise to greater complexity of structure; it may give rise instead to greater 'complexity' of the performer" (255) (i.e., professional service providers). This complexity is influenced in part by the political and social power of the professional group. Scott distinguishes between autonomous professional arrangements and heteronomous arrangements, in which "professional employees are clearly subordinated to an administrative framework" (255). An example is teachers, who are given considerable discretion over instructional techniques. The problem of measuring "good education" "makes it difficult or impossible for education administrators to know what they are doing—and their controls, as a result, threaten to be ill suited to the ends they want to achieve" (Chubb and Moe 1990, 36). However, "the people at the bottom of the hierarchy do not have a serious measurement problem. . . . The organization as a whole has a serious measurement problem only to the extent that there are people at the top who try to control the people at the bottom" (37).

An argument we have encountered already is that an enacting coalition may favor structures that cannot be rationalized on technical grounds. The implication is that the primary work of a public agency may be as much a reflection of statutory mandates as of the nature of the needs being addressed.[13] Statutory mandates often conflict with professionally derived treatment theories unless (as may be the case with medical care) the relevant professional groups dominate the enacting coalition. Stakeholders differ in the emphasis they place on efficiency, access, and quality of services (Black 1986). The state and third-party payers seek efficiency (Black's "corporate rationalist" model) and efficiency-enhancing lower recidivism rates—the latter implying greater service effectiveness and, in turn, enhancing legitimacy. Landlords and community members seek more "quality" of the kind that makes mental health patients/ex-patients manageable by keeping them in "mental patient roles" (drugged, nonautonomous)—in other words, social control (Black 1986). Stakeholders with the greatest commitment to human functioning—clients, families, and parents—often have the least power, however.

Thus, adaptations of primary work to contextual factors should be especially significant in organizations that are responsive to and shaped by public authority. As Moe (1995) and others have argued, public bureaucracies do not arise from voluntary contractual relationships; they are a product of interest group-dominated politics. Enacting coalitions are apt to become deeply interested in the details of administration, including the definition and performance of primary work.

Institutional political economy provides a useful framework for viewing any series of interactions, programs, or arrangements as part of a larger system of laws, rules, judicial precedents, and administrative practices that constrain, prescribe, and enable government activity. Furthermore, such a framework helps organize and integrate potential contributions to the study of governance from many different disciplines and fields and is essential to achieving theoretically sophisticated and empirically rigorous understanding of governance.

In summary, we urge the use of an approach to governance research that recognizes the interrelationships among institutional, organizational, and primary work domains of governance; between governance and outcomes or performance; and between performance and results and the political preferences of citizens and stakeholders. This "logic of governance" can serve as the foundation for the empirical study of governance and the collection and analysis of data.

Notes

1. A managerial role incorporates formal authority over subordinate actors, multiple tasks, and programmed and unprogrammed activity, as well as an opportunity to exercise judgment in selecting actions carried out by others.

2. The view of public managers as proactive participants in coalition politics is less well-developed in the literature than the first type of approach we describe. An exception is Kingdon (1984).

3. The manager's formal role in deck-stacking is a separate matter—relatively easy to depict in spatial models but difficult to study empirically.

4. The effectiveness of such mechanisms is suggested by experimental evidence. See the discussion of research by Nalbantian and Schotter (1997) in chapter 7.

5. Smith and Lipsky (1993) argue that the state co-opts the nonprofit sector in the interest of eliminating agency problems (see also Sabel 1993, 66).

6. Within the principal-agent framework, a low-powered incentive scheme (see discussion earlier in this chapter) is one in which the agent bears only a small fraction of risks associated with agency performance. The existence of monopoly further reduces the power of performance incentives. Furthermore, agents' tastes are heterogeneous and inconsistent over time. Thus, commitment possibilities in the public sector generally are lower than in the private sector. According to the property rights variant of principal-agent theory (Hart 1988), an owner of an asset can skim profits from its use, undetected by the manager who controls it. Ownership by outsiders dulls the incentives of dispossessed managers and workers to use the assets they control efficiently. Thus, creation of property rights is an incentive mechanism: Governments create political property rights.

7. Similarly, highly fluid "issue networks" of emotionally committed and knowledgeable activists may shape public policy (Heclo 1979).

8. Some research traditions consider culture and climate to be unique concepts; we do not attempt here to distinguish between them.

9. This range of constructs has contributed to the sense that climate "includes everything" (Denison 1990, 24). Lack of clear guidance on the measurement of culture and climate is mirrored in their operationalization; see Pfeffer (1997) for a review and critique.

10. There is a meaningful difference between "leading" and "managing": between an emphasis on "doing the right thing" and on "doing the thing right," between focusing on the ends of human activity and focusing on designing and executing the means.

11. Variations in technologies across time or organizations should be associated with variations in the relationships among the three levels of control and among organizations (Thompson 1967, 12).

12. Based on evidence from loosely structured case studies, Handler (1996) adduces a similar concept to account for the tendency to push bureaucratic discretion downward from federal to state and local levels of administration.

13. As Max Boisot has suggested (in private correspondence), private-sector organizations discover and build on their distinctive competencies. In public-sector organizations, distinctive competencies are prescribed by fiat.

5

Designing Research: Applying a Logic of Governance

How can a conceptual logic of governance be translated into designs for empirical research? This translation encounters the generic challenges of social science research, such as the difficulty of accounting for complexity in a reductionist model. Understanding policy effects and public program performance in a context of hierarchical governance systems introduces additional challenges, however. No single, parsimonious theory can account for influences through the hierarchical structure of institutional, organizational, and primary work levels of governance. The value of an integrating logic is even greater, then, for designing research that identifies the determinants of program outcomes with sufficient clarity that the findings will be useful to policymakers and public managers who seek to improve system performance as a whole.

Questions and Issues

Researchers of public-sector activities analyze a vast array of topics—a specific program (e.g., the Job Training Partnership Act), an organization or bureau (e.g., the New York City Agency for Children's Services), or a policy (e.g., family preservation policies). Underlying the substantive focus and driving the analysis are core questions of the form: Why? How? With what consequences? These research questions have many origins:

- Observed facts or descriptive statistics that call for explanation (e.g., variations in performance among schools in a school district)
- Theories that have potentially interesting empirical implications (e.g., do economic incentives alter the behavior of workers or clients?)
- Limitations in the models and methods of other studies that might have distorted their findings and conclusions (e.g., reliance on office-level averages when individual-level data are available)
- The practical needs of policymaking and program administration (e.g., strategies for improving the performance of low performing schools)
- Informal intuitions about causal relationships (e.g., collaboration among actors produces higher performance than uncoordinated action).

Governance research may focus on dependent variables that represent "intermediate" outcomes—such as managerial strategies or teachers' responses to a district-wide policy—or on outcomes or performance, such as:

- organizational outputs (e.g., service levels, patterns of treatment, or unit costs);
- outcomes for individual service recipients or administrative units (e.g., client earnings one year following program exit or student scores on standardized tests); and
- the work products of an intermediate level of administration (e.g., implementation structures, or types of activity such as performance contracts or characteristics of network relationships).

How might researchers design their analyses in ways that more explicitly take into account the many influences implied by the levels of the game described in chapters 3 and 4? The question, outcome, or substantive area of interest may point to particular models, methods, and data that must be considered if causal insights are possible. Theory-based models, applied and interpreted within a broader logic, enhance the chances that empirical research on governance questions of interest can provide robust information for policymaking.

A Reduced-Form Model

In work on the uses and misuses of models and data in the social sciences, Bradley and Schaefer (1998) encourage a cautious assessment of the link between social sciences research and policy making: "[P]olicy making needs to recognize the limits of data and models and use them as fully as possible within these limits" (189). Bradley and Schaefer underscore some of the important benefits of positivist, empirical research—objective inference, more precise empirical distinctions, identification and analysis of error, predictive power, and confidence in research findings—but caution that the realization of these benefits depends on accurate measures of social and human phenomena. Obtaining reliable measures of these phenomena can be extraordinarily difficult in practice, reflecting the complexity of social and human processes and the limitations of one's ability to fully observe and quantify them. For example, measuring and accounting for the influence of politics in local governance processes, the effects of case worker actions on clients' responses to social services, or the role of teachers in raising student achievement may be difficult.

A key to successfully balancing the many considerations at stake in designing research is the power and precision of the theory guiding the work, where "theory" constitutes *explanation,* using either deductive or inductive methods, based on concepts or principles independent of what is observed or explained. Thus, theory encompasses "classifications"—the *ordering* of entities based on their similarities or dissimilarities—or "concepts" (abstract representations). Furthermore, the explanation may be derived deductively or inductively. A researcher may use an organizing framework that uses deductive or *a priori* reasoning and test predictions derived from this reasoning. The researcher may use a logic of explanation that is assumed to be applicable and apply this logic to a policy or situation of interest (the *heuristic* use of theory). Alternatively, the researcher may derive a concept or classification from examination of observations *post hoc,* using inductive reasoning.

Use of theory-based models thus plays an indispensable role in securing understanding of the social phenomena of interest, a convincing conceptualization of their relationships to other measured and unmeasurable factors, and a strong justification for their correspondence to a particular measurement scale. Many theories, of course, are refutable, and there are likely to be some limitations to modeling and measurement that even the most carefully elaborated models cannot overcome. By approaching the complexity of social and human phenomena with theory accompanied by a logic of governance, however, we can enhance the usefulness of research for policy designers who must implement programs and policies in a policy environment that is more complex than any research design can accommodate. An abstract parameterization of a logic of governance provides a framing device for this complexity:

$$O = f(E, C, T, S, M)$$

where[1]

O = outputs/outcomes (individual-level and/or organizational outputs/outcomes)
E = environmental factors
C = client characteristics
T = treatments (primary work/core processes/technology)
S = structures
M = managerial roles and actions.

Previous chapters emphasize the distinction between a logic of governance and the specific theories that researchers use to investigate questions within this logic. By extension, this reduced-form expression is a parameterization of a logic that includes categories of variables that are included *a priori* in any logic or model of governance. It is not a "theory of governance"; it identifies an array of dependent and independent concepts that investigators encounter in empirical governance research, whether they analyze those concepts through lenses of political economy, network analysis, systems models, or institutional approaches such as that of Wilson

Table 5.1. Reduced-Form Logic of Governance

Reduced-form component	Examples of concepts
O = Outputs/outcomes (individual-level and/or organizational-level)	• precisely defined, empirically measured variables • broadly defined, not necessarily client-oriented variables
E = Environmental factors	• political structures • level of external authority/monitoring • performance of the economy • market structure/degree of competition • funding constraints/dependencies • characteristics of eligible or target population • legal institutions/practice • technological dynamism
C = Client characteristics	• client attributes/characteristics/behavior
T = Treatments (primary work/ core processes/ technology)	• organizational mission/objectives • determination of target populations, recruitment or eligibility criteria • program treatment/technology (including scope/intensity of services)
S = Structures	• organization type • level of integration/coordination • centralization of control • functional differentiation • administrative rules/incentives • budgetary allocations • contractual arrangements • institutional culture/values
M = Managerial roles and actions	• leadership practices—characteristics, attitudes, behavior (e.g., innovation and goal-setting, worker motivation, recognition and support, problem solving, and delegation of authority or work tasks) • staff-management relations, communication and decision-making tools and arrangements • professionalism/career concerns • monitoring/control/accountability mechanisms (including performance standards, incentives, and sanctions)

(1989). Table 5.1 lists examples of these reduced-form model components; certainly, there are many other examples.

A complex causal structure undoubtedly underlies the reduced-form components: Interdependencies often exist among (and within) E, C, T, S, O, and M. Many, although not all, social scientists would argue that theory-based empirical research should seek to identify a parsimonious model for estimating key causal relationships. To establish a causal relation, researchers must demonstrate association, or some relationship between cause and effect; isolation, in which the presumed cause is isolated from extraneous influences, confounding variables, and measurement error; and directionality, or the direction of the association (Hoyle 1995). The classic scientific approach to establishing causality is the controlled experiment, in which random assignment to levels of the causal variable produces isolation and allows for the identification of necessary and sufficient conditions for causality.[2] The particular logic, theory, or research design (in the case of randomized experiments) that is applied typically specifies the direction of the association being modeled and measured.

Social scientists and governance researchers are unlikely, however, to come close to attaining controlled, laboratory-like conditions for conducting empirical research. Bradley and Schaefer (1998) argue that there is not "a single situation in the social sciences in which a set of necessary and sufficient causal conditions have been found for an empirically observable phenomena" (162). By extension to governance research, models that focus on particular stages or processes of a governance regime may be informative building blocks for understanding the larger processes of governance, but such models are unlikely to capture adequately the configurational, political, and loosely coupled nature of governance.

The "true" model, of course, may be one in which the marginal effects are zero for some elements represented in the reduced form. There may be theoretical reasons for believing that this is the case, thus excluding these theoretically irrelevant factors from model specifications. Indeed, like natural scientists, social scientists frequently begin the modeling process by assuming or submitting some reasonable evidence that the model accounts for the most influential factors. In addition, researchers commonly assume (implicitly or explicitly) that the influence of unobserved or omitted factors is, on average, small, random, and/or unpredictable—and of no import to the relationships specified in the model. In some studies, researchers attempt to approximate random assignment and eliminate possible sources of systematic bias to justify claims of causality. Making these strong assumptions, particularly in the social sciences, requires a significant amount of detailed information—qualitative as well as quantitative—about the situation being modeled.

Designing governance research involves explaining results, outcomes, impacts, or performance in ways that allow for separate identification of governance arrangements and public management on outcomes of interest and recognize the configurational, political, and loosely coupled character of administration. Ideally, investigators follow the well-traveled paths of theory-based, empirical social science in constructing models such as those we review in chapters 3 and 4, from which they deduce parsimonious causal explanations of program outcomes. They test hypotheses or predictions with a relevant data set (i.e., one that includes appropriate and accurately measured dependent and independent variables).[3] Ultimately, they interpret the results of statistical tests in the context of their models to draw conclusions about correlational or causal relationships between explanatory and outcome variables and about how decision makers can use this knowledge to manage toward higher performance.

In practice, governance research shares with all social sciences research the difficulties of modeling and measuring causal relationships. Placing theory-based research in a logic of governance encourages investigators to provide a broad context for their models and empirical analyses when they draw conclusions from necessarily incomplete data and information. Sorting out and identifying factors over which policymakers and public managers might exercise leverage requires, in addition to good data, the use of appropriate theoretical and statistical models to specify and identify significant causal relationships that link governance and performance.[4] At the very least, investigators who apply a particular theory or set of theories (political economy, socialized choice, or some other logic) to a research question are more likely to produce useful—possibly generalizable—insights, particularly when the relationship is transparent to other levels of the game (institutional, managerial, technical). Such analyses have a higher likelihood of being adapted or tested for robustness by other researchers and being useful to policymakers.

Different Logics

Although our premise is that a logic of governance that is based on positive political economy constitutes a particularly sturdy framework for designing research, careful theorizing is paramount whether the investigator is using a logic of governance based in rational choice, socialized choice, or any other broad approach. In this section, we discuss examples of theory-based empirical work that reflect elements of different logics of governance. Not all make reference to a wider logic. Nonetheless, the studies make explicit or implicit claims about components of the governance regime and thus allow consideration of what the theory or model implies about exogenous factors or about factors that other logics or theories identify as important.

A logic of governance that is based in political economy builds on the individual as the unit of analysis and constrained optimization as the individual's method of choosing. This logic requires investigators to recognize the formally hierarchical, essentially political, and loosely coupled nature of policy enactment and program implementation structures and processes.[5] Moe (1984) succinctly framed the "new economics of organization" for scholars of public bureaucracy; economists such as Tirole (1994), Dixit (1996, 1999), and Williamson (1995, 1997) have made specific attempts to relate the theories of incentives and firm-level behavior to public-sector governance questions across levels of government and within bureaucratic organizations. These works extend the application of political economy theories for understanding public-sector activity more generally, beyond those that focus solely on Congressional roles and actions in shaping public activity. Principal-agent models, transaction costs, incomplete contracts, game theory, and collective action theory (which we discuss in chapter 4) may be adapted to analysis of different levels of governance.

For example, Potoski (1999) tests hypotheses about political control of agency actions through the use of policy analysis requirements, fire alarm oversight, and deck-stacking. Using data from 36 states, Potoski's dependent variables are administrative procedures (policy analysis, oversight, or fire alarm) that state legislatures require for state clean air agencies. Some of these procedures may be considered "environmental factors" in the reduced-form model (i.e., oversight procedures); others may be considered the primary work of the agency (i.e., cost-benefit analysis, economic impact analysis, or consulting with environmental or industry groups). Independent variables include measures of the strength of environmental and industry groups in the state (E or C variables in the reduced form), the complexity of the policy problem (through an interesting operationalization of "entropy"—a type of T variable), political uncertainty (E), and the strength of legislative staff (E). Potoski finds little support for the desk-stacking hypothesis, but he does find that politicians in states with more political uncertainty are more likely to "use policy analysis to hardwire agencies" (634). Furthermore, when policy problems are more complex, politicians grant more autonomy to agency technical experts.

The point of this review is not to categorize the variables used in Potoski's study or any other study; reasonable people could differ concerning categorization of variables in the analysis. The point is that Potoski's study presents clear predictions from political economy literatures and constructs empirical tests of these hypotheses. Mapping the study's variables into the abstract parameterization of a logic of governance also places the study's results within a wider scope. The robustness of Potoski's findings could be tested by using this framework applied to other policy problems, across states or other political units.

Another study that can be placed in a political economy logic of governance is Heinrich's (1999) analysis of the use of performance standards by Job Training Partnership Act (JTPA) local office administrators. Heinrich employs principal-agent literatures on contracting to predict that "if local program administrators are strategically using the information they have obtained through service provider performance reviews, they should base their service provider selection decisions in part on contractors' performance relative to the standards they set" (376). Two dependent variables examined (both O type variables) are the ranking of service providers' performance—as measured against the contract standard for clients' entered employment rate—and the ranking of service providers' cost per job placement performance relative to the maximum cost per placement specified in their contracts. Independent variables include clientele/target population characteristics (E or C variables), types of program activities (e.g., vocational training or remedial education—T or S variables), and service provider performance in the past program year or over time (lagged O variables).

Heinrich finds that agency officials used cost-per-placement standards in making resource allocation decisions, but higher job placement performance was negatively related to those decisions. A broader logic of governance prompts Heinrich to discuss possible explanations for the negative relationship to job placement performance, even though she cannot explicitly model these explanations. These explanations include the limited control that program managers may have over job placement rate performance (compared to control over program costs), political factors that influence selection of providers, the possible overriding importance of a stable system of property rights, the realization of program administrators that job placement performance is a poor proxy for long-run performance, or simply the fact that program managers do not use performance information effectively in making contracting decisions.

Empirical tests of political economy theories are not limited to quantitative analyses: Political economy logics may be reflected in the heuristic use of theories to analyze a small number of cases or situations. For example, Koremenos and Lynn (1996) apply the logic of game theory to analyze the success of Victor Wirth, the director of the Illinois Department of Aging (IDOA). In games at each level of a hierarchy, Koremenos and Lynn broadly define the strategy of *noncooperation* as "emphasizing monitoring and control or formal procedural compliance in behalf of narrowly-defined operational goals" and the strategy of *cooperation* as "behavior that is dedicated to fulfilling the organization's broad mission and that is characterized by openness, trust, and forthrightness" (Koremenos and Lynn 1996, 222–23). Using information from interviews to construct and interpret their model of strategic interactions among IDOA staff, Koremenos and Lynn's interpretation of Wirth's success was necessarily embedded in the internal dynamics of the agency:

> Wirth's problem was noncooperation originating at the top of the agency and institutionalized primarily at the division manager level, from where it was transmitted downward to the field. At lower levels, Wirth had ideological allies whom he could easily mobilize to squeeze division managers into line. This is not a universal principal of public management, however. In a social service agency where noncooperation originates at lower levels, Wirth's walking around nattering about goals might well fail (Koremenos and Lynn 1996, 235).

Empirical studies that build on socialized-choice theories may reflect altogether different logics of governance. A logic grounded in network analysis focuses on multiple actors (organizations) embedded in social relations, where "a fruitful analysis of human action requires us to avoid the atomization implicit in the theoretical extremes of under- and oversocialized conceptions" (Granovetter 1985, 487).[6] Empirical research in public-sector governance that uses the logic of networks might construct interpretations of policymaking that emphasize the centrality of continuing social and political relationships and communication among communities of stakeholders and other actors internal and external to executive agencies. Laumann and Knoke (1987) consider how elite structures affect policymaking activities and construct an

> orienting framework [as] a *set of consequential corporate actors,* each possessing (1) variable *interests* in a range of *issues* in a national policy domain and (2) relevant mobilizable *resources.* These actors are *embedded* within communications and resource exchange *networks.* The flows of specialized communications and resources among the actors enable them to monitor, and to communicate their concerns and intentions in, relevant decision-making *events* that, in turn, have consequences for their interests. These events, both in themselves, as unique historical occurrences, and in their interrelationships, have critical import for explaining the behavior of individual actors and their interaction (Laumann and Knoke 1987, 5).[7]

Empirical investigations that reflect a socialized choice logic of governance, such as Uzzi's (1996) analysis of apparel firms in New York, may find that standard concepts in political economy such as "self-interest maximization, generalized reputation, and repeated-gaming fade into the background, [and] issues of how social relationships promote thick information exchange, rapid and heuristic decision-making, and the search for positive-sum outcomes take the fore. In this logic, the network acts as a social boundary of demarcation around opportunities that are assembled from the embedded ties that define membership and enrich the network" (693). A study by Gulati and Gargiulo (1999) makes the point that "while exogenous factors may suffice to determine whether an organization should enter alliances, they may not provide enough cues to decide with whom to build those ties" (1440). Using data on 166 Japanese,

U.S., and European firms over 20 years, the authors found evidence of both endogenous and exogenous influences on network partnerships: "On the one hand, the emerging social structure progressively shapes organizational decisions about whether and with whom to create new ties. On the other hand, this social structure is produced by the (structurally shaped) decisions of individual organizations to establish relations with one another. . . . [A]ctors not only react to the conditions of their own making but in the process reproduce and change those very conditions" (1481–82).

In another analysis of private-sector networks, Lincoln, Gerlach, and Ahmadjian (1996) use a panel data set of 200 Japanese firms to examine the links between corporate performance and membership in *keiretsu* networks. Their primary dependent variable is firm profitability (measured as return on assets—an O variable). Independent variables include environment/interest E variables (e.g., industry composition, year dummies, measures of network ties), structure/organization S variables (e.g., date of company founding, financial status, and other measures of network ties), as well as lagged O outcomes from previous years. They find that long-term collective welfare seems to be stressed in *keiretsu* networks; performance variability is lower for firms in *keiretsu* networks than for independent firms.

Although network analyses of private-sector firms and market relationships are numerous, network analyses of public-sector governance structures are less common (although researchers often study collaboration among agencies or programs).[8] Exceptions to the dearth of network analysis in public-sector governance studies are the work of Provan and Sebastian (1998) and Milward and Provan (1993, 1998, 2000), who have examined the performance of mental health networks in four sites.[9] Provan and Sebastian (1998) investigated whether program effectiveness—measured by client outcomes in mental health programs—is positively influenced by smaller cores of integrated relationships, instead of by systemwide network integration. They argue that "outcomes for a particular clientele are likely to be more affected by the activities of a small group, or clique, of tightly connected providers than by the activities of complete networks" (454). Provan and Sebastian's analysis was exploratory, addressing clique relationships and client outcomes in just three networks; they conclude that the most effective network substructures are "intensive, involving multiple and overlapping links both within and across organizations that comprise the core of a network" (460). Their research indicates that integration per se is not the primary determinant of effectiveness; instead, they emphasize the importance of identifying the level and type of integration that would be expected to affect performance. In this sense, the analysis echoes a basic conclusion of Koremenos and Lynn (1996), who emphasized the importance of context in applying and interpreting their game theoretic analysis of a manager's success.

Socialized-choice theories also might be used to examine the primary work level of governance, including structure/technology relationships, the roles of professionals in organizations, or resource dependence and isomorphism. For example, Barley (1986) analyzes the implementation of a new scanning technology in hospital radiology departments and argues that technology does not determine structure but is socially mediated. This understanding about the relationship between primary work and structure has potentially important consequences for understanding governance systems: "[B]y treating technology as an occasion for structuring, researchers will confront contradictory results head-on because of structuring's central paradox: identical technologies can occasion similar dynamics and yet lead to different structural outcomes" (105).

Professionals in organizations with complex or uncertain technologies often may have autonomy or considerable discretion. Potoski's (1999) analysis links complex problems with greater delegation from state legislatures to bureaucratic expertise. Eisner and Meier (1990) test whether presidential control (from a principal-agent model) or bureaucratic discretion (from a bureaucratic politics model) better explains antitrust policy in the U.S. Department of Justice's Division of Antitrust over the years 1959–1984. In particular, they focus on the apparent shift in antitrust policy emphasis during the Reagan years. Their dependent variables are the percentage of antitrust cases filed each year that involved monopolies, price fixing, or mergers (T or O variables); their independent variables include environmental variables (economic indicators and political variables such as liberalism scales and presidential administrations) and structure/organization variables (the ratio of economists to lawyers in the antitrust division and indicator variables for the creation of an Economic Policy Office in the division). They find that policy priorities did not originate during the Reagan presidency but were put in motion earlier "by a professionalization process;

economists were brought into the division and provided with a crucial position in the policy process. The economists' professional norm and values . . . came to play a central role in the definition of policy" (Eisner and Meier 1990, 283). Furthermore, however, they find that "[b]ecause economics had become central to the administration of policy, changes in the body of economic knowledge were transmitted into the policy process. The agency, as a result, was vulnerable to changes in economics that it could neither control nor foresee" (284).

Resource dependence and primary work are addressed by D'Aunno, Sutton, and Price (1991), who analyze the response of drug treatment units to competing forces when community mental health centers have diversified to include them. D'Aunno, Sutton, and Price construct hypotheses from theories of myths and ceremonies in organizations (Meyer and Rowan 1977), isomorphism (DiMaggio and Powell 1983), and structural inertia (Hannan and Freeman 1984). D'Aunno, Sutton, and Price interpret their results as "consistent with Meyer and Rowan's (1977) views on the adaptation of organizations to conflicting institutional demands. Further, the results provide little support for the view that organizational ability to change core features is limited and that organizational adaptation is contingent on task environments" (D'Aunno, Sutton, and Price 1991, 656). D'Aunno, Sutton, and Price also find that their results are "consistent with Hannan and Freeman's (1984) assertion that organizational inertia is rewarded and that change is risky (D'Aunno, Sutton, and Price 1991, 656). In addition, "resource dependence may be a necessary but not sufficient condition for conformity" (658).

Keiser's (1997) study of the child support enforcement bureaucracy provides another example of resource dependence and its role in performance of primary work. Keiser examined dependent variables of either substantive enforcement (dollars collected) or symbolic enforcement (cases processed); independent variables such as federal amendments to child support law, state electoral competition, and interest group pressures; client characteristics with proxies such as the male unemployment rate and the Aid to Families with Dependent Children (AFDC) take-up rate; and organizational variables of bureaucratic capacity. She found that the child support bureaucracy was relatively autonomous, with little response to the environmental factors she examined. Greater expertise of state legislators was correlated with pressuring the bureaucracy for more substantive enforcement; value agreement and tractability were also important.

Beyond political economy and socialized-choice logics, another logic derives from general systems theory, a specific expression of which can be found in price theory and the economic theory of production. Systems models may frame governance regimes as production or transformation processes that link inputs to outputs via organizations, managers, and technologies (Scott 1998; O'Toole and Meier 2000). These production function, or input-output, studies are common in K–12 education research, in which student achievement often is modeled as a function of inputs that include student characteristics, teacher education and experience, teacher/student ratio or class size, and expenditures.[10] Barnow (1979) extends these ideas to training programs in which the outcomes of interest are a "set of skills and attitudes possessed by the participant after completing the program," produced by "program inputs . . . , the levels of skills and attitudes possessed by the participant prior to the training (which may be thought of as 'raw materials'), and . . . other personal characteristics that may influence the training process" (299).

In summary, governance research at institutional, managerial, and primary work levels may be approached via different theories and methods, which reflect different logics of governance. Awareness of a wider logic—whether it is based in political economy, socialized choice, or other perspectives—provides an overarching framework with which governance researchers assess the research strategies and explanatory power offered by different logics, as well as theories within logics. Broadening the intellectual reach of governance research in this way can add to the conceptual depth of analysis in the field, but multidisciplinary governance research is not an end in itself. In fact, such reach may not be advisable within a single study without due caution. For example, testing theories that originate from different disciplines by examining two different regression coefficients in the same model may not faithfully execute a logic of governance consistent with either theory.

An integrating logic can draw the investigator's attention to influences on operations and outcomes that originate at various levels of administration—for example, formal mandates in legislation, administrative guidelines, or discretionary strategies chosen by managers. Studies such as Koremenos and Lynn (1996) and Gulati and

Gargiulo (1999) show how well-specified governance research can encourage the investigator to take into account the endogenous nature of factors that researchers often assume are exogenous, such as local implementation structures or service and resource provider behavior. The value of such an approach is evident in the interpretation of a body of research that examines similar sets of questions but focuses on different aspects of the issue. We discuss specific examples in the context of welfare research in chapter 8.

Summary

The intellectual distance between theories and concepts on one hand and causal models that are appropriate for an investigator's data set on the other hand often is considerable. Inevitably, governance researchers make simplifying assumptions, use methods that are less suited to the "true" model than to the data available, or measure crudely something we know is much more complex. Reference to a wider logic of governance is even more crucial under such conditions: An abstract representation of such a logic—whether it is viewed in terms of institutional, managerial, and primary work levels or in a reduced-form representation of E, C, T, S, M, and O variables—provides a bridge for designing and interpreting research on complex governance processes.

This placement underscores the endogeneity of many complex governance processes. Furthermore, it encourages transparent and focused discussion of limitations on findings that are attributable to the models, methods, and data used, as well as comparisons with other, competing explanations that also may be consistent with the evidence. In chapter 6, we consider in greater detail the challenges and possibilities involved in designing governance research—in particular, the models, methods, and data that governance researchers employ in the effort to produce robust findings for understanding and designing governance systems.

Notes

1. The terms we apply to each reduced-form component show our interest in human services governance. The components are broadly applicable, however: "Clients" become "customers" or

"citizens"; "treatments" might be primary work or production of any kind. For example, O'Toole and Meier (2000) refer to C as "target population characteristics" and suggest that "treatments" may be divided into exogenous and endogenous aspects.

2. A necessary condition for causality is one that must be present for an event to occur, although its presence does not guarantee occurrence; a sufficient condition for causality is one that guarantees that the event will occur whenever it is present, although the event may occur even in its absence.

3. The "ideal" data set for this research might include individual-level data on outcomes, clients, and treatments, as well as rich information for multiple sites and multiple environments; such data sets are rare, however.

4. We discuss methods in greater detail in chapter 6.

5. The application of rational-choice theories to public-sector activities has not been without critics or debate; see essays and critiques in Monroe (1991); Green and Shapiro (1994); Friedman (1996); Zey (1998).

6. In his critique of under- and oversocialized views, Granovetter (1985) states that "both have in common a conception of action and decision carried out by atomized actors. In the undersocialized account, atomization results from narrow utilitarian pursuit of self-interest; in the oversocialized one, from the fact that behavioral patterns have been internalized and ongoing social relations thus have only peripheral effects on behavior" (485).

7. Emphasis in original.

8. The spring 1999 issue of *Policy Studies Review* (vol. 16, no. 1) included papers from a symposium on "The Impact of Collaborative Efforts: Changing the Face of Public Policy through Networks and Network Structures."

9. We discuss the first of these studies, Provan and Milward (1995), in detail in chapter 7.

10. See, for example, Hanushek (1996) and Hedges and Greenwald (1996) for reviews of this literature.

6

Designing Research: Models, Methods, and Data

Throughout this book, we describe useful frameworks and approaches for designing, carrying out, and interpreting governance research. Our assessment of governance research necessarily draws from diverse sources across many disciplines, subdisciplines, professional fields, and subfields. The research and findings of these communities, however, typically are remote from one another, and many researchers may not envision their purpose as contributing to governance research per se; that is, an overarching concern with *governance* may not motivate a particular work or research agenda. Nonetheless, the findings from these disparate sources may be relevant to others interested in governance questions.

In this chapter, we identify conceptual boundaries for a "literature of governance" from several disciplines and professional fields. Then, making reference to the governance literature, we discuss issues related to models, methods, and data and identify problems and promises of various analytical approaches to the study of governance.

Identifying a Literature of Governance

To assess the contributions, challenges, and possibilities of theory-based governance research, we reviewed a large sample of studies that we collectively describe as a "literature of governance." These studies explore aspects of governance from a range of viewpoints and research traditions, in different policy areas, with diverse methods, and with different levels of technical complexity. We aimed to include research that conceptualized a hierarchical logic of governance—broadly construed, explicit or implicit—and exhibited certain individual characteristics of quality or rigor. In choosing the types of studies to highlight, for example, we gave less emphasis to primarily descriptive accounts of events, laws, regulations, relationships, or processes that did not attempt to frame research questions with some kind of theory, conceptualization, or other framework.

Our analysis of the governance literature is distinct from works that attempt to define the boundaries, functions, or development of particular disciplines or fields (e.g., Kettl 1996, 2000; Bendor 1994; Frederickson 1997). To capture the essence of governance research from many different perspectives, we employed a more catholic approach that favored breadth instead of depth in many cases. Our analysis is wide in scope and seeks to identify commonalities of empirical governance research, including strengths and weaknesses, across theoretical and disciplinary bases.

The undertaking of a broad, multidisciplinary review of the governance literature would have been ill-advised, however, without some specific criteria about which works to review. We developed the following criteria that we applied in identifying works to include in a literature of governance:

- Did the research frame questions or propositions in a way that advanced theoretical or empirical modeling of some part of the governance process?
- Did the research develop multicomponent models or frameworks as a step toward testing hypotheses empirically?
- Did the research define and operationalize specific concepts or variables that are common to governance research at a general level, or that might be useful for governance researchers working in diverse policy areas?
- Did the research provide guidance for data collection or suggest appropriate methodologies for empirical governance research?

- Did the research present convincing and appropriately framed findings that were neither overgeneralized nor underconceptualized?

We selected more than 500 studies that appeared to satisfy one or more of these criteria. Because these criteria involve some subjective as well as objective assessments and because we chose to capture breadth rather than depth, our literature review is illustrative, rather than exhaustive.[1] We did not review the *population* of governance studies across theories, methods, disciplines, policy areas, or time. Other researchers might include additional or different contributions in a similar endeavor to define a literature of governance.

Thus, our approach to a literature review may come at some cost in terms of the generalizability of the models, measures, and findings we discuss to specific research traditions within the domain of governance research. Our review does not define a narrow sampling frame, measure particular aspects of the sample, or formally test for the prevalence of particular characteristics. Perry and Kraemer (1990) and Wright, Black, and Flournory (1999), for example, identified a sampling frame of specific journals over a specific period of time, coded particular aspects of each study, examined patterns, and made generalizations about the specific types of research they examined. In addition, reviews of empirical and theoretical research in specific areas of interest to governance research appear in sources such as Bendor's (1990) study of formal models of bureaucracy or Shelanski and Klein's (1995) review of empirical research that uses transaction cost analysis.

We also did not aim to include the collected works of any one particular researcher or analyst in our review. Although some of the observations we make may apply to one particular work of a researcher, that researcher may address the specific issue in another paper or publication. In general, we attempted to review and assess each piece on its own merits.

Finally, many of the works we examined did not clearly employ any logic of governance even though a particular theory, associated with a broader logic, may have been used. Research on governance regimes and problems requires transparent and focused discussion of exactly what is assumed, predicted, measured, and explained in these models, as well as the limitations on findings attributable to the models, methods, and data employed.

Critiquing a Literature of Governance

In this section, we discuss models, methods, data, and findings of governance research, highlighting problematic and exemplary approaches and works. Many of the analytical challenges and problems we confront in empirical governance research are generic to social sciences research; therefore our discussion places some of these issues in broader context.

Models

Having a broad yet detailed understanding of a governance regime or situation—drawn from different disciplinary perspectives and across multiple levels of analysis, if possible—helps to identify variables or components that are integral to a logic or framework, regardless of whether measures are available for all potentially important factors.

Scope and context. In the governance literature we reviewed, researchers frequently develop theories or models that focus on a particular aspect of a governance process or unit of analysis, decoupled from a wider context or directed more narrowly within what our reduced-form model indicates might be a "full" account of the governance process (i.e., one that progresses from legislative enactment to policy implementation)—reflecting either the specific focus of the theory employed or a need to scale the analysis to tractable proportions. A researcher may concentrate, for example, on a particular policy (e.g., child protection), a specific program (e.g., Temporary Assistance for Needy Families), an organization (e.g., the Illinois Department of Children and Family Services), a type of activity (e.g., performance contracts or network ties), or individual outcomes. Analytical reduction and restrictions on the focus of models are imperative for investigating many aspects of governance.

A theory or model applied narrowly, however—with subsets of rules, laws, interactions, practices, or outcomes not linked to or interpreted in the context of a broader framework of the governance problem or situation—might lead to mismeasurement of a concept or relationship, inappropriate aggregation (or disaggregation) of data, or lack of consideration of important variables. Furthermore, analyses that use restricted models may give not merely a partial account but a *biased* partial account of the complex, configurational workings of governance. For example, production functions for student achievement seldom contain state- or district-level political environments or financing structures that may affect school-level governance (Lynn and Tepper 1998). Moe (1985) discusses this problem in the context of regulation studies:

> [P]opular models of regulation as well as quantitative empirical work have tended to focus only on very small parts of the whole—in the former case for reasons for clarity and mathematical tractability, and in the latter because of data collection and measurement problems (and because they are often guided by these same models). Given the very real difficulties that comprehensiveness entails, these approaches are entirely reasonable short-term research strategies. But it is important to remember that they threaten to yield biased inferences about the causes of regulatory behavior. They clearly omit factors whose causal effects may overwhelm or distort the "special" relationships on which they singularly focus (Moe 1985, 1095).

Although the fact that modeling choices are influenced by temporal, data-related, and theoretical constraints probably is unavoidable, policy design and evaluation could be better informed by research that explicitly discusses models and findings within a broader governance context. For example, several researchers have evaluated the problem of "cream-skimming" in federal job-training programs—in which participants who are perceived to be more employable are more likely to receive program services. In most of these studies, researchers do not distinguish between cream-skimming by job-training agency staff and self-selection decisions by those eligible for services (Heckman, Heinrich, and Smith 1999). Anderson et al. (1992) and Anderson, Burkhauser, and Raymond (1993), for example, compare data on program enrollees with those who were eligible for services and determined that enrollees were much less likely to be high school dropouts compared to the eligible nonparticipants; they interpreted their findings as strong evidence of cream-skimming. Similarly, Sandell and Rupp (1988) find that adult high school dropouts are significantly underserved in JTPA programs, although they concede that the absence of stipends or the correlation of low formal education with age also could have contributed to lower participation rates for this group.

With better data on participant self-selection processes, including information on awareness and application decisions, and a broader context or analytical framework that considers the influence of performance standards, local-level management, and service delivery processes, others present evidence of a much more complex governance system that determines access to program services (Cragg 1997; Heckman and Smith 1997; Heckman, Heinrich, and Smith 1999; Heinrich, forthcoming.) The findings of these latter studies showed how the decisions of individuals who are eligible for services, of program staff who are charged with screening applicants and assigning enrollees to program services, and of managers who are concerned about efficiency and measured performance contributed in various ways and at different levels of program administration to the resulting participant population. In addition to producing a more accurate account of the cream-skimming problem, the results of these studies generated more specific and useful policy guidance to program administrators and policymakers who are concerned with this problem. Parsons (1991) studied similar issues but in the social security disability program; he finds that strategic manipulation of initial eligibility determination policies, which prompts administrative delays and self-screening on the part of program applicants, serves as a "short-run control mechanism" for the flow of applicants and transfer expenditures.

Operational definitions of model components. Having a thorough understanding of the problem or situation being modeled and corresponding data for empirical analyses does not, however, guarantee that a researcher will be able to thwart all modeling problems. Developing operational definitions of model components in governance—and in social sciences research more generally—frequently is challenging. Operational definitions that are used to describe human and social phenomena inevitably involve simplification and formalization in a way that attempts to capture the essential features of these phenomena; that is, they are positivistic, or expressed in terms of what we can concretely and directly observe. Simplicity, precision, and tractability come at a price, however, in that the concept being defined is removed from its context, and misrepresentation is possible. In education research, for example, a common operationalization of economic disadvantage is receipt of a free school lunch; with little trouble, most of us probably could think of several essential features of economic disadvantage that this measure neglects. The poverty level measure is another example; as an indicator, it is an objective and unambiguous measure, but it may not be a useful operational definition of poverty because it fails to capture many essential features of impoverishment.

In addition, Bradley and Schaefer (1998) point to the problem of circularity in operational definitions. Social phenomena are complex and embedded in complex contexts. To gain an understanding of what we cannot fully observe, we rely on proxy measures; thus, measurement precedes definition. The theory requirement of measurement demands, however, that a concept first be unambiguously defined. Thus, in modeling complex governance problems or phenomena, multiple operational definitions of the same concept are not only plausible but likely—making the replication of research models and results more challenging.

In our review of governance literature, for example, we identified many different operational definitions of the concept of *discretion*. Although an essential feature of discretion—described as making judgments regarding policy actions that are not prescribed by formal rules, legislation, or other agreements (Ringquist, 1995)—was common among most definitions, the measures themselves were primarily context-specific: for example, "deliberate over- or under-diagnosis of clients by clinical social workers" (Kirk and Kutchins 1988); "departure of agency decisions from positions agreed upon by the executive and legislature at the time of appointment" (Calvert, McCubbins, and Weingast 1989); "provision of any information, advice, or assistance that reflected clients' circumstances by adapting or interpreting formal protocols and eligibility determination forms" (Meyers, Glaser, and MacDonald 1998); or the benefit approval rate, exemption rate, and community work experience assignment rate in a study of welfare reform (Schiller 1999.) In terms of model specification and replication, one concern might be, for example, that a "benefit approval rate" modeled as discretion in one welfare reform study might be used as a proxy for an administrative policy emphasis on income support in another, representing a distinctly different concept.

In most cases, the analysts in the works we reviewed did not adequately discuss other possible operational definitions of the concepts they were measuring, if at all. For example, in a study of how the presence of private schools in a state affects the level of public school resources and performance, Arum (1996) offers considerable detail about the data and measures for state- and student-level variables in his analysis. Arum's discussion does not address other possible measures of the concepts he was trying to capture, however, or whether other possible interpretations were possible for the variables he chose to use. Keiser and Meier's (1996) use of the number of female state legislators as a measure of women's political strength at the state level is another example of this type of problematic operationalization.

Examples of research that helpfully frames operational definitions of concepts include Nohria and Gulati (1995), who offer a thorough discussion of their measures for "innovation" and "slack" (see Nohria and Gulati 1995, 34). They describe and defend their measures, comparing them to other operationalizations of these concepts. A comprehensive review of all possible alternative operationalizations or interpretations for variables in a study typically is unnecessary, however. In some cases, a footnoted comment may provide essential details behind the author's reasoning. For example, Sabatier, Loomis, and MacCarthy (1995) examine professional norms, hierarchical controls, and budget maximization behavior in U.S. forest service planning. They acknowledge other possible operational definitions of these concepts or variables in a footnote: "An [*American Journal of Political Science*] reviewer argues that the [1974 Resources Planning Act (RPA)] alternative is not a good indicator of hierarchical controls, given that it is not absolutely binding on the forest. While the latter is true, the output levels in the RPA alternative are *quantitative performance indicators* for field offices, a relatively rare phenomenon among federal agencies. And these certainly are at least as good an indicator of hierarchical controls as the [National Labor Relations Board] precedents to regional office staff used by Moe (1985) or the vague policy guideline to 'go slow on enforcement' issued by the Reagan Administration to [Environmental Protection Agency] regional offices and used by Wood (1988)" (Sabatier, Loomis, and McCarthy 1995, 212, footnote 4).

In practice, operational definitions that capture all of the essential properties of a social phenomena or characteristic and justify their correspondence to a particular measurement scale are rare. Greater acknowledgment of these difficulties and consideration of alternative interpretations could increase the chances that findings are not overgeneralized.

Alternative specifications and interpretations.   Given that social science researchers frequently rely on imperfect data and variable operationalizations in developing models, attempts to investigate other possible specifications or interpretations of the models are particularly important.

MacCallum (1995) describes three basic modeling strategies in social sciences research—strictly confirmatory, model generation, and model comparison—that are useful in considering how approaches to modeling in governance research might be improved in general. In the *strictly confirmatory* approach, a researcher formulates one model of interest and evaluates the model by fitting it to appropriate data. If the model produces interpretable parameter estimates and fits the data well, it is considered a plausible model. Lowery's (1983) study of the effectiveness of tax and expenditure limit policies, which uses data from four states that adopted these policies (in addition to comparison states that did not adopt them), appears to follow this approach. Limited data are the major impediment to exploration of alternative models of policy effectiveness in his study. An important drawback of a strictly confirmatory approach is that it provides little flexibility to address unanticipated results or assess their generalizability.

In the *model generation* approach, in contrast, a specified model is fit to appropriate data, and the model results are subsequently evaluated with the purpose of modifying the model to improve its parsimony or fit to the data. In the absence of a strong theoretical foundation for the model, however, the basis for modifications typically becomes inspection of parameter estimates, examination of residuals matrices, and the use of statistical tests to evaluate changes in explanatory power as a result of respecifications. The danger of this approach lies in the possibility that if modifications to the original model are not *substantively* meaningful and justifiable, the subsequent modifications may be determined primarily by chance characteristics of the observed sample and may result in models that are not generalizable to other samples (unless they are derived with extremely large sample sizes for a broad-based sample). Model generation approaches are most appropriate in exploratory model development, as long as the researcher acknowledges it as such and any model derived is evaluated using new data.

Keiser and Meier (1996) engage in model generation analyses in their study of organizational learning in child support enforcement bureaucracies, using state-level data ($N = 50$). The primary objective of their study is to compare standard regression model results with "a new quantitative technique that better fits public administration's need for prescription" (459). They suggest that standard regression diagnostic techniques downplay the potential usefulness of unusual cases and introduce an alternative modeling approach: "substantively weighted least squares." In this particular article, the theoretical justification for model modifications is methodological. Meier and Gill (2000) present substantively weighted analytical techniques in greater detail.

The third approach to modeling that we argue should be more commonly and explicitly applied in governance research is model comparison—specification of several alternative models *a priori* that are fit to the same set of data. The alternative models might represent competing theoretical explanations or reflect conflicting research findings in the literature. Among the modeling efforts we probed in the governance literature, we found a tendency to neglect alternative models, explanations, or ways of knowing the phenomenon under study.

Not every research effort need conduct at least two analyses—one using the "primary" approach developed by the author and others that address all possible alternative explanations—to be insightful or helpful. Consideration of alternative explanations may be particularly important, however, for understanding governance in a wider framework and deriving more generalizable study findings. This point is particularly true of studies that use unique data sources. In such cases, the researcher's failure to place his or her model in a larger context that might allow for alternative model designs and interpretations leaves unclear to an audience that is unfamiliar with the data whether alternative processes might be at work.

An example in which alternative explanations are usefully considered is Weingast's (1984) study of "theoretical perspective and empirical support for congressional dominance of agency decisions" (181). Weingast makes very clear that his point is to show that agency dominance is a misguided account and that his own argument also may be flawed; he argues the extreme of the congressional dominance view, however, to point out the flaws in an alternative interpretation. Such a rhetorical placement of the argument contextualizes Weingast's research in a way that is helpful for making sense of both views.

Another example of research that make helpful comparisons to alternative interpretations of findings is Denison and Mishra's (1995) analysis of organizational culture and effectiveness. They state:

> [A]s a cross-sectional study, there is a familiar set of limitations on inferring causality. The case studies develop plausible explanations for the linkage of culture and performance in the five firms, but provide little basis for inference. The quantitative study generates results that are consistent with the hypotheses, but those results are also consistent with the hypothesis that effectiveness determines the cultural traits, or that the two are simply coincident in time. Clearly, the ideal research design would not only incorporate in-depth measures of cultural traits, but would examine those with appropriate lag time, and a broad range of effectiveness measures (220).

Similarly, in an empirical study of Environmental Protection Agency (EPA) policy actions, Wood (1988) tests the robustness of a principal-agent model in explaining agency monitoring and abatement activities and then considers alternative explanations for why this model fails to adequately explain the longitudinal variations in EPA clean air outputs.

In general, modeling efforts are more likely to produce robust, generalizable results when there is full awareness of what might be important to measure in the situation under study (made explicit by a logic or theory): a precise understanding of competing theories or explanations for the observed phenomena and access to data and methods necessary to test them. Acknowledging that modeling choices and familiarity with alternative "ways of knowing" are influenced to at least some degree by the researchers' disciplinary backgrounds and experience with particular methodological approaches to research also is important, however. In the following section, we discuss how methodological choices may similarly affect what can be learned about governance regimes, policies, processes, and outcomes.

Methods

As the foregoing discussion suggests, modeling and methodological choices frequently are considered simultaneously. Recent calls for strengthening the cumulative governance knowledge base have highlighted the need to advance the methodological tools applied, with a particular interest in expanding the use of empirical research strategies that attempt to relate the measurable effects of public programs and policies to the specific governance features that seem to produce them (Gill and Meier 2000; Mead 1997, 1999; Milward and Provan 1998; Roderick, Jacob, and Bryk 2000; Smith and Meier 1994).

Quantitative and qualitative approaches. Although the governance studies we reviewed employ a diverse range of quantitative methodologies, ordinary least squares (OLS) regression and slight variations of OLS approaches clearly are the most common statistical methods applied. Qualitative methodologies include observations, semi-structured interviews, surveys, case studies and comparative case studies, grounded theory, and other field research techniques. There is relatively little use of more complex modeling techniques—such as two-stage least squares, simultaneous equations, structural equation modeling, interrupted or pooled time series models, seemingly unrelated regressions, or hierarchical linear modeling—that might more appropriately account for the hierarchical, configurational, and time-varying nature of governance processes.

Some of the most convincing studies combine quantitative and qualitative approaches to data analyses.[2] In conducting theory-based, empirical research, qualitative studies aid in the formulation of research hypotheses, the specification of statistical models, and the interpretation of model findings, as well as informing policy discussions on the basis of empirical results. In addition, particularly when data are drawn from administrative records, surveys of program administrators, or other public archives, having in-depth knowledge of the government program or service system that typically can be gained only through qualitative techniques frequently is essential to appropriate use of these data.

Research by Brock and Harknett (1998); D'Aunno, Sutton ,and Price (1991); Hasenfeld and Weaver (1996); Heinrich and Lynn (2000); Riccucci, Meyers, and Lurie (1999); Roderick et al. (1999);

Sandfort (2000); Selden (1999); and Uzzi (1996, 1997)—among others—illustrates the value of qualitatively derived knowledge in empirical studies of public program processes and outcomes. Roderick et al. (1999), for example, use observations and interviews of teachers, students and their families, and school personnel to gain a clearer understanding of the implementation of Chicago's educational reforms aimed at ending social promotion and their effects (quantitatively measured through test scores) on students and classroom instruction. Focusing on experimental evaluations, Sherwood and Doolittle (1999) similarly discuss the value of ethnographic research that, combined with typical quantitative measures of program implementation, shows how program services are viewed and experienced by participants, as well as by those who choose not to participate, improving understanding of observed program impacts. In some cases, a particular study may not report a qualitative component, but the understanding of the variables and model are built on personal experience with or observation of the organization or process being studied (e.g., Heinrich 1999; Sandfort 2000).

On the other hand, not all studies that include a qualitative component use the information effectively to guide model development and estimation. For example, in a study of the implementation and effectiveness of a five-year, school-based program to improve "social competency" and reduce problem behaviors among at-risk students, Skroban, Gottfredson, and Gottfredson (1999) develop a conceptual model of the program intervention and use structural equation modeling in a comparative evaluation of the program's effects. Through their qualitative study of the program's implementation, however, they learn that "the program was never implemented according to initial expectations" (11), and their assumptions about the comparability of the two schools chosen for the non-experimental evaluation were violated.[3] Despite these revelations, Skroban et al. estimate their structural equation model—including characteristics of the school populations and a program impact indicator—and find, not surprisingly, that the intervention had no significant effects. They make no effort to adjust their methodological approach in recognition of the fact that at least two important underlying assumptions of their original specification were shown to be false.

In other studies we reviewed, researchers appeared to include large numbers of potentially important variables without giving adequate consideration to what the underlying structural model or interrelationships might be or whether the model focused on the appropriate level of analysis. In a study of child support enforcement, for example, Keiser and Meier (1996) include the *state* unemployment rate for males as a *client* characteristic under the category "implementation variables." Other researchers might view this variable as an economic indicator, and there is no discussion of how the male unemployment rate might influence or interact with other characteristics of noncustodial parents/clients (e.g., their earnings or earnings potential and their willingness to comply with child support collection efforts) that also might affect policy outcomes.

Many studies are noteworthy, however, in their exception to these general criticisms of haphazard or inadequately informed modeling and methodological choices to governance research. Marcoulides and Heck (1993), for example, develop a structural equation model that is based on socialized-choice assumptions to test whether organizational culture influences organizational performance.[4] They measure organizational culture as five interrelated latent (unobserved) variables—organizational structure/purpose and organizational values (assumed to be exogenous) and organizational climate, task organization, and worker attitudes/goals (assumed to be endogenous), all of which correspond to sociocultural, organizational belief, and individual belief subsystems—and relate that culture to organizational performance. The findings of their model suggest specific factors that managers can manipulate at the organizational level to influence organizational performance.

In another well-designed study, Forder (1997) applies an institutional economics framework to generate propositions about "optimal governance structures" in the provision of community care services, focusing in particular on alternative incentive contracts between public purchasers and private providers of residential care for the elderly. Forder tests hypotheses about the relationships between contract/pricing arrangements, service provider organizational form (for-profit versus nonprofit), service quality, and client dependency levels, using ordinary least squares regression analyses of data from a population of registered residential care homes for the elderly. He finds that misrepresentation of client dependency was more likely to occur where contract arrangements linked cost reimbursement with client characteristics and that for-profit providers were more likely to engage in misrepresentation practices. Following his presentation of empirical findings, Forder considers at some length alternative models and observed contract/pricing arrangements and how they might be explored in future analyses.

A third illustrative study, by Hser et al. (1999), begins with the development of a conceptual model that hypothesizes a positive relationship between individuals' drug use and their treatment "careers" and investigates organization influences on individual outcomes. Using structural equation modeling techniques, the researchers examine relationships among individuals' drug use, their cumulative treatment experiences or characteristics of the treatment they received, and post-program outcomes across four primary organizational/treatment modalities. They find significant differences in individual treatment outcomes by organizational type and relate specific characteristics of treatment practices (e.g., length of stay) to individual outcomes. They conclude, however, that the processes that underlie or mediate cumulative treatment practices and effects are poorly understood; a better modeling approach that uses data on how client characteristics interact with treatment processes and organizational features to produce the observed differences in outcomes is needed.

Levels of analysis. In specifying more sophisticated models that take into account complex organizational processes and the configurational, political, and loosely coupled nature of governance, methods that allow for the opportunity to explore heterogeneity across sites, offices, or programs, as well as at different operational levels within sites or programs, are needed. Although some studies appear to explicity recognize these fundamental aspects of governance and select methodological approaches that accommodate them, many studies do not or cannot attempt a more technically advanced strategy to model estimation (as in the case of Hser et al. 1999). In their study of professional norms, hierarchical controls, and budget maximization behavior in U.S. forest service planning, for example, Sabatier, Loomis, and MacCarthy (1995) obtain survey responses from *individuals* within a forest service office, but an individuals-within-offices modeling design is not specified; instead, group means are derived from the individual responses and analyzed. In other studies, such as Mead's (1999) analysis of welfare caseload declines in Wisconsin, individual-level or other multilevel data simply may not be available.

When theoretical conceptualizations, data, or methods are limiting, many researchers choose to focus their analysis of relationships in governance regimes at a single organizational (or individual) level. Some studies group individuals or other units of analysis and attempt to explain *average* effects or outcomes for higher levels of aggregation (e.g., Mead 1999). Although aggregate analysis may be the only option available, aggregation can exacerbate other modeling problems, such as omitted variable bias—particularly when the omitted variables are at the level of aggregation (Hanushek, Rivkin, and Taylor 1996). Care in interpreting study findings is needed to avoid using the results of regression models at one level of hierarchy to infer what might be going on at lower levels.

Other studies, including experimental and nonexperimental program evaluations, analyze the influence of organizational or structural factors on individual or lower-level unit outcomes by controlling for these factors in individual-level regressions; estimating separate individual-level regressions for different organizational units; or using a single program indicator variable, such as a "school" or "local office" indicator. Many of these studies explain only a small percentage of the total variation in individual outcomes and contribute little to our understanding of the interactions and influence on program outcomes of specific organizational or structural factors.

In general, a major problem with making these compromises in the chosen level of analysis is that the resulting analyses typically do not provide adequate information to address questions that are critical to governance researchers. Jennings and Ewalt (1998), for example, study the influence of increased coordination and administrative consolidation in JTPA programs on 10 JTPA participant outcomes while controlling for demographic and socioeconomic characteristics of participants. Their models account for 5 to 29 percent of the total variation in individual outcomes, and the administrative variables are statistically significant in about half of these models. Some questions linger, however: How much of the total variation in client outcomes is attributable to policy or program design and implementation factors? What portion of variation attributable to such factors is explained by the two administrative variables? Might other potentially important administrative or policy variables that are not incorporated in these models change the observed effects of the coordination and consolidation variables? Without answers to these questions, one is left not only with uncertainty about how much of a difference the organization of these programs makes but also with unclear policy prescriptions for program designers and administrators. Should they consolidate or not?

In light of the limitations of ordinary least squares in modeling and identifying causal relationships in government systems, Gill and Meier (2000) suggest some quantitative research methodologies that they believe are more compatible with observed relations in the administration of public organizations and policies, as well as with theoretical formulations of them. These methodologies include *advanced time series techniques*, such as distributive lag models of the cumulative effects over time of initial policy or program changes; *Bayesian approaches* that use prior knowledge to assign *a priori* probability on unknown parameters; and their latest technique, *substantively weighted least squares*. They point out that all of these approaches are special cases of the generalized linear model, which should be more accessible to researchers.

Another statistical methodology that is based on the generalized linear model is the hierarchical linear model—a multilevel model that allows researchers to formulate and test hypotheses about how factors or variables measured at one level of an administrative hierarchy might interact with variables at another level. Because most relationships in governance systems involve activities and interactions that span multiple levels of organizational or systemic structures, multilevel models are more likely to be consistent with formal and informal models of governance.

In multilevel models, the assumption of "independence of observations" in the ordinary least squares (OLS) approach is dropped, and relationships in the data are allowed to vary (rather than assumed to be fixed over varying contexts). The extent to which multilevel modeling improves statistical estimation in comparison with standard OLS models depends on *cross-level effects* in the data and the corresponding extent of variation in the dependent variable at different levels of analyses (see Bryk and Raudenbush, 1992; Heinrich and Lynn 1999, Krull and MacKinnon 1999). Lee and Bryk (1989), for example, find significant differences in mean student achievement between public and private (Catholic) school sectors, with statistically significant cross-level effects between sector and student social classes and the minority gap—implying that the magnitude of the sector effect depends on the social class and minority gap of the schools compared. The existence of cross-level interactions is at the crux of the development of multilevel modeling techniques. Potentially severe problems—including reduced (or inflated) precision of estimates, misspecification and subsequent misestimation of model coefficients, and aggregation bias—may arise when statistically significant cross-level interactions are present but ignored in OLS specifications.

Education researchers such as Goldstein (1987) and Bryk and Raudenbush (1992) have led social science efforts in developing and applying multilevel models to analyses of public service delivery systems. In early research, Bryk and Raudenbush (1987) apply these techniques to analyze school-level effects on students' mathematics achievement scores. More recently, the application of multilevel modeling strategies has been extended to other areas of public policy research. For example, using data collected during the national JTPA study on participants' characteristics, earnings, and employment outcomes, along with administrative and policy data, Heinrich and Lynn (2000) estimate hierarchical linear models of participant outcomes. They find that site-level administrative structures and local management strategies (including performance incentives) had a significant influence on participant outcomes.

For governance researchers, the most important advantages of multilevel modeling are the expanded possibilities it creates for investigating hierarchical relationships and the influences that policy, administrative, and structural variables might have at the client level. Bryk and Raudenbush (1992) criticize the neglect of hierarchical relationships in traditional OLS approaches as fostering "an impoverished conceptualization" that has discouraged the formulation of hypotheses about effects occurring at and across different levels. Although Goldstein (1992) also regards multilevel modeling as a potential explorative tool for theory development, he cautions—and we strongly concur—that exploratory analyses should not be substituted for theory-based research and that multilevel models should not be regarded as a panacea for all types of complex data analysis problems. Complex methods cannot overcome weak conceptualizations in poorly designed research.

The breadth of qualitative and quantitative methods in governance research, as well as the technical complexity of some of the methods, raises a question regarding interpretation and access to these studies. As research reaches across disciplines or fields that may have widely accepted and understood methodologies, the issue of methodological explanation becomes important. We do not argue that each paper should bear the burden of providing a "textbook" presentation of the methods it uses, but adequate references, at least, should be included. For example, Perry and Miller (1991) use structural equation modeling and implement model revisions to improve the fit with their data. They do not provide information to the reader about the theories or information they use to guide the modifications they employ in this model generation approach, making it difficult for readers to evaluate consequences of possible alternative specifications. Marcoulides and Heck (1993), on the contrary, not only explain their approach to structural equation modeling and the statistical tests they perform; they also discuss the appropriate application and limitations of the LISREL[5] methodology and other possible sources of measurement error and model misspecification in their study. As Wright, Black, and Flournory (1999, 5) point out, "without an adequate understanding of the research process, one can hardly expect to understand, replicate or build upon the research findings of others."

Data

Empirical studies are only as good as their data. All of the benefits of empirical social sciences research—objective inference, more precise empirical distinctions, means for identifying error, predictive power, and replication of and confidence in research findings—are predicated on accurate measurement, which is inevitably challenging for researchers working with social and human phenomena.

Sources and uses. The data in the studies we reviewed exhibit eclectic range and type, including administrative data from public programs, survey and interview data, Congressional records and other data from public archives, and data collected during randomized experiments. Examples of specific sources include state-level information on child support collection; surveys of research and development laboratory staff; federal court cases; surveys of case managers overseeing children in state custody in Tennessee; interviews with individuals in federal reinvention labs; case studies of federal agencies; interviews with utility company executives; firm performance of Japanese firms; surveys of citizens in Illinois counties; surveys conducted by the Merit Systems Protection Board; case observations from the Boston Water and Sewer Commission and the Boston Housing Authority; National Forest Management Act plans and surveys of U.S. Forest Service officials; radiology exams in two different hospitals; and surveys of supervisors and directors of drug abuse treatment organizations. Even within a narrower segment of the diverse governance literature (public administration), Wright, Black, and Flournory (1999) find that a variety of data sources were used in the 143 journal articles they reviewed over four months, including self-administered surveys (55.2 percent), archival or secondary data (35.7 percent), interview or telephone surveys (7.0 percent), laboratory experiments (7.0 percent), observations by researchers (4.2 percent), and other data that were not always explicitly described to readers.

In a review of econometric methodologies for investigating the effectiveness of public programs, Heckman, LaLonde, and Smith (1999) suggest that more effort should be invested in improving the quality of data used in studying program effects than in the development of methods to overcome problems generated by inadequate data. Gill and Meier (2000) also attribute some challenges of building a cumulative body of research in public administration to a lack of data; they argue that common data sets might promote interaction among researchers and opportunities for collaboration and replication of research. Other fields of study do not face the replication or collaboration issues raised by lack of widely available data: Economists, sociologists, and other social scientists often use large data sets such as the Current Population Survey, the National Longitudinal Surveys, the Panel Study of Income Dynamics, and the General Social Survey. Some larger data sets are available to governance researchers, including the International City Management Association survey of personnel, the Bureau of Census Survey of Local Government Finances, and The State of the Nation's Cities: A Comprehensive Database on American Cities and Suburbs.

Governance research, however, is characterized far more by unique instead of common data sources. These unique sources can make acquiring knowledge about governance difficult, not just across governance regimes but also within policy areas. In assessing the use of administrative data for policy research, Hotz et al. (1999) are motivated in part by a concern that the recent devolution of family-related policies and programs to states and localities will make it difficult for the federal government and others to monitor these programs and their outcomes. As they point out, state and local governments have mixed experiences in producing reliable intrastate information on the effectiveness of alternative policies and very little experience in collecting reliable and valid data for interstate comparisons. Hotz et al. discuss administrative data issues in detail; they describe the advantages and disadvantages of working with these data, as well as the implications of their limitations for producing reliable policy recommendations.

Combining administrative and survey data, along with data from public records, may provide a broader range of information about legislative and policy directives, rules and procedures, and some other parameters of program or agency operations, as well as about the contexts or political environments within which the programs operate. These types of data combinations may best capture the configurational, political, and loosely coupled nature of governance regimes.

Many of the studies we reviewed, in fact, do combine multiple sources of data. For example, Blau and Schoenherr (1971) gathered data from the administrative records of state employment security agencies, interviews with program administrators, and census data in an empirical study of organizational structure in these agencies. Jennings and Ewalt (1998, 2000) link administrative data with surveys of state job-training and welfare-to-work program administrators about program goals, priorities, and implementation strategies to generate empirical measures of political and policy variables. Ferguson (1991) uses administrative data from Texas school districts, along with census data, to evaluate the influences of structural, technological (teaching), and environmental factors on students' test scores. We could mention many other examples of similar research in the study of education, including the application of these data in multilevel modeling studies.

Although combining data from multiple sources to expand research possibilities can be useful, some caution is warranted. In a discussion of data collection for experimental and nonexperimental evaluations, Sherwood and Doolittle (1999) suggest that mixing of data from different sources (such as data from management information systems and surveys) may not produce accurate measures across observations or levels, particularly when data are obtained from different sources for experimental and control or comparison groups. If measures of individuals' earnings are obtained from employment security data for some cases, for example, and survey data are used to construct earnings measures for persons whose earnings are not available from employment security records, researchers should attempt to verify the comparability of these measures.

Problems and restrictions. Although combined data sources can offer unique opportunities for in-depth analyses of governance problems and issues, many of these data are obtained with conditions for restricted access, creating barriers to collaboration in and replication of research. Governance research that is based on these kinds of data also may be difficult for readers to consume, interpret, and assess across unfamiliar or inaccessible data. For example, anticipating or identifying alternative interpretations of survey responses, possible omitted variables in an analysis, or alternative interpretations for the findings an author presents may be difficult. This conclusion suggests that if researchers are to communicate and facilitate the replication of their research models and findings more effectively, they must bear the burden of framing their models and results in a context that includes discussion of potentially important variables that could not be incorporated into their models.

In our review of governance research, we found that few researchers even acknowledge the possibility that important variables might be missing from their models. For example, one group of authors points out that their analysis is "rather coarse"—but they provide no details about how serious the problem of "coarseness" is (Palmer, Danforth, and Clark 1995). Among other works that make reference to omitted variables, such omitted variables sometimes are described in a footnote or in one or two sentences near the end of an article. For example, Chubb (1985, footnote 9) and Heinrich (1999, footnotes 6 and 8) list variables that are likely omitted from their analyses. Of authors that do mention potentially important variables or concepts that they are unable to model, very few take the extra step to interpret their model results in light of these omissions. Masten, Meehan, and Snyder (1991) is one of the few articles we came across that discusses possible omitted variables *and* their likely effects on the model.

Whether research fails to discuss omitted variables at all or the variables are only briefly mentioned, the burden is on the reader to interpret the model in the context of potentially important but omitted factors. In the first case, the reader has the additional task of identifying important omitted variables; in the second case, the reader knows at least some of the omitted variables that the author considers important but is left to do the analysis herself or himself, potentially misapplying the framework that underlies the researcher's model. Although expecting researchers to address every possible contingency and concern in print would be unreasonable, it would be helpful if they were more forthcoming about what is and is not included in their models and how the models and their interpretation might be driven by the specific data employed.[6]

There also is the complementary concern about communicating to readers the properties or characteristics of the social phenomena that are measured and justifying their correspondence with the choice of measurement scale. Wright, Black, and Flournory (1999) conclude in their research review that "the field of public administration frequently has failed to provide information that would allow the reader to judge the adequacy of the research measures"; particularly troublesome, they add, is "the nearly complete neglect of issues regarding the reliability or validity of the research measures" (21).

Summary

As we suggest at the beginning of this chapter, many of the analytical challenges we confront in designing governance research—constructing empirical models that are based on a theory or logic of a governance, identifying appropriate methodologies for analysis, and applying them to reliable data—are common to social sciences research. Throughout this chapter, we urge greater communication among researchers across disciplinary boundaries regarding the context, analytical frameworks, strategies for empirical analyses, and limitations of their empirical modeling efforts. We also think it is important to acknowledge, however, the constraints imposed on researchers who are compelled to condense extensive research efforts into papers of publishable length or into brief conference presentations in making their work more widely accessible.

In sessions at the National Public Management Research Conference (Texas A&M University, December 1999) and the Midwest Political Science Association Meetings (Chicago, April 2000), researchers raised concerns similar to those we discuss in this chapter about effective social sciences research and the communication of research findings. At both of these conferences, scholars indicated their dismay at being obligated to abbreviate or omit discussion of important details or elements of their research, such as information about variable construction, the statistical methodologies they used, and alternative model specifications they may have attempted. At the same time, editors of prominent journals that publish public policy, public management, political science, and other social sciences research continue to implore researchers to produce shorter articles. We believe that this issue warrants further attention and discussion across research communities; a potential objective would be the development of broader, interdisciplinary (likely Internet-based) networks for the distribution of full-length/working paper-length essays that comprehensively address modeling, methodological, and data issues.

Notes

1. For each study, we recorded the levels of analysis and the components of the reduced-form model that the study's empirical analysis incorporated (i.e., E, C, T, M, S, O). This approach allowed for easier comparisons across studies of the types of modeling strategies and data or variables employed in the research. Second, when applicable, we described the theoretical or conceptual basis for the study, and we indicated whether the research was empirical and involved qualitative and/or quantitative methods of analysis. Finally, we listed the data sources and sample sizes and briefly noted the study's major findings

2. *Poverty Research News* 1, no. 4 (January/February 2000), published by the Joint Center for Poverty Research of the University of Chicago and Northwestern University, is devoted to issues and problems of combining quantitative and qualitative research strategies.

3. Skroban et al. assumed that any shifts in the population would be similar for the two schools and that the intervention would be the only major change introduced in either school during the period.

4. A distinctive advantage of structural equation modeling is the ability to estimate and test relations between latent or *unobserved* variables and measured factors, as specified in a conceptual model informed by theory and/or previous research.
5. LISREL (LInear Structural RELations) is a computer program.
6. Such obstacles are less of a factor for users of common data sets such as the Current Population Survey, National Longitudinal Surveys, Survey of Income and Program Participation, or other individual-level data sets.

7

Governance Research: Scholarly Applications

In preceding chapters we describe the theoretical bases underlying different logics of governance, argue for possible advantages of using a logic derived from political economy literatures, and point out the need for multidisciplinary research to understand the complexities of governance systems. Chapter 6 reviews many of the problems researchers encounter in building models of specific governance processes or complex interactions of governance regimes. A diverse group of researchers has applied an eclectic set of theoretical frameworks and empirical tools to confront these problems; the ultimate goal is to understand governance systems—including why they work (or don't work), how they work, and with what consequences.

In this chapter, we undertake a more in-depth review of empirical governance research, following two approaches. First, we begin with a review of governance research in three prominent public policy domains: federal job training programs, public schools, and publicly funded drug abuse treatment programs. Our primary objective is to draw together the findings of diverse, multidisciplinary, empirical studies of governance systems and bring into focus the cumulative insights they generate for the study of governance. In this endeavor, we synthesize the work of some "noncommunicating" researchers; thus, we also try to point out their backgrounds or methodological approaches to addressing basic questions of governance in these three policy areas. Our reviews are illustrative rather than exhaustive, with an emphasis on deriving insights for scholars rather than practitioners.

Second, we engage in a more extensive analysis of individual studies to examine more specifically the challenges governance researchers face in modeling research questions and interpreting data in light of these questions. For this analysis, we have selected seven studies that embody many strong features of empirical governance research and approach research questions in rigorous and sometimes novel ways. Although these studies are not without shortcomings, they demonstrate the possibilities of careful, theory-based explorations of consequential questions of governance.

Governance Research in Three Policy Domains

We begin our broader, policy-focused review of empirical studies of governance systems with a selection of studies concerned with publicly-sponsored employment and training programs.

Public Training Programs

The Job Training Partnership Act (JTPA) of 1982 was a major initiative of the Reagan administration's agenda to reduce the size of government and broaden the role of the private sector in the management and operation of public programs. The JTPA program was distinguished from its training program predecessors, as well as other social programs, by three important features: the extension of formal authority for program administration to private-sector representatives (on Private Industry Councils, or PICs), the introduction of a performance standards system that was based on monetary (budgetary) incentives, and a highly decentralized administrative structure that allowed substantial discretion at the state and local levels for the development of programs and the use of performance incentives. These essential structural features of JTPA programs have been preserved in the design of the new Workforce Investment Act (WIA) programs, which replaced the JTPA in July 2000.

Most scholarly research on JTPA programs has focused on the performance standards system, which recently has drawn increased attention with the initiation of reform efforts under the Government Performance and Results Act (GPRA). Like the GPRA, the JTPA performance standards system was regarded as a policy tool that would demand accountability for results (i.e., program outcomes) and lessen the government's need for costly process and compliance monitoring. Romzek (1998) describes four types of accountability that require differing strategic management focuses: hierarchical accountability for inputs (e.g., administrative rules guiding routine tasks), legal accountability for processes (e.g., audits, site visits, and other monitoring tasks), political accountability for outputs (e.g., responsiveness to stakeholders and constituencies), and professional accountability for outcomes (which best characterizes the focus of the JTPA performance standards system). As Romzek explains, an emphasis on professional accountability allows continued scrutiny of administrative discretion but defers to the discretion of managers "as they work within broad parameters, rather than on close scrutiny to ensure compliance with detailed rules and organizational directives" (Romzek 1998, 204).

The development of the JTPA performance standards system may help to explain Congress's confidence in expanding the administrative authority of private-sector representatives (through PICs) to the entire JTPA program, including authority for planning and program administration—which some observers believe should have remained a public responsibility. As Orfield and Slessarev (1986) note, a primary objection to an expanded administrative role for PICs was that power would lie with "those not accountable to any constituency through the democratic voting process" (46). Although the legislation allowed the extension of *formal* administrative authority to PICs over all program/administrative functions, it was a charge of local service delivery areas to define the extent of *real* authority or control that PICs would have over key program functions/processes.[1] These core primary work processes included defining target populations and selecting JTPA program participants, determining the scope of program services and the "network" for service provision, and monitoring program performance and developing policies/incentives to motivate program improvements. The potential for a strong role for the PICs, combined with minimal provisions for political accountability, made the JTPA program extraordinary among social programs in its emphasis on professional (or outcomes) accountability.

Our review of JTPA research shows the progression of scholarly efforts to identify the effects of performance standards, to get inside the "black box" of state and local program implementation, and to understand how bureaucratic discretion—in the selection of program participants, the structuring of administrative and service delivery arrangements, and the use of performance incentives—influenced JTPA program outcomes and impacts. The differentiation in management structures and performance incentive policies that evolved in local JTPA service delivery areas provides a unique opportunity for researchers to model and assess their effects for program operations and performance.

One of the first influential studies of JTPA programs and the performance standards system used interviews and observations of state and local JTPA program staff in Illinois; the authors conclude that the performance standards system was generating unintended consequences—specifically, an "overwhelming emphasis on placement rates and low-cost training" and screening on education levels (i.e., "cream-skimming") to produce low-cost placements (Orfield and Slessarev 1986, 5).[2] In a multisite process evaluation study that covered nine states, Dickinson et al. (1988) also found that states with policies that emphasized exceeding performance standards and placed more weight on cost standards discouraged services to hard-to-serve eligibles, provided less basic skills training, and reduced the average length of services for adults. Not all of the service delivery areas they studied emphasized high performance levels, however—suggesting the importance of examining other factors that might influence management decisions about performance objectives as well as service delivery.

To examine in greater depth how bureaucratic factors might relate to program outcomes and impacts, Heckman and various colleagues studied program implementation at several study sites in conjunction with the national JTPA study experimental evaluation. They interviewed case workers and JTPA program administrators and combined qualitative data analyses with econometric work to analyze the influence of performance standards in applicant acceptance, service assignment, and participant termination decisions, as well as the implications of these bureaucratic decisions for program outcomes (Heckman, Smith, and Taber 1996; Heckman and Smith 1995, 1997; Courty and Marschke 1997; Heckman, Heinrich, and Smith 1997; Heckman, forthcoming).

Using conditional probability models to decompose JTPA participation rates into components related to eligibility, awareness, application, and acceptance into the programs, Heckman and Smith (1997) show that voluntary choices and lack of information about JTPA programs account for more of the demographic disparities observed in program participation than bureaucratic preferences (or cream-skimming). Heckman, Heinrich, and Smith (1997) describe how differences in local management policies and social and professional norms among caseworkers might have influenced the responses of JTPA staff at different sites to performance incentive policies. They cite Heckman, Smith, and Taber (1996), who report that JTPA caseworkers in Corpus Christi manifested "social worker" preferences—that is, the caseworkers preferred to serve the least employable, in apparent defiance of the performance standards system. In contrast, Heinrich (forthcoming)—which includes econometric models of JTPA participant selection and service assignment processes—describes a service delivery area in which performance incentives were strongly reinforced in performance-based contracts, with service providers and caseworkers acutely aware of contractually defined performance expectations and the administrative emphasis on achieving high placement rates at low costs. This research contributes to our understanding of how institutional factors and bureaucratic discretion at the local level shape key programmatic decisions and influence the potential for and extent of cream-skimming.

Courty and Marschke (1997) also make important contributions in the study of JTPA performance incentives, elaborating on the moral hazard problem and potential consequences for program outcomes. They use data from the national JTPA study and information on state performance incentive policies to develop econometric models of how program administrators might use "private information" on participant outcomes, as well as their own discretion, in implementing procedural and accounting rules to influence performance outcomes and awards. Courty and Marschke present evidence suggesting that program administrators engaged in "gaming" activities, delaying formal discharge of participants in the effort to boost measured program outcomes—and inefficiently expending program resources in the process. Responding to these and related findings, Heckman, Heinrich, and Smith (1999) use a formal model to show how designers of performance standards systems might choose performance measures and reward functions that discourage local agencies from maximizing their measured performance in ways other than improving their actual performance.

Heckman and Smith's (1995) research further shows that the performance standards used to guide state and local JTPA program administrators were not effective measures of progress toward the legislative goals of increasing participants' earnings and reducing welfare dependency. They compare estimates of JTPA program earnings impacts with federal performance measures of adult participants' earnings levels at termination and 13 weeks later. Heckman and Smith found that the short-run performance measures were only weakly (and sometimes negatively) related to long-term program gains and that the relationship between earnings levels and impacts worsened over a longer period. Heckman and Smith conclude that this finding reflects a fundamental weakness of the JTPA performance management system; they argue that a positive link between the short-run measures employed and the long-term effects that are the true goals of a program is a critical prerequisite to an effective performance management system.

Although some of these studies of performance standard systems in public training programs have drawn on principal-agent theories and institutional theories of bureaucracy in interpreting results, few have framed their empirical analyses in the context of organizational theories that might contribute to a broader perspective on and interpretation of the diverse governmental factors operating within these systems. In a more recent study of JTPA programs, Heinrich and Lynn (2000) employ the reduced-form logic of governance to guide their formulation of hypotheses and specification of models for testing. They consider two main policy questions: What implications do administrative or structural arrangements in JTPA programs (e.g., performance-based administration versus traditional bureaucratic control) have for program outcomes? Does an administrative emphasis on measured performance induce agencies to change program priorities and primary work processes in ways that influence program outcomes (either positively or negatively)?

Using data from the national JTPA study, Heinrich and Lynn examine the degree to which power and authority were shared among local JTPA entities involved in program administration, as well as the extent to which public-sector versus private-sector administrative authority or control are related to the structure of local service delivery networks. For example, they find that when private-sector representatives assume more formal authority—through the role of PICs as administrative entities and recipients of federal job-training funds—they place more emphasis on measured performance and adopt administrative practices (e.g., more performance-based contracting and contracts with for-profit organizations) that also demand accountability for results.

Drawing from previous research, Heinrich and Lynn formulate two hypotheses about the relationship between governance and performance in JTPA programs: Increased levels of coordination and/or centralization of authority in the provision of employment and training services will increase program performance, and an outcomes-oriented approach and a stronger emphasis on performance requirements in administration will be positively related to measured program performance. They estimate multilevel models to disentangle and explain the roles of administrative structures and performance management policies in producing JTPA participant earnings and employment outcomes, controlling for the characteristics of participants, the services (treatment) they received, and other environmental factors.

The results of Heinrich and Lynn's models show that organizational structure is important (as is management) to the extent that managers choose the structural arrangements governing program operations. They find that centralization of authority within JTPA programs through a strong role for PICs (i.e., not requiring PICs to share power equally with local political executives) had the largest positive effect on program outcomes. According to a paradox attributed to Amartya Sen (see Miller 1992 for a discussion), delegation of administrative authority to more than one subordinate entity often leads to incoherent behavior or to inefficiency with respect to *a priori* preferences—the more so when subordinate entities have specialized (or different) functions. Milward and Provan (2000) similarly find that when mental health services networks are coordinated by a "core" agency with direct, unitary control over funding (e.g., as in the role of PICs with centralized authority), they achieve better results. Even more directly relevant are the findings of Jennings (1994) and Jennings and Ewalt (1998), who examine the effects of administrative coordination patterns on JTPA program outcomes and find that increased coordination and administrative consolidation had significant, positive effects on program outcomes.

The second main finding of Heinrich and Lynn's (2000) research is that managers also drive performance through their choices about policies that guide program operations (such as reliance on performance-based contracts, emphasis of particular performance goals, and targeting of services to specific eligible groups). Performance management policies that strongly emphasize straightforward, easily monitored program objectives appear to contribute most to a coherent focus on program goals among management and staff and to higher earnings levels and employment rates for program participants. (We discuss the practical implications of findings from the numerous studies of job-training programs reviewed in this section further in chapter 8.)

Public Schools

One of the deepest veins of literature concerning policy control of public bureaucracies addresses the problems of governing public schools. The "effective schools" literature in general is particularly broad in its topical, disciplinary, and methodological range, and studies focusing on school governance are a mere subset of this large body of research. In providing context for the research we discuss, we draw on several extensive reviews of the school effectiveness literature that more comprehensively address theoretical and empirical modeling, as well as methodological and data issues.

In a far-reaching review of earlier school effectiveness research, Purkey and Smith (1983) assess a variety of studies—including case studies, surveys, program evaluations, and implementation studies—as well as theories of the organization of schools. They determine that most of these studies generate a "list of ingredients, and rather divergent ones at that," for increasing school effectiveness, without indicating how the ingredients might be combined to produce positive student achievement (440). Purkey and Smith comment:

> How does one school have teachers with high expectations for achievement, whereas another does not? Why does one school have clear goals, whereas a second muddles through with conflicting ideas of success? Unfortunately, available research does not yet provide an answer. Most current school effectiveness research lists a variety of potential ingredients but offers little direction for mixing them together (441).

Lee, Bryk, and Smith (1993) similarly criticize early school effects research for its "black box" conception of school organization and its lack of concern with "the internal workings of schools, the process through which schools produce desired outcomes, or how their organizational structures might influence the distributions of these outcomes (either within a particular school or across the population)" (172).

Purkey and Smith (1983) appear to embrace March and Olsen's (1976) theory of schools as "loosely coupled systems" rather than the classical bureaucratic perspective of schools. The bureaucratic perspective of schools as formal, rationally controlled organizations that are characterized by a functional division of labor, teaching roles defined by subject and student type, rule-governed social interactions, and limited individual discretion undervalues informal, personal, and communal aspects of schools as well as some larger environmental factors (Lee, Bryk, and Smith 1993). The early findings of school effectiveness research—that characteristics common to similarly effective schools do not necessarily operate and interact in the same way within the schools—also negate a bureaucratic view. "Our view," Purkey and Smith assert, "is that most successful school change efforts will be messier and more idiosyncratic than systematic" (446). Noting the dearth of longitudinal studies, the lack of empirical data, and small and unrepresentative samples in many studies, they argue for more longitudinal studies that adopt a conception of schools as nested layers (classrooms within schools) within functioning social systems that embody distinctive cultures.

One of the earlier empirical studies by Meyer, Scott, and Deal (1981), for example, espouses a view of school governance that is similar to that urged by Purkey and Smith. Meyer, Scott, and Deal analyzed data collected from multiple layers of a San Francisco Bay-area school system, including surveys and interviews with superintendents from 30 school districts, 103 elementary schools in these districts, and 469 teachers in a subsample of 16 schools in these districts. On the basis of simple correlational analyses of these data and analysis of variance, they conclude, "Schools exist in environments that are highly elaborated in their institutional structures but relatively poorly developed in their technical systems" (170). For this reason, survival is better pursued through conformity to "wider institutional rules" rather than through "coupling of the organizational structure with the technical activities." In other words, the instrumental use of formal authority may have little real influence over the activities of teaching and learning and how they are organized and evaluated by school personnel and their constituencies.

Chubb and Moe (1990) also review effective schools research, in which the organizational foundations of effective performance are identified as "clear school goals, rigorous academic standards, order and discipline, homework, strong leadership by the principal, teacher participation in decisionmaking, parental support and co-operation, and high expectations for student performance" (16). They also point out that questions regarding how public policy can be used to promote such effective organizations are not adequately addressed in the literature. Chubb and Moe argue that "institutions of educational governance [are] fundamental causes of the very problems they are supposed to be solving" (18). They reject the "open systems" theorizing that one finds, for example, in Scott (1998) and Meyer and Rowan (1977). According to Chubb and Moe (1990), "Different institutions constrain and aggregate individual choices in very different ways, and this, in the end, is why different kinds of organizations emerge, prosper, or fail within them" (21)

More recent school governance studies are concerned with large- and small-scale efforts to reform educational organizations and processes and, in particular, with their implications for schools' and individual student's performance. Cohen (1995), for example, studies the effects of public education reform efforts in California, Michigan, and South Carolina. In his case-study analyses, he describes school reform in terms of providing "guidance for instruction": Reformers seek to strengthen it and render it coherent. Reformers seek more intellectually demanding instruction; new purposes for schools, such as critical thinking, intellectual independence, and cultivation of students' ideas and interests; and stiffer standards for performance. Cohen concludes that policy goals such as lean, focused, coherent, and demanding education are transformed at the school level into "an astonishing profusion of varied reform ideas and practices" (Cohen 1995, 32). He argues that "systemic reform has been promoted as though it were chiefly a matter of policy," but "policy can work only if it is surrounded by an enabling politics" (32). A "working policy" in this context presumably means an observed low variance around a designed model of how primary work should be performed at school sites.

In a similar spirit—but with a somewhat different finding— Bimber (1993, 1994) investigates the connection between institutional structure and organizational performance by exploring the extent to which variance in "governance systems" in high schools was associated with differences in school activities and performance. Bimber employs a case-study approach to compare patterns of decision making in four high schools "chosen to represent four points along a spectrum of decentralization" (1994, 4). The four governance models he assesses are "traditional, centralized school governance"; "modest decentralization," involving local school control of a discretionary budget; an *avant garde* form of decentralization, involving extensive devolution of authority to the school site and a form of school site democracy; and complete independence from central authority. "Evidence from the three public schools," Bimber says, "shows that there is not much variation in the nature of decisionmaking under different degrees and forms of decentralization . . . " (1994, 46)—in stark contrast to decision making at the independent school. He concludes, "[D]ecentralization efforts can fail to produce meaningful governance changes. To be effective at removing constraints and creating environments in which schools take responsibility for the education process, decentralization should address the need for comprehensive changes across all interrelated categories of decisionmaking" (Bimber 1994, ix).[3]

Lee, Bryk, and Smith (1993) describe the Chicago Public Schools' reform efforts, beginning in the late 1980s, as "a response to unrepresentative bureaucratic systems" and one of the "most visible and fundamental current reform effort[s]" (195). Lynn and Kowalczyk (1996) study the effect of two shifts in governance regimes in Chicago Public Schools: from so-called traditional, top-down administration through the introduction of discretion and local democracy at the school site to the recentralization of administration at the district level under the control of the mayor. Their analysis of formal authority within these regimes is "mapped" from official documents, primarily the pre-reform School Codes of 1985 and the post-reform School Codes of 1994. Lynn and Kowalczyk (1996) observe a general tendency for the various stakeholders to defend against loss of influence. As a result, governance changes tended to be undercut or nullified by offsetting adjustments in the system as a whole. They reach the preliminary conclusion that "Chicago public schools are probably becoming less, not more, governable; the job of principal is probably harder, rather than easier, to perform in a focused, goal-oriented way; and the leverage of local communities over the quality of teaching and learning in the schools has not obviously been enhanced in any predictable sense" (31).

Elmore, Abelman, and Fuhrman (1996) also studied changes in educational governance regimes; they focused on reforms to increase educational accountability in Kentucky and Mississippi. They argue that "all attempts to change relationships among actors in complex governance structures entail three distinct types of problems: . . . the *design* of the new systems . . . the *implementation* of new systems . . . [and] the *politics* of the new systems" (3). As examples of design elements in the "new accountability systems" for school reform, they identify state accreditation of districts (or assessments of individual schools), mandatory testing of students (general performance or performance in specific domains), and a version of relative performance assessment or measured improvement against performance-based proficiency thresholds. They use the term "implementation" to refer to features such as public reporting of results, rewards or penalties for performance, and exemptions from process regulations. Examples of political elements include constituency pressures, resource constraints, and political stability.

Elmore, Abelman, and Fuhrman (1996) consider the challenges states confront in designing accountability systems, including "whom to hold accountable, for what levels of performance, on the basis of what types of performance indicators, with what consequences" (4). They analyze information from administrative databases such as the Kentucky Instructional Results Information System and the "Mississippi Report Card," as well as information from interviews and other qualitative data sources. They find that "constituency pressures moderate policymakers' initial stances, resulting in efforts that provide more local leeway than originally planned; resource constraints affect policy design and implementation; and the instability of the political environment threatens the stability of policy and its translation into practice" (45). On the basis of their analysis, they suggest that creating incentives that promote improvements in student learning, over and above basic maintenance types of oversight, is an extraordinarily complex task that poses challenges even for well-developed state systems. Performance-based accountability systems require high levels of technical expertise and competence to manage and aid districts and schools in improving performance, as well as ongoing support from elected officials (or political stability). States' ambivalence about these systems lies partly in their concern that performance criteria are being substituted for process regulations that "protect constituencies and serve as important statements about minimal services to be provided to all children . . . and serve important interests, such as the state's desire to limit corruption, inefficiency, and waste" (57).

Hanushek, Rivkin, and Taylor (1996) also consider questions of local management, discretion, and accountability in public schools. They note that if schools are effective in using their resources to produce higher student achievement, policymaking is simplified in that one can focus on the appropriate level and distribution of resources and allow local school districts to determine their use. If schools are not effective in translating resources into good student performance, however, policymakers must contend with choices about particular approaches for increasing school effectiveness or for developing incentive mechanisms to guide local choices. On the basis of their review of the large body of school effectiveness research, Hanushek, Rivkin, and Taylor find little evidence that local school districts are effective in converting additional resources into higher student achievement. Even more pertinent to the issues considered in this book, however, is their finding that "virtually none of the previously identified studies considers how the state structure for schooling affects outcomes or . . . the estimates of resource effects" (9). Furthermore, they determine that researchers' neglect in appropriately accounting for the influence of these regulatory, financial, and other governance factors on student achievement results in biased estimates of the effects of school resources on student outcomes.

Some of the research on school governance analyzes the influence of institutional structures and public policies on students' educational outcomes (addressing the questions we posed above) and ameliorating the level-of-analysis problem through the use of multilevel statistical modeling. As we discuss in chapter 6, multilevel statistical methodologies applied in governance research may facilitate empirical tests of hypotheses about how factors or variables measured at one level of an administrative hierarchy might interact with variables at one or more other levels within government and social systems. Goldstein (1995), one of the leaders in developing and applying these methods to education research, emphasizes the

long-recognized fact that school systems are one of the more obvi-
ous examples of a hierarchical structure, with students grouped or
nested within classrooms, schools, districts, and states. Multilevel
statistical analyses that explicitly model this grouping are more
likely to disentangle the influences of factors such as regulatory policies, organizational practice, and management on student achievement from those of student, family, and other environmental
characteristics.

Roderick and Camburn (1997) and Roderick, Jacob, and Bryk
(2000)—who have been examining the Chicago public school system's decision to end "social promotion" and increase student
achievement—demonstrate how these modeling techniques can be
applied to address educational governance and policy questions at
the school district level. Roderick and Camburn (1997) test hypotheses about students' likelihood of failing courses and their likelihood of subsequent recovery from grade failure. Their models allow
them to assess the potential effectiveness of three alternative strategies (individual- and system-focused) for improving student performance: improving the educational preparation of students before
they enter high school; creating "transition years" to ease stress and
increase support for students; and instituting large-scale, school-
wide restructuring and reform efforts to improve teaching practices
and school environments. They find several important relationships among individual- and school-level variables and generate
strong evidence of school-level effects that suggest that "governance
and instructional environments . . . matter" (32).

Roderick, Jacob, and Bryk (2000) use three-level hierarchical linear models to analyze the effects of new policies regulating student
promotion and retention in public schools. They model students'
short-term and long-term achievement gains and educational attainment as a function of school demographics and characteristics, measures of policy implementation and teachers' classroom strategies,
parental involvement within the schools, and the school environment and "prior school development." Their study also includes a
qualitative component with intensive case studies of each school's
approach to promotional policy implementation and a longitudinal
investigation of students' experiences under the policy.

Roderick, Jacob, and Bryk (2000) explore, with rigorous empirical
and qualitative methods, relationships across and within schools,
classrooms, students, and parents to address key questions: How do

the magnitude of these policy effects vary by school characteristics, and to what extent can they be linked to teachers' and principals' responses to the policies or to the underlying quality or structure of the school environment? How does variation in the implementation of the policies shape student achievement? These questions are precisely the type that Purkey and Smith (1983); Chubb and Moe (1990); and Smith, Scoll, and Link (1995) argue have been seriously neglected in school effectiveness research.

Substance Abuse Treatment Programs

Following dramatic increases in illicit drug use in the 1960s, including high levels of drug abuse among American soldiers in Vietnam, President Nixon introduced the first major federal policy initiative to expand the availability of drug abuse treatment. In 1971, Congress unanimously supported the creation of a Special Action Office for Drug Abuse Prevention to coordinate federal resources for drug abuse prevention, treatment, and research. A simultaneous, massive increase in federal funding of drug abuse treatment spurred the rapid development of community-based treatment programs—which expanded from just 6 centers in 1969 to 300 treatment programs in 1973 and to more than 3,000 programs by 1977 (Fletcher, Tims, and Brown 1997). The earliest large-scale study of drug abuse treatment effectiveness—the Drug Abuse Reporting Program (DARP), which collected data from approximately 44,000 clients and 52 federally funded treatment programs between 1969 and 1972—also was initiated during this period. DARP was followed by the Treatment Outcome Prospective Study (TOPS), which was intended to expand the data collected in DARP and involved more than 11,000 patients in 41 programs between 1979 and 1981.

Longitudinal, nonexperimental analyses of the cost-effectiveness of drug abuse treatment programs in DARP and TOPS showed that drug abuse treatment programs were effective in reducing illicit drug use during and after treatment across all three major treatment modalities—long-term residential, out-patient drug-free, and methadone maintenance. Analyses of data collected in these studies focused on relating client histories of illicit drug use and participation in treatment to their observed illicit drug use and criminal activities in the follow-up period. As Gerstein and Harwood (1990) emphasize, however, drug treatment "is not a single entity but a variety of different approaches to different populations and goals" (132). Although TOPS obtained more program-level data, information collected about treatment programs or organizations was limited in focus to the types of services delivered and program environments.

In the early 1980s, federal funding for drug abuse treatment was significantly reduced while new problems emerged—different patterns of drug use (e.g., crack cocaine use), AIDS, and inadequate resources for treatment, along with changes in the organizational structure of the treatment system—that limited the applicability of previous study findings. The 1981 Omnibus Budget Reconciliation Act not only decreased funding for these programs by 25 percent, it also converted public monies for drug abuse treatment into state block grants. Research showed that within the primary treatment modalities, differences in program size, setting, organizational structure, philosophy, therapeutic approach, and funding were becoming more apparent (Hubbard et al. 1997). Little was known, however, about how these treatment programs were adapting to changes in federal funding and illicit drug use or whether progress was being made in translating earlier research results into more effective treatment practices.

In an effort to address some of the more complex questions about drug abuse treatment effectiveness, two additional large-scale studies were initiated in the mid- to late 1980s: the Outpatient Drug Abuse Treatment Systems (ODATS) study and the Drug Abuse Treatment Outcomes Study (DATOS). ODATS, which is ongoing, surveys unit directors and supervisors in drug abuse treatment programs to obtain extensive organization-level data on the characteristics of drug abuse treatment programs, their environments, and their clients. ODATS has progressed through four waves of data collection from a total of more than 600 programs since 1984, although no client-level data are collected. In contrast, a major strength of the DATOS research is the extensiveness of client-level data obtained from more than 10,000 adults in 99 drug abuse treatment programs between 1991 and 1993. Research using ODATS and DATOS data is attempting to evaluate how changes in program resources and the financing of treatment, organizational structure and program design, and treatment practices and treatment duration relate to client outcomes (controlling for client and environmental characteristics).

D'Aunno, Folz-Murphy, and Lin (1998), for example, use multiple and logistic regression analyses to study the extent to which key methadone treatment practices—dosage levels, treatment duration, and client influence in dose decisions—changed from 1988 to 1995 in a panel sample of methadone units, as well as which treatment practices were related to improved client outcomes. Although they determined that treatment practices improved significantly, they also found that many units continued to use practices that did not meet desired standards (e.g., the average methadone dose level was still less than the recommended minimum in 1995). Government regulation of methadone treatment had a positive effect on treatment practices; the more that treatment units reported their practices were influenced by regulation, the higher their dose limits and average methadone dosage levels (D'Aunno and Vaughn, 1992).

In an earlier study on the effectiveness of methadone treatment for heroin addiction, Attewell and Gerstein (1979) had come to a different conclusion about the effectiveness of federal government regulation of drug abuse treatment. They drew on organizational theory to develop a conceptual model of policy implementation that "link[ed] the macrosociology of federal policy on opiate addiction to the microsociology of methadone treatment" (311). Using a case-study approach—including observational research in clinics, interviews with clients, and analyses of program records from clinics over several years—they investigated managerial responses at the program level to government policy and institutional regulation, as well as clients' behavior and responses to subsequent program changes. Based on qualitative analysis of these observations, they conclude that compromised federal policies resulted in ineffective local management practices and poor outcomes for clients.

In considering alternative explanations for the divergent findings of Attewell and Gerstein's (1979) and D'Aunno, Folz-Murphy, and Lin's (1998) studies, one might investigate whether government policies have changed over time to become more effective in guiding local methadone treatment practices. Both studies suggest that more information is needed about what influences treatment unit responses to government regulation or what types of treatment units or managers of these units are more likely to alter their practices in response to regulatory mandates. Because the ODATS data were obtained at a single organizational level and at cross-sections in time, assessment of the complex, hierarchical relationships among chang-

ing government policies, drug abuse treatment organization practices, and managerial and client responses is impossible. The
ODATS researchers acknowledge that data are not available from individual staff members about treatment practices, nor from individual clients about their characteristics and outcomes.

Although the DATOS data are comparatively rich in client-level
information, the limited amount of data collected about programs
(i.e., their structures, environments, and other relevant characteristics) and linked to client-level data likewise diminishes their usefulness for exploring issues of program governance and management, as
well as their relationship to client outcomes. Hubbard et al. (1997),
for example, analyzed the DATOS one-year follow-up data; they
found that treatment duration was one of the most significant correlates with positive treatment outcomes across different treatment
modalities. They also conclude, however, that the full potential of
treatment is not achieved for all clients, and that "more complex
questions of access to, use of, and effectiveness of core comprehensive therapies and services for diverse client sub-populations with
different lengths of exposure to treatment" should be investigated
(276).

In studying the relationship of counseling and self-help activities
to DATOS client outcomes, Etheridge et al. (1999) similarly point
out that although treatment duration, treatment retention, counseling, psychological impairment, and regular participation in 12-step
self-help groups have been associated with post-treatment outcomes in a multitude of studies, the ability of programs to provide
these services effectively varies considerably. Etheridge et al. suggest that the inconsistent relationship between treatment services
and outcomes may be explained in part by variation in program administration or the extent to which programs are able to target treatment and services to patients' needs. In their regression models that
predict service receipt and program outcomes, Etheridge et al.
found that the simple "program attended" indicator is one of the
most significant explanatory factors. In discussing this finding, they
speculate as follows:

> Although the investigation of the influence of specific program
> characteristics on patient outcomes was outside the scope of this in-
> vestigation, the significance of program as a predictor in two of the
> modalities suggests that patients' participation in self-help after

leaving the formal treatment episode is related to certain structural, philosophical practice features of these treatment programs (109).

Etheridge et al. (1999) go on to suggest that drug abuse treatment researchers should investigate program-level influences on patient outcomes, using statistical techniques such as hierarchical linear modeling that facilitate analyses of nested or multilevel relationships. Specifically, they argue that the development of more complex, multilevel models is an important next step in extending our understanding of the separate and combined contributions of patient, program administration, and treatment process variables to treatment outcomes and for providing "the kinds of policy- and practice-relevant information necessary to improve the effectiveness and efficiency of drug abuse treatment in this era of increased cost constraints and accountability" (111). Broome, Simpson, and Joe (1999) add that poor treatment results are commonly assumed to be a patient problem and that little attention has been given to the way program staff, administrative policies, and resources are used to respond to patient needs.

Substance abuse treatment research in the past three decades has involved numerous large-scale, multi-site, clinical studies and has produced some clear findings about some aspects of substance abuse treatment that facilitate positive post-treatment outcomes. These findings include consistent associations between program effectiveness and retention in treatment, counseling intensity, methadone dosage levels, regular participation in 12-step self-help groups, and provision of psychiatric and vocational services to clients with specific deficiencies in these areas. Yet researchers understand comparatively little about why these programs vary so much in their *implementation* of effective service strategies and treatment practices—that is, in applying the relevant results of clinical and "best practices" research to the management of their programs. The major research questions identified by Gerstein and Harwood (1990) still await cogent answers:

What client and program factors influence treatment-seeking behavior, treatment retention and efficacy, and relapse after treatment? *How can these factors be better managed?* (194, emphasis added)

What are the relations of treatment performance (that is, differential outcomes, taking initial client characteristics into account), the content and organization of treatment (specific site arrangements, service offerings, therapeutic approaches, staffing practices), and the costs of treatment? (195)

The lack of useful research on the governance and management of drug abuse treatment programs is partly a consequence of limited data on structural and management factors in the DARP, TOPS, and DATOS studies. In the ODATS study, considerable data are available on organizational factors, but there are no client-level data that would allow for analyses of the interrelationships and possible cross-level interactions between treatment service delivery and individual client characteristics (which define the primary clinical level) and institutional factors and administrative policies that operate at one (or more) levels above the clinical domain.

One additional drug abuse treatment study—the National Treatment Improvement Evaluation Study (NTIES)—was designed specifically to measure and learn from the cross-level linkages that might exist between post-treatment outcomes and institutional and programmatic factors—including administrative and financial structures, external organizational relationships, program policies, treatment philosophies, administrative procedures, staff characteristics, and others—as well as between these variables and client-level characteristics. The NTIES data were collected from more than 500 drug abuse treatment service delivery units and more than 6,500 clients during the years 1993–1995; the service delivery unit and client-level data sets can be directly linked for multilevel statistical analyses. A new research agenda using the NTIES data is being developed by researchers at the National Opinion Research Center and the University of Chicago, with the goal of increasing our understanding of the main levels of policy, administration, and management that might either block or facilitate the implementation of effective drug abuse treatment practices.

More Extensive Reviews of Individual Governance Studies

In this section, we shift our focus to more extensive reviews of individual studies, with greater attention to specific modeling, methodological, and data issues confronted by the authors of these studies.

Carpenter (1996) develops a formal model of agency behavior under funding uncertainty. He points out that significant coefficients

on aggregate budget variables (regressed on some measure of performance) often are interpreted as support for the "budgetary control
hypothesis."[4] He raises three primary conceptual shortcomings in
these interpretations, however: First, the conclusion does not specify whether resource constraints or political signals constitute the
causal mechanism that influences agency action. Second, such conclusions are not specific about whether budgetary control emanates
from the president or from Congress. Third, existing interpretations
of support for the budgetary control hypothesis do not explore the
timeliness of agency responsiveness to budgetary control or how
such responsiveness compares to other possible control efforts. Carpenter's analysis confronts the conceptual imprecision of model
components (in this case, "budget" variables) across studies, as well
as the need for specificity in modeling, measurement, and interpretation of budgetary control.

Carpenter develops a model with two primary components:
"adaptive expectations"—in which agency officials make "con-
scious and direct use of transmitted information older than that
available at present" (Carpenter 1996, 287)—and a model of linear
information processing in the agency, adjusted to account for levels
of hierarchy, which reflects "the signal processing behavior of a hierarchical agency in which each level of hierarchy exhibits expo-
nential response delay" (289). Carpenter's analysis is grounded in
behavioral approaches for analyzing organizations (Simon 1947),
and he draws from and responds to theoretical models—empirical
and nonempirical—that address budgetary control, uncertainty, and
signaling (e.g., Bendor and Moe 1985; Fenno 1966; McCubbins
1985; Weingast and Moran 1983; Wildavsky 1988; Wood and Waterman 1991, 1993).

Carpenter separately applies his model to data from the Food and
Drug Administration (FDA) from 1938–1990 and to the Federal
Communications Commission (FCC) from 1933–1990. Dependent
variables that measure agency performance are product samples
taken and inspections conducted (FDA) and the number of broad-
cast station inspections and the number of discrepancy notices
given to ship radio operators (FCC). All four of these dependent
variables might be considered either outcome O or primary work T
variables in the notation of a reduced-form model of governance. Independent variables include lagged dependent variables, three measures representing different budget hypotheses (S), presidential

party indicators (*E*), party balances of Congressional oversight committees (*E*), and the size of the regulated industry (*E* or *C*). The FDA analysis also controls for amendments that strengthened the agency's visibility and funding (*E*), and the FCC analysis controls for the party balance of commission members (*S*).[5]

Carpenter's modeling strategy reflects model generation that "emphasizes thorough diagnostic testing and model reduction" (Carpenter 1996, 290) and model comparison strategies. His model generation process is extremely careful and clear: He conducts auxiliary analyses as diagnostics, then estimates the corrected, reduced models and presents them along with the initial models. Carpenter concludes that existing models of budgetary influence are misspecified and that "control over regulatory programs exercised by elected authorities through agency budgets may best be characterized as signaling influence" (298). He proposes a new measure that incorporates budget information as an explanatory variable in such models, allowing for delays in inference and screening effects by the agency. Thus, Carpenter conducts model comparisons—different interpretations of budget control influences—within the model. He also conducts a wider model comparison in which he identifies—but argues against—three alternative explanations of his findings: one based on "a mechanical adjustment model" of administrative complexity in the agency's regulatory process, another derived from a "slack resources" hypothesis, and the third employing a "strategic delay" interpretation of these findings.

Carpenter comments that "[s]tudents of organization have long recognized that public bureaucracies are not monolithic institutions of the sort that simply translate aggregate resources into output or choice, yet all our statistic models portray regulatory agencies as if they acted in precisely this fashion" (Carpenter 1996, 299). The theories, models, and methods that Carpenter employs constitute an exemplary exploration that addresses these shortcomings.

Provan and Milward (1995) argue that studies that link network structures and effectiveness have received little attention. Furthermore, many network studies build primarily from theoretical bases of resource dependence (Pfeffer and Salancik 1978) and transaction cost economics (Williamson 1985), which encourage a focus on the "organizational antecedents and outcomes of network involvement, with little attention paid to the network as a whole, except for its governance and structure" (Provan and Milward 1995, 1). Provan and Milward directly address this dearth of research, asking "[w]hat, if any, is the relationship between the structure and context of mental health networks and their effectiveness?" (4)—where they measure effectiveness as enhanced client well-being (O).

Provan and Milward use questionnaire and interview data from 1991–1992, drawn from individual health and human service agencies in community mental health networks at four sites (Providence, Tucson, Akron, and Albuquerque); they draw client outcomes from a sample of all client outcomes. Their study employs primarily qualitative methods, utilizing a case survey approach, in which "multiple levels of analysis (individual, agency, and network levels) are used to develop an in-depth picture of a single case" (Provan and Milward 1995, 4).

Provan and Milward use a multi-constituency approach for assessing effectiveness, building on work by Zammuto (1984), and consider explanatory variables related to network integration (Freeman 1979; J. Scott 1991) that include network density (the extent to which agencies are operationally linked to one another), centralization (whether links and activities are organized around any one or small group of organizations), resource munificence (per capita state spending on mental health services for the population studied), degree of state fiscal control of agencies, and system stability (of the environment where service delivery occurred). State fiscal control and system stability may be regarded as environmental components of a governance model; the network measures might be considered environmental, primary work, and/or structure components.

Provan and Milward generate four propositions for future network research. They predict that network effectiveness will be greater when the network is integrated through centralization, when external control is direct, when the network is more stable (though they do not expect stability to be a sufficient condition for effectiveness), and when resources are sufficient (they point out that availability of resources does not guarantee network effectiveness, but the lack of resources is likely to limit effectiveness).[6]

Provan and Milward provide an exhaustive justification for their model measures, although they do not always consider alternative interpretations of these measures. They do discuss limitations of the analysis, including possible omitted variables (e.g., "historical patterns of funding, system evolution, patterns of treatment, or the mix and distribution of services among providers" as well as client characteristics or organizational level variables). They do not speculate, however, about how their model findings might have changed if they had taken these factors into account.

Provan and Milward's research links network studies to issues of interest to policy makers: Are network structures effective in improving client outcomes? If so, what aspects of the network enhance or impede effectiveness? This exploratory study takes an important step in the "understanding of networks and network effectiveness that goes beyond the commonly heard but unsubstantiated claim that network involvement is a good thing" (Provan and Milward 1995, 30).

Chubb (1985) argues that previous empirical research on intergovernmental relations that was based on models of federalism and implementation emphasize a system's complexity and make it "difficult to generalize about the political and bureaucratic factors associated with different implementation outcomes; complexity confounds parsimonious explanations and demands the introduction of special considerations that can only be gleaned from careful case study" (994–995). In addressing these lines of research, Chubb's main goal is to show the possibilities for formal specification and quantitative analysis of these relationships.

Chubb employs theoretical perspectives from principal-agent analysis (with multiple principals), the new economics of organization and political economy literatures (e.g., McCubbins and Schwartz 1984; Miller and Moe 1983; Moe 1984, 1985; Weingast and Moran 1983), and fiscal federalism. Chubb aims "to show that political as well as economic influences by the national government on state and local governments can be conceptualized within the single theoretical framework of principal-agent theory and analyzed empirically with the rigorous quantitative methods of public finance" (Chubb 1985, 999).

The analysis uses data from 1965–1979[7] and examines dependent variables of total educational expenditures for local school districts, and total state and local spending for vocational education (with a separate analysis for spending on disadvantaged students). These funding measures may be considered structure variables from a reduced-form model of governance. Explanatory variables include environmental and political influences such as oversight committee membership and ideology for the different programs; the need or taste for education at the local or state level; presidential administration indicators; other funding sources (*S*); and private income and the client's taste for education (*C*). Using a three-stage generalized least squares method (involving seemingly unrelated regressions), Chubb finds that "a grant without the benefit of matching incentives, and despite local disincentives against cooperation with redistributive programs, was more stimulating than a grant that suffered more of these problems; . . . differences in grant performance related in a straightforward fashion to variations in the interests of politicians overseeing the agencies that monitored the grants" (Chubb 1985, 1011).

Chubb offers little discussion of alternative interpretations of his findings or alternative interpretations of the variables he uses in the analysis. Other aspects of the model, however, are carefully detailed and defended. For example, Appendix 1 of the paper discusses potential problems with using data pooled across time and states, as well as the strategy for addressing these problems. In a footnote, Chubb addresses some possible omitted variables in the analysis and defends their exclusion from the model.[8]

Chubb points out that "the study of contemporary federalism has developed along two lines, one economic and the other political, that fortuitously have complementary strengths and weaknesses. By bringing these two lines together it may be possible to progress substantially further, analyzing the role of politics formally and quantitatively, and the role of economics in the context of administrative and political constraints that plainly matter" (Chubb 1985, 1011). His analysis is a good example of the possibilities of such eclectic, multidisciplinary empirical governance research.

Goodrick and Salancik (1996) examine the effects of organizational constraints and institutional norms on primary work practices. Building on neoinstitutional theory (e.g., DiMaggio and Powell 1983; Meyer and Rowan 1977; Meyer, Scott, and Deal 1983), Goodrick and Salancik argue that "organizational interests play a role in selecting practices, but as an addition to the constraint provided by prevailing institutions rather than as an alternative to them. Interests play this role when institutions are uncertain and, hence, insufficient for constraining choices" (Goodrick and Salancik 1996, 3). They expect that institutional norms will be most uncertain when means for pursuing goals are unspecified, when a knowledge base for primary work is not clearly defined, or when institutional values are conflicting.

Goodrick and Salancik analyze physicians' decisions to perform Cesarean section deliveries, which represent the second situation they identify in which institutional norms will be uncertain, allowing for organizational influences on practice. Their dependent variable is a hospital-level construct: the primary Cesarean section rate (a T or O variable in the reduced-form governance model). Cesarean sections are "regulated by a core set of institutional standards about the need or lack of need for the procedure, as well as standards at the margin, where uniform agreement does not exist (Goodrick and Salancik 1996, 5–6). Because agreement is lacking at these margins, they argue, the "knowledge base for practices is incompletely specified" (6). When mothers face very high or very low risks, institutional norms are clear concerning whether to perform a Cesarean. Goodrick and Salancik hypothesize that organizational influences on practice will be most salient at intermediate levels of risk and that these organizational influences are likely to vary by hospital ownership (for-profit, nonprofit, government), financing (fee-for-service or prepaid insurance), and teaching status. All of these variables represent structural (S) components.

Using 1978–1986 data from all California hospitals with delivery services, Goodrick and Salancik also construct independent variables of risk, which might be considered measures of client characteristics. They use ordinary least squares (OLS), generalized least squares (GLS), and Poisson regressions (to appropriately model the rareness of the outcome of interest for most hospitals) in a series of analyses and provide details about model diagnostic tests for autocorrelation and heteroscedasticity. They conclude that "[h]ospitals' differential responsiveness to treatment standards for cesareans . . . are primarily exhibited when those standards are most uncertain, at intermediate levels of measured risk. . . . And . . . there is little evidence that hospitals' discretion in responding to inferred risk factors interacts with the level of risk faced" (Goodrick and Salancik 1996, 23).

Although Goodrick and Salancik did not discuss alternative interpretations of their variables, they do raise three possible limitations of their study. First, "risk measures are not exhaustive (i.e., we had no data on high birth weight), leaving open the possibility that unmeasured risk may compromise interpretation of our results" (Goodrick and Salancik 1996, 24). Pointing to evidence from one of their regression specifications, however, they argue that the absence of main effects for hospital type (after entering interaction terms with risk) indicates that unmeasured risks are not a serious concern. Second, they raise the possibility that their findings represent an ecological fallacy because they used hospital-level data to understand individual-level (physicians and patients) interactions. They point to results from previous research, as well as results they would have been more likely to find had an ecological fallacy been a problem, to argue that their findings are likely not affected by ecological fallacy. Finally, the HMO hospitals in the sample were all part of the same organization, and the authors cannot disentangle the effects they found for HMOs from the management of that particular network of hospitals.

Goodrick and Salancik's study represents a strictly confirmatory approach to modeling in governance research. It also conveys a logic of governance grounded in socialized choice: "Institutional forces set the very framework within which technical forces operate . . . technical practices are embedded in institutional frameworks and . . . these frameworks resolve uncertainty by specifying the logic upon which the rules about the 'correct' use of a practice are based" (Goodrick and Salancik 1996, 25). Furthermore, they model and test the importance of organizational influences when institutional norms are uncertain. Finally, the study is of interest for the role of public management in governance systems, "exploring how institutional theory and strategic management can inform each other by specifying the constraints under which strategic choice is exercised" (25).

Nalbantian and Schotter (1997) conduct experiments to explore individuals' responses to group incentives for compensation. They argue that formal economic models of behavior under group incentives have not been complemented by methodologically sound empirical explorations. In addition to the lack of variation among different incentive schemes, which prohibits sound empirical tests, Nalbantian and Schotter point out that many empirical studies that attempt to examine participatory or other schemes are "suspect due to methodological weaknesses, most notably, the frequent failure to control other potential explanatory variables and for feedback relationships" (316). Their research tests the influence of partnership payment schemes (revenue sharing), target-based schemes (based on the work of Holmstrom 1982 and others), tournament-based schemes that rely on intraorganizational competition, and individual monitoring schemes that vary in probability of monitoring by the principal.

To conduct the study, Nalbantian and Schotter divided 400 persons into groups of 12 (group members did not know other members of their team and did not have information about individual effort levels of other team members).[9] They conducted two phases of the study; each phase involved two experiments. In each experiment, subjects participated in different kinds of incentive schemes, with 25 repeated interactions (for the same kind of scheme). In the second experiment in each phase, the incentive scheme was switched. The different phases allowed the researchers to test whether participants behaved differently with regard to certain incentives schemes if the order in which they participated in a basic revenue-sharing plan was switched.

From regression analysis of the experiments' results, Nalbantian and Schotter conclude that "the history of a group and its performance in the past is an important predictor of how that group will perform when a new incentive program is introduced. In addition, . . . one effective way to increase group effort is to introduce some within-firm competition between work units performing the same task" (Nalbantian and Schotter 1997, 335). Furthermore, they find that monitoring can be effective—but is costly—and that subjects shirked when monitoring probabilities were low.

Because this study was conducted under controlled conditions, it did not account for many other factors that might affect outcomes in a workplace setting. Nalbantian and Schotter acknowledge this point but argue that the research represents an initial empirical foray into understanding the theoretical implications of group payment schemes: "[O]ur experiments provide at best a bare-bones economist's view of the incentive problem. They characterize productive performance as the outcome of a noncooperative game and are concerned solely with the incentive properties of the various reward formulae as the explanation for behavior. Psychologists, compensation practitioners, and others certainly would protest that life is far different in the workplace than in our experiments" (Nalbantian and Schotter 1997, 335–36).

Nalbantian and Schotter's study is an example of a model comparison approach, in which competing models of individual behavior under group incentives are put to an experimental test. Although the model, stripped of institutional context, may strike many observers as stark, the authors argue that it establishes "an economic baseline which helps determine how much more of observed behavior under group incentives needs to be explained" (Nalbantian and Schotter 1997, 336–37). Furthermore, although public-sector governance researchers might overlook such a study because it examines pay-for-performance schemes in for-profit organizational settings, the findings about intrafirm competition and establishment of group norms may provide useful insights for public-sector managers.

Uzzi (1996) examines firms' links with other firms in networks of relationships and the influence these links may have on firm survival or failure. He argues that the concept of embeddedness "does not explain concretely how social ties affect economic outcomes" (674). In particular, Uzzi examines structural embeddedness, which "focuses on the relational quality of interactor exchanges and the architecture of network ties" (675).

Uzzi bases his analysis in organization theory and social network theory (e.g., Burt 1992; Granovetter 1985; Hannan and Freeman 1989; Powell 1990). Uzzi conducts an ethnographic analysis of 23 New York apparel firms (described in Appendix A of the paper) and uses these findings to construct hypotheses for a quantitative analysis of network ties among about 480 union firms. He identifies key elements of embeddedness as trust, "fine-grained information transfer," and "joint problem-solving arrangements." He predicts that firms involved with others through embedded ties (instead of arm's-length transactions) will be more likely to survive but that relationships that include arm's-length and embedded ties will enhance firm survival more than if firms' relationships consist of just one kind of tie.

The dependent variable is firm survival or failure during calendar year 1991 (an O variable). Explanatory variables include measures of embeddedness (measured by first-order network coupling, social capital embeddedness, and second-order network coupling); network size, network centrality; organization age; organization size; and whether the firm was a "generalist" (i.e., the firm made multiple products). These variables might be considered environmental and structure components of a governance system. Explanatory variables also included indicators for the location of the firm (E components).

Uzzi finds support for his main hypotheses about the links between embeddedness and firm failure (summarized effectively in

Uzzi 1996, Figure 5). He finds that "embeddedness increases economic effectiveness along a number of dimensions . . . —organizational learning, risk-sharing, and speed-to-market" but that embeddedness "yields positive returns only up to a threshold point. Once this threshold is crossed, returns from embeddedness become negative" (Uzzi 1996, 694).

Although Uzzi spends some time describing his measures of embeddedness, he does not describe in great detail the control variables in the analysis (e.g., organization age) or the measurement or other possible interpretations of these variables. He acknowledges that the limited time frame may limit his approach, yet he argues that statistical controls account for many of the factors that panel data would provide.

Uzzi more effectively discusses the links between his theoretical approach and alternative theoretical approaches to the question he examines. For example, he argues that "[f]rom a sociological perspective, fine-grained information exchange cannot be explained as a special incident of information asymmetries or asset specificity because the *identity* of the individuals and the quality of their social ties are as important as the information itself" (Uzzi 1996, 678). In discussing his quantitative results, he notes that "resource dependence theory predicts the *opposite* of my results—that firms reduce dependence to increase desired outcomes, such as autonomy and survival" (695, footnote 5).

Uzzi's study applies a socialized-choice approach that is based in organization and social network theories to understanding firm-level outcomes of survival or failure. Uzzi's models and methods demonstrate an interesting hybrid of strictly confirmatory, model generation, and model comparison approaches to governance research.

Moe (1985) examines the regulatory activities and environment of the National Labor Relations Board (NLRB) from 1948 to 1979. He argues that "popular models of regulation as well as quantitative empirical work have tended to focus only on very small parts of the whole," which can lead to distorted views of the regulatory systems of governance (1095). Moe identifies an "endogenous core" of relationships that characterize NLRB outcomes—consisting of final Board decisions, staff filtering decisions, and constituent filing decisions. He argues that each is made up of a formal process and "mutual adjustment" in which "each step in this three-step process is a potential cause of each of the others" (1097). Furthermore, exogenous variables of political authority (presidents, Congressional committees, and the courts) and the economic environment can influence decisions by all three types of actors in the endogenous core of relationships.

Moe's analysis is rooted in two primary theoretical bases: Adaptive adjustment of actors in his model stems from the behavioral literature in organizational analysis (e.g., Cyert and March 1963; Simon 1947), and hierarchical control, information asymmetries, and conflicts of interest stem from agency theories (e.g., Jensen and Meckling 1976; Moe 1984). Although Moe (1985) does not examine all elements of the endogenous core in a single model (he uses OLS models to separately examine Board decisions, staff filtering of cases, and constituent filing decisions), and he admits that he is oversimplifying the core (see Moe 1985, 1097, footnote 3), he makes the case for "mutually adaptive adjustment" among the elements of the core. He finds, for example, that constituent filing decisions (which determine the case mix) are strongly related to staff filtering and Board decisions; that economic conditions (unemployment and inflation) shape all three components of the endogenous core; and that the Board is responsive to exogenous political influences of the president, the courts, and Congress. Thus, reactions to outcomes have a direct link back to primary work, and environmental factors (political and economic) shape the primary work of the NLRB.

Moe extensively describes his selection and measurement of dependent and independent variables (see primarily Moe 1985, footnotes 8 through 18). For example, footnote 8 describes the measure of pro-labor tendencies of the Board as Board vote scores ratio. Moe suggests a plausible alternative, reports tests of it in his models, and argues for the measure he finally chooses. Furthermore, he details in the text and in footnotes model diagnostics and comparisons of these diagnostics with the final model he presents. He argues that the simple model captures well the processes of mutual adjustment among the endogenous core actors, but he is unable to measure the specific "perceptions" and "bureaucratic control mechanisms" that underlie these processes.

Moe's model represents a hybrid of strictly confirmatory and model generation approaches: Basing his study in behavioral and agency theories, he tries to strike "a compromise between comprehensiveness and dyadic simplicity, constructing a framework that mirrors the literature's emphasis on the variety of causal factors and their systemic interconnection while imposing a simple, coherent structure" (Moe 1985, 1115). Although Moe develops a framework suited to a particular regulatory agency, he argues that such an approach can prove useful for understanding other bureaucratic processes as well.

Concluding Comment

The examples in the preceding sections depict generic problems or issues of governance and public management, including control of bureaucracies, resource allocation, and performance management, as well as generic problems of empirical social sciences research. A logic of governance guided our efforts to frame the questions of how and why these issues are of interest and our efforts to sketch the consequences of exogenous and endogenous factors suggested by this logic. In mapping these issues to existing empirical research in a literature of governance, the following framing questions guided our work: What is the research question? What methods may be used to address it? What data are used? What are the findings? The studies we cite are by no means the only ones that might be adduced with respect to the issues under discussion. Our discussion of each substantive and methodological issue is not exhaustive; it is intended to illustrate how a logic of governance can frame inquiry, analysis, and assessment. The logic we employ and the research resources that assist in its application direct us away from either atheoretical eclecticism or deficient specifications and toward more rigorous, theory- and problem-based governance research.

Notes

1. Aghion and Tirole (1997) define formal authority as "the right to decide" and real authority as "the effective control over decisions."

2. The performance standards used in the JTPA included measures of participants' entered employment rates (i.e., job placement rates), hourly wages, and weekly earnings at the termination of program participation and 90 days later; cost per entry into employment (or per "entered employment"); welfare recipients' en-

     tered employment rates; the entered employment rates for youth; and cost per entered employment for youth.

3. Bimber identifies as models for decentralized systems McDonald's regulation of its franchisees, where strict standardization is the objective, and the administration of national parks by the National Park Service, where considerable variation in local administration is an objective.

4. The budgetary control hypothesis "holds that elected authorities manipulate agency budgets to achieve desired policy outcomes, and that when they do so, agencies respond behaviorally in the way authorities wish, by decreasing performance in response to budget cuts, and by increasing performance in response to funding boosts" (Carpenter 1996, 283).

5. Appendix B of Carpenter (1996) provides extensive details about variable definitions and sources.

6. The approach of Provan and Milward (1995) was primarily model generation. Subsequent work by these authors using these same data, however, represents a series of model comparisons.

7. Analysis strategy, data sources, and variable measures are described in Appendices 1 and 2 of Chubb (1985).

8. This footnote identifies relevant omitted variables as "1) school finance equalization decisions by state courts or legislators that produce higher tax burdens to equalize school expenditures, and 2) federal civil rights legislation generating state compliance costs in all state and local policy fields from the mid 1960s onward. However equalization decisions were not implemented until the late 1970s, and even then, in only a minority of states. Federal civil rights legislation is the more probable specification problem, but its effects are difficult to specify" (Chubb 1985, 1004, footnote 9).

9. The experiment is described in detail in the article, and instructions that participants received are reproduced in the article's appendix.

8

Governance: Research and Practice

We have assumed throughout this book that the scientific study of governance can assist or inform the practice of governance. Is this assumption reasonable? A substantial literature reveals the uncertain, even controversial, relationship between the world of science and the world of social, political, and administrative action—that is, between knowledge and power (Aaron 2000; Bradley and Schaefer 1998; Brudney, O'Toole, and Rainey 2000). The notion that research can be useful for practice raises many issues. How much skepticism about usefulness is related to the arcane properties of research and how much to the disinclinations and skill deficiencies of practitioners? Do practitioners—policymakers, managers, primary workers—have much influence on governmental performance (Brudney, O'Toole, and Rainey 2000)? Could practitioners be more influential if they had more applicable knowledge? To what extent should the problems and preoccupations of practitioners influence the content and direction of research, and to what extent should research shape the agendas, decisions, and actions of practitioners? Do the answers to these questions differ across policy domains, hierarchical levels, and political and administrative contexts?

Kingdon (1984) has argued, for example, that policymakers have significant influence on issue and action agendas. Wilson (1989) argues that what government actually does and why is determined primarily by middle and lower level personnel; in contrast, Kaufmann

(1981) argues that the influence of middle managers is quite limited. Noll and Weingast (1991) suggest that policymakers and subordinate personnel take their cues from elected officials to the extent that governance can be said to be under effective legislative oversight. Gruber (1987), on the other hand, believes that the lack of bureaucratic accountability is a significant problem, and Skocpol (1985) similarly claims that bureaucrats can have a significant independent impact on public policy.

Addressing all of these questions and issues in depth is beyond the scope of this book. Instead, we take as an article of faith that research ought to influence the practice of governance; officials whose actions affect the well-being of others in fundamental ways should actively seek out potentially useful knowledge and possibly relevant ideas from research.[1] We believe, moreover, that research is influential even if the paths of influence are far from well marked out. From the influence of the old bureaus of municipal research on the design and practice of urban governance in early 20th century through the influence of universities, think tanks, and contract research organizations on policy agendas, public resource allocation, and administrative behavior in recent decades, the heuristics, findings, conclusions, and prescriptions of systematic research have affected governance in practice (Price 1954; Orr et al. 1994).

The pathways along which this influence travels are labyrinthine, however. Our purpose in this concluding chapter is to attempt to gain perspective on the labyrinth by sketching salient aspects of research and practice that sometimes obscure or obstruct the paths by which they ultimately connect. Our primary audience for this endeavor is the multidisciplinary community of governance researchers. In this regard, we seek to clarify what we mean when we say that the quality of governance research has a positive bearing on its usefulness. In addition, we present what we hope are useful examples of research with relatively clear implications and insights for enlightening the practice of governance.

The Nature of Research

Well-known tensions pervade the relationship between researchers and practitioners. Practitioners often argue that much research—especially academic research—is irrelevant, ambiguous, or incomprehensible. Out of impatience or indifference to academic scholarship and its purveyors, practitioners are apt to turn to more customer-oriented contract research organizations; to the ideas and recommendations of ideologically motivated researchers; or to advocacy research, which they admire because it is infused with the values of constituencies. Ideally, and if possible, practitioners will turn to their policy analysis or policy planning units to interpret and synthesize research literature, although such units often are nonexistent or inaccessible to practitioners at managerial and operational levels.

For their part, many members of the governance research community are wary of unduly close affiliations with practitioners. Leiserson and Morstein Marx (1959) warned:

> [A]dministrative research must be oriented toward actual behavior and the working problems of administrators; continuous efforts must be made to encourage such research and to bring its results to the attention of busy administrators. But administrative research must not be turned into the handmaiden of officials to justify their preferences in any given moment (48).

More recently, Brudney, O'Toole, and Rainey (2000) have argued that "the best scholarship on public management is not constrained and controlled by the immediate needs on the front lines of management in government but should offer insights and findings that carry implications for altering and improving practice over the longer haul" (254; cf. Bozeman 1993). Many researchers, especially those in universities, would argue that consultants are available to satisfy the instrumental needs of practitioners; researchers should take a broader, more fundamental perspective on governance, while remaining duly concerned for its implications for practice. This exhortation still begs the question, however, about how to increase practitioners' access to and use of knowledge generated through academic research.

Research Strategies

Governance research takes three general forms: "best practices" research, which seeks out exemplary administration; applications of social science theories and methods, primarily for an academic au-

dience; and policy/implementation analysis—that is, policy- or pro-
gram-oriented investigations of administrative problems and
practices and management strategies and their consequences. We do
not regard these categories of research as mutually exclusive; in
fact, some of the more sagacious research efforts combine more than
one of these research strategies (see, e.g., Attewell and Gerstein
1979; Provan and Milward 1995; Roderick, Jacob, and Bryk 2000;
Sandfort 2000).

Much of the recent literature on public management has been
prescriptive and oriented toward identifying and advocating the
adoption of "best practices" in organizational management or program administration.[2] Although such research may employ various
conceptual heuristics (e.g., principal-agent models or colorful meta-
phors) as a guide to data interpretation, for the most part it is inductive and based on observation or accounts provided by practitioners
of specific cases, episodes, or experiences. Because best practices
research has considerable verisimilitude, practitioners tend to regard it as highly credible—much more so than arcane, highly qualified findings from social science research. The implicit assumption
of best practice researchers, as well as many practitioners, is that the
diffusion of best practice examples to other contexts, with practitioners learning from other practitioners, is an effective way to improve governance.

Although best practices research is seductive and, at its best, illu-
minating and insightful, it usually makes little effort to situate management in a conceptual framework that incorporates other
determinants of government performance or considers competing
explanations for the apparent success of a "best practice." Furthermore, even in studies that explicitly consider the context in which
managers operate, explanations for performance typically are
underidentified; disentangling the contributions of different variables or configurations of variables to organizational or management effectiveness is simply impossible. For this reason, such
research can seldom claim to produce the consummate causal understandings necessary to justify its application in other settings,
particularly where variables omitted from the research may be influential. For the most part, the lessons and prescriptions offered
under the heading of "best practices" have not survived systematic
tests of their validity. For this reason, they are little more than af-

ter-the-fact interpretations of particular experiences that may have many other interpretations.

Social science theories and methods are designed to address many of these challenges to validity. Although such work has long been in disrepute for its inability to model the complexities of governing institutions, the theories, models, and methods of social science disciplines have been evolving toward the sophistication needed for governance research, as we elucidate in chapters 6 and 7. Lynn (1996a) also notes that "several veins of inquiry originating within the social science community seem to have considerable promise as sources of explanatory heuristics bearing on the motivation, strategies and choices of public managers. A number originate in the use of rational choice theories to model economic, political, and social behavior . . . " (Lynn 1996a, 114). These developments underlie the logics of governance and their application as discussed throughout this book.

The quality of this kind of research—by which we mean its claims to validity—has a significant bearing on its claims to influence with practitioners. For example, in chapters 5 and 6 we argue that analysts who frame their research questions in a broader context of the governance problem, investigate alternative operational definitions of the concepts they measure, and explore different specifications or possible interpretations of the models they develop are more likely to generate robust results with useful implications for practitioners. Although nearly all researchers struggle with tradeoffs between precision and parsimony in modeling, as well as data constraints, studies that fail to deal forthrightly with the limitations of concepts, methods, and data deserve the disrespect of practitioners.

The third, relatively recent research/administrative technology, policy/implementation analysis, draws considerably on social science methods and has been considered a means of overcoming the inherent differences between the worlds of research and practice. Schultze (1968) expresses the frustrations of the social scientist in public life as follows:

> The most frustrating aspect of public life is . . . the endless hours spent on policy discussions in which the irrelevant issues have not been separated from the relevant, in which ascertainable facts and re-

lationships have not been investigated but are the subject of heated debate, in which consideration of alternatives is impossible because only one proposal has been developed, and above all, discussions in which nobility of aim is presumed to determine the effectiveness of the program (75).

With a more effective link between research and practice, for example, practitioners might be more likely to develop multiple proposals for policy action that represent alternative models or interpretations of a particular policy problem, as framed and analyzed by a competent social science researcher.

Sundquist (1978) coined the term "research broker" to describe the role of packaging and retailing to policymakers the intellectual products of the research community with positions either inside or outside of government (e.g., university-based professional schools or organizations such as the Brookings Institution). Sundquist's view was that although knowledge that may be useful to policymakers often is available in the research community, it is inaccessible to or unrecognizable by them. Hence, policymaking often is less thoughtful and well informed than it might be. By identifying, assembling, and translating potentially relevant bodies of knowledge into intelligence that is relevant to the immediate needs of policymakers, research brokers perform an essential role in the governance process (Lynn 2000b).

Policy analysts and research brokers must have good research to interpret and synthesize for practitioners. Governance researchers can contribute to shortening the pathway from their work to enlightened practice by addressing issues that bear on effective governance and by being forthright concerning the implications and limitations of their findings.

The Nature of Practice

One's view of the world of practice affects one's views of the potential usefulness of different kinds of research. Many scholars of governance, for example, have sought to identify or deduce generic aspects of organizational and managerial structures and behavior. Their message is that the complexity of the real world can be penetrated and fundamental aspects of governance identified (e.g.,

Bozeman and Strausmann 1990; Gulick 1937; Knott 1993). Such efforts have considerable heuristic value in promoting reflection on and analysis of the practice of governance, although they may neglect important contextual aspects.

In contrast, our inclination is to view the world of governance practice as quite differentiated. Theory and observation suggest that this is so, and propositions to the contrary ought to be forced to survive tests of validity. Logics of governance such as those we discuss in this book—even a reductive one based in political economy—impel investigators to confront complexity as potentially significant and to model the contexts of governance (rather than treating contexts as generic) to approach the consummate causal understanding urged by Mohr (1996, 1999) (see chapter 1).

In chapters 3 and 4 we review possible approaches for modeling the institutional, managerial, and technical levels of governance regimes. In this section, we revisit some of these issues in light of practitioner concerns—especially those at the managerial or primary work level. Of particular interest in addressing the question of practitioner influence are the relative contributions to performance of contexts (including structures, norms, rules, and the like) and individual characteristics.

Influences of Contexts and Individuals

Many scholars have sought to differentiate administrative agencies and the demands on their administrators in a systematic way, often focusing on different missions, functions, or tasks. For example, Wilson (1989) identifies four types of public bureaucracies, based on differences in information asymmetries between managers and workers (principals and agents). He argues that managerial strategies are likely to differ for production organizations (in which both agent effort and outcomes are observable by the principal), procedural organizations (in which agent effort is observable but outcomes are not), craft organizations (in which outcomes are observable but effort is not) and coping organizations (in which neither agent effort nor outcomes can be reliably observed and evaluated).[3] Managers in procedural organizations may design compliance systems that are based on agent effort, but they must know the links between effort and outcomes; managers in craft organizations are most successful if they design compliance systems that are based on outcomes. In coping organizations, however, "effective management is almost impossible" (Wilson 1989, 175).

Wilson's typology focuses on the relationships between managers and workers. Other efforts to differentiate management practices point to more external factors. For example, Hargrove and Glidewell (1990) focus on the agency's relationship with the public and stakeholders to identify aspects of "impossible" jobs in public management:

- The agency's clients are difficult to serve and often unpopular and controversial.
- There is intense conflict between stakeholders and other constituencies over what, how, and why the agency does its work.
- Front-line workers are not held in high regard by the public and have low professional standing.
- The agency has a weak "myth" or reputation for reliable service in the common good.

Jobs characterized to a great degree by these dimensions are impossible "because logically the difficulties are too extreme, and empirically the incumbents have uniformly been unable to perform the job to the constituents' or to their own satisfaction" (Hargrove and Glidewell 1990, 5).

Knott (1993) attempts to account for internal and external factors in modeling the contexts in which managers operate and argues that public and private managers share these concerns. The internal factors he identifies are information asymmetries between managers and workers, interdependence of tasks and actors, and conflicts of interest among units in an organization. Key external constraints on managers are the degree to which the organization participates in economic exchange or is subject to political authority, the degree of competition in the market for its goods or services, and the number of stakeholders. Specific combinations of these internal factors and external constraints, Knott argues, create contexts that require different management practices.

Governance practice also may differ systematically by hierarchical level, as we suggest in chapter 2. Creating and sustaining governing relations at the institutional, managerial, and operational levels of governance involve distinctive emphases or demands on practitioners and the influence they might have on governmental performance.[4] At the institutional level of governance, likely issues of concern are the purposes and rationales for governmental action. At the managerial level, in contrast, issues of concern are the choice of administrative strategies and instruments and the allocation of budgetary resources. At the operational level, practitioners are preoccupied with the design and use of structures and instruments and the use of resources.

Further differentiation may be appropriate. Within the managerial level, for example, administrative behavior is likely to depend on the practitioner's place in the organizational hierarchy. Dunleavey (1991) argues that collective-action problems inside bureaucratic organizations govern practitioner behavior. Lower-level personnel at every level are likely to be more committed to strategies that affect the attractiveness and rewards of their work than to strategies that improve the performance of the regime or organization as a whole; achieving the collective benefits of privatization or innovation, for example, is unlikely to generate enthusiasm among personnel who might feel threatened by such changes or unaffected by their success.

Practitioner roles differ with regard to the constraints that circumscribe them. Practitioner discretion is restricted in numerous ways: by formal or informal rules, by guidelines, and by norms or other socialized beliefs and practices. The concept of constraint is not absolute, however. Constraints can be overcome—albeit at a cost in time, effort, and compromise on other goals.[5] Thus, contexts might be described in terms of their malleability or susceptibility to exogenous or endogenous change.

Individual influence in the face of constraints may be an important factor because practitioners' own goals and circumstances affect their inclinations to incur the costs of overcoming rather than adapting to constraints. Thus, practitioners' responses to constraints in a given structural context are likely to differ (Lynn 1991). The questions of constraints and how the possibilities of overcoming them affect practitioner orientation introduce the distinction between short- and long-run strategic behavior. Prescriptive public management studies often finesse this distinction by appeals to a short run inhabited by political appointees or program managers for whom contextual and structural factors are assumed to be (or are urged to be taken as) given. Too often, such studies give short shrift to a more malleable longer run inhabited by officials who see themselves as confronting a wider array of variables, circumstances, and opportunities (Knott and Hammond 2000; Lynn 2000a).

Beyond their varying reactions to constraints, individual practitioners are likely to differ in many other ways—for example, demographic characteristics, human capital, social relationships, and personal values. Such variation in characteristics can lead the general focus of public managers to differ, regardless of their roles. Following Moore (1995), we might usefully distinguish between managing "outward" toward the organization's environment; managing "upward" toward superior authority; and managing "downward" toward the organization's work, workers, and outputs. In principle, a practitioner's orientation might be upward, downward, outward, or any combination of the three, depending on individual inclination.

The interaction between structures and managerial inclinations and strategies might be significant, however. For example, an outward orientation probably tends to be associated with more senior hierarchical roles (Haass 1999). An outward or horizontal orientation might be expected in networked or especially politicized structures, a bidirectional upward/downward orientation in more traditional hierarchies, and a downward orientation in decoupled managerial or supervisory contexts. The management practices associated with Knott's (1993) categorization of internal factors and external constraints also might be interpreted as generating predictions for upward, outward, and downward orientations.

Given the endogeneity of the structural and personal aspects of practice contexts, sorting out the extent of practitioner influence on governmental outcomes is difficult. Doig and Hargrove (1987) have argued that managerial influence is associated with a favorable match between individual attributes and organizational tasks within a historical/political context that is conducive to change. Lynn (1985) elaborated on this notion in arguing that four factors interact to account for practitioner influence: the practitioner's personality or orientation, the practitioner's instrumental skills, the strategic judgments of the manager, and the difficulty of the challenges presented by the organizational/political/historical context. In other words, many factors count toward the performance of government; the relative significance of these factors depends on the values of all factors in the configuration (Lynn 1996a). As Heclo

(1985) has argued, "The appropriate unit of analysis is the cluster of interrelated parts that produce the results by which we are governed" (374).

Views of the type and extent of practitioner influence in governance systems necessarily affect the kinds of research considered "useful" for practitioners and policymakers. At an individual level, characteristics of practitioners—school principals, agency heads, elected officials, or service workers—may have a significant bearing on governance in practice. Alternatively, if organizational and social structures and roles dominate or reduce the scope of individual attributes in accounting for governmental performance, research that yields robust findings concerning structures and roles is more likely to influence actual performance of government than research that is preoccupied with leadership, managerial strategies, and best practices. Located between these individual and structural extremes is a perspective that practitioner characteristics and context interact in complex ways (where "context" encompasses the configurational, political, and loosely coupled nature of a governance regime). An approach to research that incorporates a logic of governance assumes that contextual influences on performance—perhaps interacting with individual characteristics—are at least possible, if not likely. Although variation in contexts may be insignificant in practice, this perspective holds that it is advisable to discover this variation through empirical analysis rather than to assume it. For these reasons, governance research that incorporates explicit awareness of contextual factors and allows for their causal influence on governmental performance should have a greater claim on practitioner attention than research that disproportionately focuses on individual-level factors and places contextual considerations into a conceptual black box.

Enlightening Practice: Utilizing a Logic

One approach to understanding whether and how governance research may guide practice—by policymakers or by street-level bureaucrats—is to examine studies that focus on different aspects of a policy. The scope of possible implications for practitioners may be expanded or reduced for "people-changing" policies in which clients can react to and thus affect the service that is performed. In this section, we review—against a background of a logic of governance—four empirical studies that examine different aspects of the complex implementation contexts of welfare-to-work programs (Henly 1999; Levine 1999; Meyers, Glaser, and MacDonald 1998; Sandfort 2000). These studies' implications for practice range from suggesting little or no emphasis on local governance of these programs to emphasizing a critical role for governance arrangements in affecting client outcomes. Table 8.1 lists the data, methods, and units of analysis for each of the studies.

Henly (1999) uses interviews of welfare recipients, similar workers, and job supervisors and ascribes a crucial role to informal networks that help welfare recipients find and keep jobs. She argues that formal job placement programs cannot replicate the contacts of these networks for identifying possible jobs and providing employers with references about applicants from current employees. Henly focuses primarily on environmental and client characteristics (i.e., network relationships, job characteristics, child care needs) as determinants of whether welfare recipients find and keep jobs. For example, the job supervisors she interviewed stigmatized welfare recipients; thus, financial incentives to employers who hire welfare recipients probably would not be successful. The role of the welfare office and the scope for managers to influence outcomes are virtually nonexistent in Henly's account. A policy's incentive effects are not mediated by a local governance structure; instead, they are consumed directly by recipients and balanced through their personal networks and their job experiences. Overall, Henly argues that helping welfare recipients find and keep jobs should provide additional "formal supports" such as child care and transportation assistance and should focus on reform of the workplace—the ultimate point of "outcome" for these welfare recipients.

In another study of welfare recipients and their experiences in leaving welfare for work, Levine (1999) provides insight into how recipients view work incentives. She points to several major influences over welfare recipients' decisions to work and concludes that unstable policy environments mute incentive effects; that bureaucratic errors undermine recipients' attention to incentives; that child care that mothers can trust is needed; that conflict at work creates disincentives for working; that limited social networks reduce job possibilities; and that many recipients want to work, but working may involve negative as well as positive experiences.

Table 8.1. Data and Methods of Selected Studies of Welfare-to-Work Programs

Study Author and Date	Data	Method	Unit of Analysis
Henly (1999)	Interviews from Workplace Environment Study in Los Angeles County Interviews conducted from mid-1996 to mid-1997 44 current welfare recipients with work experience, 30 women who had never received welfare but held jobs similar to those that welfare recipients were qualified to hold, and 30 job supervisors	Empirical—qualitative, semi-structured interviews	Welfare recipient
Levine (1999)	Interviews with 30 current or former welfare recipients in a Chicago neighborhood	Empirical—qualitative, semi-structured interviews	Welfare recipient
Meyers, Glaser, and MacDonald (1998)	Observations of 66 interviews between clients and caseworkers Semi-structured interviews with 43 caseworkers and supervisors Observations and interviews conducted in 1993–1994	Empirical—qualitative, semi-structured interviews and observations; backward mapping	Interaction between welfare clients and Work Pays case-workers
Sandfort (2000)	County-level measures in Michigan, using census data, administrative data October 1996–September 1997	Empirical—quantitative, logit regression	County

Like Henly, Levine emphasizes the importance of personal networks for finding and keeping jobs. Levine's analysis allows more of a role for case managers: Levine argues that negative interactions between welfare recipients and caseworkers produce positive incentives for recipients to find work. What, then, of caseworkers who apply rules consistently and who treat welfare recipients with respect? The converse of Levine's argument might imply that such positive interactions would provide *disincentives* for working; this possibility is not likely, but the implications are not clear. Levine's argument also indicates that if policies were more straightforward, caseworkers would make fewer mistakes in conveying program rules to recipients, and policies would be more effective tools for moving welfare recipients into jobs. How likely are simpler policies, however, in light of the multifarious goals of enacting coalitions? Finally, Levine notes that job training programs would be more successful if they could mimic recipients' social networks for finding jobs. Henly's analysis indicates that no such formal programs could replicate informal networks because the program would be tagged with the stigma associated with receiving welfare.

Turning to other units of analysis for welfare-to-work programs, Meyers, Glaser, and MacDonald (1998) analyze implementation of a new welfare reform program in California that expanded transitional assistance and reduced benefit reductions when recipients worked, using interactions between caseworkers and welfare recipients as the unit of analysis. In most interactions the authors observed, caseworkers provided little information to clients about the benefits of work and self-sufficiency and provided little "positive discretion"[6] or personalized attention. Meyers, Glaser, and MacDonald conclude that "[u]nder the conditions that characterized implementation of the California reforms—including limited resources, complex administrative problems, conflicting policy objectives, and ambiguous political support—modest changes in welfare policy were unlikely to transform the operations or the dominant message delivered by workers at the front lines of the system" (20).[7]

This study's findings indicate that incomplete and inconsistent messages from welfare staff can mute the intended effects of welfare reforms; Levine's interviews with welfare recipients echo these findings. Meyers, Glaser, and MacDonald (1998) claim more of a role for local welfare governance than either Henly or Levine claims, however, and they argue that it is *necessary* (though acknowledge it is not sufficient) for successful welfare reform. Thus, if policies are to have any effect on individual behavior of welfare recipients, the practice of primary work and treatment interactions in policy implementation must be considered as well.

County-level variation is the focus of Sandfort's (2000) study of whether service delivery structures and technology affect the proportion of a county's welfare caseload that combines welfare and work and ultimately moves into the workforce. In particular, Sandfort investigates immediate labor force attachment (Work First) and case management with additional supportive services (Project Zero). She finds statistically significant effects for county economic conditions and for demographic characteristics such as the proportion of female-headed families in the county and the proportion of cash assistance recipients who are white. There also is a relatively large, positive effect for the Project Zero intervention, but because the model can pick up only a fixed effect for the program, Sandfort is unable to disentangle which specific aspects of the program—"the increased child care and transportation, the mentoring program, the altered role of frontline workers, or the interactions in the public welfare office that stressed work"—may be driving the overall result (155).

Sandfort's study examines the role of county-level governance structures in welfare-to-work transitions. Possible influences of program managers are not explicitly incorporated in these models but are implied, as Sandfort suggests, in choices for service technology and service delivery structures. The county-level analysis does not accommodate measures of recipients' interpersonal networks that Henly and Levine identify as important. Although such networks may affect the outcome of interest, omission of these measures from Sandfort's model will not affect her estimates if clients' personal networks are not related to counties' establishment of particular programs or clients' utilization of county programs. Furthermore, because Sandfort's analysis examines county-level measures, ascertaining how variation in recipient and local office characteristics might affect her findings is impossible.

These studies illustrate how different research approaches and different levels of analysis applied to a particular governance area may suggest very different implications for practitioner influence. Analyses of welfare-to-work policies or outcomes may attribute little role to the local office implementation of a policy or of local office managerial choices (e.g., Henly 1999), conclude that only certain aspects of implementation or street-level practice affect client incentives or choices (e.g., Levine 1999), consider translation of the policy at the front lines to be necessary but not sufficient to influence outcomes (e.g., Meyers, Glaser, and MacDonald 1998), or attribute important effects to the policy even after characteristics of the client or environment are taken into account (e.g., Sandfort 2000).

The potential for these or other studies of welfare-to-work programs to influence practice does not depend solely on whether one considers an individual study's models, methods, and data to be appropriate for the question at hand. To the extent that governance systems are configurational, one cannot "add" the results of studies at different levels to attain an account of the regime as a whole. In the context of such complexity, best practices research or studies that reflect conventional wisdom may hold the most appeal for practitioners.

Stakes are increasing, however, for attaining greater understanding of just how structures and individuals influence outcomes, as well as for understanding the implications for local office governance and management. The Personal Responsibility and Work Opportunity Reconciliation Act (PRWORA) of 1996 has granted states increased flexibility in designing their welfare programs, while imposing additional work requirements and time limits for recipients. This expanded flexibility nearly guarantees more variation in structures and contexts across sites. From a governance perspective, the ways such new policies are implemented at the technical or primary work level and what effect these actions have on moving welfare recipients off of welfare and into jobs is crucial.

Enlightening Practice: Prospects

Distance, reservations, and tensions often impede discourse between researchers and practitioners. In this section, we suggest how the path from research to practice might be widened by selectively highlighting research that appears to have relatively clear implications for governance and appraising its prospects for enlightening practice. First, we build on the discussion of governance research in the policy domain of public training programs (highlighted in chapter 7) to illustrate research with important practical implications. Then we discuss the insights practitioners might derive from a diverse group of governance studies that address issues of incentives and cooperation in organizational contexts and the possibilities for enlightened practice that might be realized with practitioners' application of these findings.

Some Practical Implications of Governance Research

The research on public training programs that we discuss in chapter 7 endeavors to model and understand bureaucratic discretion involved in the selection of JTPA program participants, the structuring of administrative and service delivery arrangements, and the use of performance incentives, as well as the implications of these management and policy choices for program outcomes and impacts. The findings of these studies have some relatively clear implications for the governance of public training programs; in some cases, the issues addressed by researchers parallel those actively confronted in the policy arena by practitioners.

One of the most prominent and controversial areas being investigated by researchers studying public training programs concerns the issue of who gets access to training services. Studies conducted by Orfield and Slessarev (1986) and Dickinson et al. (1988), which applied survey research and other process evaluation methods, alleged that states with more aggressive performance standard policies were discouraging services to more disadvantaged program eligibles as local agencies sought to produce low-cost placements. In the period following these reports to the House of Representatives (Orfield and Slessarev 1986) and to the National Commission on Employment Policy (Dickinson et al. 1988), the federal government eliminated performance standards for program costs. In addition, the Department of Labor issued a directive indicating that it was no longer encouraging the use of performance-based contracts by JTPA administrative agencies in local service delivery areas. In 1992, amendments were made to the JTPA to prohibit further use of cost performance measures and mandate the formulation of separate measures for enrollees identified as "difficult to place in employment."

As Dickinson et al. (1988) suggest, however, achieving high performance levels is not the primary goal of all local service delivery areas. Research by Heckman, Smith, and Taber (1996) (reviewed in chapter 7) describes a local JTPA agency in which front-line workers exhibited explicit preferences for serving the least employable, in apparent defiance of the early performance standards system incentives. The follow-up study by Heckman, Heinrich, and Smith (1997) sought to explain how differences in local management policies and social and professional norms among caseworkers might have contributed to the differential responses of JTPA staff to performance incentive policies across sites. Research by Heinrich (1999) also shows how at least one local agency continued to use performance-based contracts that included program cost standards even after the 1992 JTPA amendments prohibited these practices. These studies make clear that local managers were exercising the discretion accorded them in a decentralized system of program administration and augment our understanding of how institutional factors might have played a role in aiding or limiting individuals' access to training services.

The foregoing research also has relevance for the new policy of "universal access" in public training programs, in which *all* adults (not solely economically disadvantaged adults) are eligible for "core" or basic workforce development services, regardless of their eligibility for specific categorical programs. One might expect that universal access, interpreted simply, would eradicate all concerns about equity in access to services. Although the 1998 Workforce Investment Act (WIA) provisions eliminate targeting requirements, however, individuals are granted access to more intensive levels of services at One-Stop Career Centers through a sequential process. For example, if a client is unable to obtain employment or becomes unemployed again after receiving core services, he or she may apply for additional services at the next (more intensive) level. When program funds are sparse, legislative guidelines encourage local administrative boards to give priority for intensive and skills training services to public aid recipients and other low-income persons. Researchers such as Eberts, O'Leary, and Wandner (1999) have raised the concern that local career center staff might lack the necessary "tools" to properly target or "funnel" a significantly larger number of participants into appropriate levels of employment and training assistance.

One policy implication of this research is that monitoring individuals' paths through the workforce development system and their receipt of different levels of core as well as more intensive training services will be an important public responsibility for state and local program administrators because a universal access approach is unlikely to eliminate the possibility that access to varying levels of services still might be constrained locally. In addition, the expanded role of performance management information in WIA—in certifying service providers and allocating WIA funds on the basis of the numbers of job placements—is very likely to generate incentives similar to those in JTPA programs that encourage one-stop centers and other providers to maximize job placements and limit access to more costly services.

Another prominent area of public training program research has focused on the design of the outcomes-based performance standards system in JTPA and its effectiveness in improving JTPA program outcomes. As we indicate in chapter 7, this research generally suggests that the performance standards that guide state and local JTPA program administration have not effectively measured progress toward the legislative goals of increasing participants' earnings and reducing welfare dependency (Heckman and Smith 1995; Orr et al. 1997; Barnow 2000). More specifically, these researchers have shown that federal performance measures of adult JTPA participants' earnings levels at termination and 90 days later were only weakly (and sometimes negatively) related to long-term program gains. Heckman and Smith (1995) imply that a positive link between short-run performance measures and long-term program effects is essential to the effectiveness of a performance management system—a finding that is particularly important given the goal of increased accountability for service provider performance through the continued use of outcomes-based performance standards under WIA.

A significant change in the performance standards utilized under WIA is the addition of measures of participant outcomes at 6 and 12 months following job placement. A question that arises with this new provision is whether the extension of the follow-up period to as long as one year after a participant's placement will generate more accurate information about longer-term training program effects. A review of the evidence on this issue by Heckman, Heinrich, and Smith (1999), however, suggests that moving from measures of earnings and employment at 13 weeks after termination to out-comes measured a year later will have little effect on the relation-ship between performance measures and program impacts. They argue that if the objective of the performance management system is to guide local government entities in maximizing net program im-pacts, the system would need changes that are substantially more far-reaching than those being implemented. The prospects for such a major revamping of government performance standards systems probably are poor, however, and achieving an ideal system of incen-tives probably is infeasible. As our discussion in this chapter sug-gests, making a connection between the paths of research and practice is one thing; turning practice around in new directions and toward untraveled paths is quite another.

Insights for Enlightened Practice

What might practitioners learn about a more generic management, program, or policy concern if they were to survey a broad gover-nance literature to help them reach a solution to a particular prob-lem? For example, human service organizations are under increasing pressure to integrate or coordinate their activities verti-cally and horizontally, in the face of continued budgetary strin-gency and growing demands for performance-oriented management by public and managed care agencies. Moreover, advances in treat-ment concepts increasingly emphasize the importance of inter-agency coordination in meeting the needs of communities, families, and individuals. Thus, human service organizations confront a vari-ety of strategic decisions associated with their actual or potential in-terdependence—including whether to coordinate, diversify, convert, or terminate specific services.

Designing and maintaining formal and informal mechanisms needed to foster cooperation are no small tasks, and an effortless achievement of cooperative relationships cannot be assumed. The scope of the problem is highlighted by U.S. General Accounting Of-fice (GAO) assessments of two different approaches to services inte-gration,[8] in which the GAO concludes that numerous efforts over a 30-year period to promote greater client orientation and flexibility in the delivery of human services have largely failed (GAO 1992). In general, changes in administrative structures failed to overcome conflict, coordination, and information problems, and administrators found little political support for overcoming barriers to change.

Recent services integration initiatives have fared no better, according to GAO (1992). Agencies and organizations responsible for enacting systematic reforms were denied authority to create new organizational structures or develop multi-agency service plans and budgets (GAO 1992, 5). Inability to alter financial incentives owing to the inflexibility of funding streams was an obstacle to reforming services delivery. In contrast, efforts that "did not attempt to change state and local organizational structures" fared much better, primarily because they required less political support and were less threatening to established interests (GAO 1992, 6).

What sources might practitioners turn to in order to improve the chances of successful cooperation? Best practices or success stories of collaborative efforts often are the primary sources of information for practitioners who must respond to formal requirements to coordinate or more general pressures to improve performance (to which service coordination is viewed as a response). Yet a wider scope of governance research may produce more durable and reliable information for practitioners. In preceding chapters, we have touched on general research frames and findings from specific studies that may provide insights for enlightened practice in the area of service coordination. For example, in chapter 4 we discuss political economy-based concepts of principal-agent models, transaction costs, and collective action theory, as well as socialized-choice concepts that emphasize embeddedness and power. In chapter 7 we review in depth Provan and Milward's (1995) study of structural determinants of mental health services effectiveness in four different cities and the predictions they generate for network effectiveness. We also review Nalbantian and Schotter's (1997) experiments that explore individuals' responses to group incentives for compensation. They demonstrate that a group's history and past performance will affect how it responds to a new incentive program, that intraorganizational competition can be effective, and that participants will shirk if monitoring is ineffective. Although public-sector governance researchers might overlook a study such as Nalbantian and Schotter's because it examines pay-for-performance schemes in for-profit organizational settings, the findings about intrafirm competition and establishment of group norms may provide useful insights for public-sector managers who seek to improve the performance of fields of administrative units, especially if they are dispersed (e.g., local offices). Of course, these examples are far from exhaustive with regard to research literature that might provide insights into issues of coordination for practitioners.

For example, Bardach and Lesser (1996) analyze the complex problems associated with achieving a greater degree of collaboration among bureaus. They note that practitioners tend to downplay the restrictive effect of institutional barriers to collaboration because they have little power to change them. Although Bardach and Lesser place considerable emphasis on the importance of individual-level motivation to collaborate, they note that institutions shape these motivations and that the removal of institutional barriers to collaboration, including the lack of mandates and insufficient resources, is important to changing individual behavior.

Chisholm (1989) examines such informal coordination in the San Francisco Bay Area Rapid Transit (BART) system. He concludes that the system "is highly coordinated and appears to be becoming more so" because of an "extensive series of informal relationships between key actors" who are seeking ways to reduce uncertainty resulting from interorganizational interdependence (Chisholm 1989, 191). Chisholm concludes in general that coordination should be no more extensive than actual interdependence warrants and that it should be informal wherever possible to minimize the cognitive and political demands of coordination. Sabel (1993, 69) makes the counterargument that informal groups can serve personal or group ends instead of institutional ones. Considering these studies together raises the question of what, other than informality, causes actors to emphasize institutional rather than the narrow purposes—a central element in achieving coordination that is consistent with policymakers' intent.

Research on the use of common pool resources (CPRs)[9] also produces findings that are potentially applicable to the problem of achieving effective coordination in human services. For example, Ostrom, Schroeder, and Wynne (1993) evaluate three different institutional arrangements for providing and producing small-scale irrigation systems, as well as the resulting transaction costs and incentives for various actors. Transactions costs include coordination costs, information gathering (e.g., scientific and location information), and various strategic behaviors—free riding, rent seeking, shirking, adverse selection, moral hazard, and corruption. The researchers conclude that the choice of structural arrangements has an important bearing on the results achieved. For example, inappropriate institutional arrangements can "generate unintended consequences such as high levels of corruption, overinvestment in large-scale projects, and underinvestment in smaller projects and in operations and maintenance" (42). Their specific advice to management analysts is to include a wide array of "intermediate performance measures" to predict the consequences of specific structural arrangements. This notion appears to have considerable research potential.

Ostrom, Gardner, and Walker (1994) also study CPRs, and their insights may have relevance for practice in areas such as human services coordination. They find:

> The capacity to design and enforce one's own rules . . . is not a sufficient condition to ensure the resolution of difficult and complex dilemmas. Without some willingness to extend reciprocity to others, while building trust and better rules, initial agreements can rapidly unravel. Without access to reliable information about complex processes, participants may not understand the ambiguous situations they face. The likelihood of crafting and sustaining rules in situations involving many exogenous changes is dramatically reduced. The capacity to design their own rules will not enhance the outcomes achieved by the nontrusting and narrowly selfish individuals of the world, but will enhance the outcomes of those who are prepared to extend reciprocity to others and interact with others with similar inclinations (328–29).

A potential application of research on cooperation is the current effort through WIA to achieve service coordination of formerly categorical programs—employment services, unemployment insurance, former JTPA programs, veterans employment and training services, and others—into a system of local one-stop career centers. Local Workforce Investment Boards (WIBs), whose members are appointed by local elected officials to supervise the operation of the one-stop career centers, have been charged with selecting one-stop operators through a competitive process or through designation of a consortium that includes at least three of the federal programs that provide services at the one-stop centers. Relevant research by Jennings (1994) and Jennings and Ewalt (1998) examining the effects of administrative coordination patterns on JTPA program outcomes and by Heinrich and Lynn (2000) on centralization of authority within JTPA programs finds that increased coordination, administrative consolidation, and a clear line of administrative authority within public training programs has had significant positive effects on program outcomes. Whether consolidating the operations of several large employment and training programs at the state level under WIA will improve coordination and promote a coherent focus within local level program administration remains to be seen, however.

The illustrative review in this section suggests that formal authority as a means of governance—that is, as a solution to problems of coordination and control in achieving the goals of public policy—is notably limited or, alternatively, contingent. When institutional rules are devoid of important resources needed by the organization (or sector) and cannot be easily enforced, they become truly symbolic and have little consequences on the actual delivery of services (Hasenfeld 1992). Preferred mechanisms for achieving cooperation, which rely on informality and the gradual emergence of trust, often are frustrated, however, by attempts to impose hierarchical controls in the name of particular policy objectives and maintenance of political property rights. Moreover, this review suggests that findings from governance research can generate insights that are relevant to enhancing coordination; yet the configurational nature of governance also implies that selectively applying findings from such research will not necessarily produce the intended results. We argue, however, that there is great potential value in expanding the scope of governance research to which practitioners may turn.

Conclusion

Whatever the difficulties arising from divergences between the worlds of research and practice, and however effective the policy analyst or research broker is in overcoming them, the fact remains that the influence of governance research on practice depends on practitioners who appreciate its potential value. Practitioners have an influence on governance only to the extent that they comprehend the institutional contexts in which they operate and the opportunities for influence these contexts afford (Lynn 2000a). Our argument throughout this book is that practitioners seeking enlightenment concerning governance questions should consult research that is likely to provide valid answers. Is anything out there worth consulting?

The most useful research, in our view, derives empirically testable propositions from a clearly developed theoretical framework or explicitly posed set of questions that reflect a logic of governance. The most useful data sets include information on subsets of these variables at two or more levels—for example, aggregate outcome, client, and treatment information for multiple sites or data on client, treatment, and site characteristics that might facilitate simultaneous analysis of sequential (i.e., stage-by-stage) or parallel (i.e., multi-site) treatment or processing of clients.

The value of an integrating logic of governance is clearest in research that seeks to identify determinants of program outcomes with sufficient clarity that the findings will be useful to policymakers and public managers who seek to improve the performance of the system as a whole. By approaching the complexity of social and human phenomena with theory accompanied by a logic of governance, we can enhance the usefulness of research for policy designers who must implement programs and policies in a policy environment that is more complex than any research design can accommodate.

Notes

1. Thus, we disagree sharply with contemporary post-positive arguments that all research is so tainted by unwarranted and undiscoverable bias that it cannot inform democratic discourse or action.

2. Such research has a long history. Discussing public administration research after World War II, V. Ostrom (1973) refers to "a new style of research reflected in case studies designed to provide a narrative about the 'realities' of administrative decision making" (9). Ostrom speaks of how the new behavioral research into goal displacement and bureaucratic dysfunction undermined the traditional model of bureaucratic rationality.

3. See chapter 4 for additional discussion of these types of organizations.

4. We do not intend to reify the discredited notion that different kinds of governance issues are or ought to be compartmentalized, with policymaking the province of elected and appointed officials and implementation the province of the permanent government. In the U.S. Constitutional regime, powers are separated and shared among branches and levels of government. Our point is that practitioner preoccupations generally differ by branch and hierarchical level.

5. An enacting coalition may structure legislation so that the costs of deviating from its preferences are high. If the cohesion of the legislative majority is weak or breaks down, however, so that officials are in effect governed by multiple principals, practitioners may have considerable latitude to pursue personal preferences.

6. Positive discretion is "provision of any information, advice, or assistance that reflected clients' circumstances by adapting or interpreting formal protocols and eligibility determination forms (on topics that included but were not limited to employment)" (Meyers, Glaser, and MacDonald 1998, 8).

7. Meyers and Dillon (1999) further explore issues of organizational structure and "inspiration" in the local offices.

8. "Services integration" generally refers to client-centered program administration in which service delivery agencies assume responsibility for directing individuals to appropriate points of service and cooperate in maintaining records of clients' use of the system.

9. Ostrom, Gardner, and Walker (1994) define common pool resources as systems (e.g., a fishery) where "excluding potential appropriators or limiting appropriation rights of existing users is nontrivial (but not necessarily impossible) and the yield of the resource system is subtractable" (4).

References

Aaron, Henry J. 2000. Seeing through the fog: Policymaking with uncertain forecasts. *Journal of Policy Analysis and Management* 19, no. 2 (spring): 193–206.

Aghion, Philippe, and Jean Tirole. 1997. Formal and real authority in organizations. *Journal of Political Economy* 105, no. 1 (February): 1–29.

Aharoni, Yair, and Richard M. Burton. 1994. Is management science international: In search of universal rules. *Management Science* 40, no. 1: 1–3.

Aldrich, Howard E., and Jeffrey Pfeffer. 1976. Environments of organizations. *Annual Review of Sociology* 2: 79–105.

Alt, James E., and Kenneth A. Shepsle. 1990. *Perspectives on positive political economy.* New York: Cambridge University Press.

Anderson, Kathryn, Richard Burkhauser, and Jennie Raymond. 1993. The effect of creaming on placement rates under the Job Training Partnership Act. *Industrial and Labor Relations Review* 46, no. 4: 613–24.

Anderson, Kathryn, Richard Burkhauser, Jennie Raymond, and Clifford Russell. 1992. Mixed signals in the Job Training Partnership Act. *Growth and Change* 22, no. 3: 32–48.

Anspach, Renee R. 1991. Everyday methods for assessing organizational effectiveness. *Social Problems* 38, no. 1 (February): 1–19.

Argyres, Nicholas S. 1995. Technology strategy, governance structure and interdivisional coordination. *Journal of Economic Behavior and Organization* 28, no. 3: 337–58.

Arrow, Kenneth. 1985. The economics of agency. In *Principals and agents: The structure of business*, edited by John W. Pratt and Richard J. Zeckhauser. Cambridge, Mass.: Harvard Business School Press.

Arum, Richard. 1996. Do private schools force public schools to compete? *American Sociological Review* 61, no. 1 (February): 29–46.

Asch, David, and Cliff Bowman, eds. 1989. *Readings in strategic management.* London: Macmillan.

Attewell, Paul, and Dean R. Gerstein. 1979. Government policy and local practice. *American Sociological Review* 44 (April): 311–27.

Bardach, Eugene, and Cara Lesser. 1996. Accountability in human services collaboratives: For what? and to whom? *Journal of Public Administration Research and Theory* 6, no. 2 (April): 197–224.

Barley, Stephen R. 1986. Technology as an occasion for structuring: Evidence from observations of CT scanners and the social order of radiology departments. *Administrative Science Quarterly* 31: 78–108.

Barnow, Burt S. 1979. Theoretical issues in the estimation of production functions in manpower programs. In *Evaluating manpower training programs: Research in labor economics,* Supplement 1, edited by Farrell Bloch. Greenwich, Conn.: JAI Press.

———. 2000. Exploring the relationship between performance management and program impact: A case study of the Job Training Partnership Act. *Journal of Policy Analysis and Management* 19, no. 1 (winter): 118–41.

Bendor, Jonathan. 1990. Formal models of bureaucracy: A review. In *Public administration: The state of the discipline,* edited by Naomi B. Lynn and Aaron Wildavsky. Chatham, N.J.: Chatham House, 373–417.

———. 1994. The fields of bureaucracy and public administration. *Journal of Public Administration Research and Theory* 4, no. 1: 27–39.

Bendor, Jonathan, and Terry M. Moe. 1985. An adaptive model of bureaucratic politics. *American Political Science Review* 79: 755–74.

Benz, Arthur. 1993. Commentary on O'Toole and Scharpf: The network concept as a theoretical approach. In *Games in hierarchies and networks: Analytical and empirical approaches to the study of governance institutions,* edited by Fritz W. Scharpf. Boulder, Colo.: Westview Press.

Bimber, Bruce. 1993. *School decentralization: Lessons from the study of bureaucracy.* Santa Monica, Calif.: RAND Corporation.

———. 1994. *The decentralization mirage: Comparing decisionmaking arrangements in four high schools.* Santa Monica, Calif.: RAND Corporation.

Bird, Edward J. 1999. Politics, altruism, and the definition of poverty. *Journal of Comparative Policy Analysis* 1, no. 3: 269–91.

Black, Bruce L. 1986. Institutional context and strategy: A framework for the analysis of mental health policy. In *The organization of mental health services: Societal and community systems,* edited by W. Richard Scott and Bruce L. Black. Beverly Hills, Calif.: Sage Publications.

Blau, Peter M., and Richard A. Schoenherr. 1971. *The structure of organizations.* New York: Basic Books.

Bolman, Lee G., and Terrence E. Deal. 1991. *Reframing organizations: Artistry, choice, and leadership.* San Francisco: Jossey-Bass.

Bozeman, Barry. 1993. Two concepts of public management. In *Public management: The state of the art,* edited by Barry Bozeman. *San Francisco: Jossey-Bass.*

Bozeman, Barry, and Jeffrey D. Straussman. 1990. *Public management strategies: Guidelines for managerial effectiveness.* San Francisco: Jossey-Bass.

Bradley, W. James, and Kurt C. Schaefer. 1998. *The uses and misuses of data and models: The mathematization of the human sciences.* Newbury Park, Calif.: Sage Publications.

Braybrooke, David, and Charles E. Lindblom. 1970. *A strategy of decision: Policy evaluation as a social process.* New York: Free Press.

Brock, Thomas, and Kristen Harknett. 1998. A comparison of two welfare-to-work case management models. *Social Service Review* 72, no. 4 (December): 493–520.

Brodkin, Evelyn Z. 1986. *The false promise of administrative reform: Implementing quality control in welfare.* Philadelphia: Temple University Press.

Broome, Kirk M., D. Dwayne Simpson, and George W. Joe. 1999. Patient and program attributes related to treatment process indicators in DATOS. *Drug and Alcohol Dependence* 57 (December): 127–35.

Brudney, Jeffrey L., Laurence O'Toole, Jr., and Hal G. Rainey. 2000. *Advancing public management: New developments in theory, methods, and practice.* Washington, D.C.: Georgetown University Press.

Bryk, Anthony S., and Stephen W. Raudenbush. 1987. Application of hierarchical linear models to assessing change. *Psychological Bulletin* 101, no. 1: 147–58.

———. 1992. *Hierarchical linear models: Applications and data analysis methods.* London: Sage Publications.

Burns, James McGregor. 1978. *Leadership.* New York: Harper & Row.

Burt, Ronald S. 1992. *Structural holes: The social structure of competition.* Cambridge, Mass.: Harvard University Press.

Caiden, Gerald E. 1991. *Administrative reform comes of age.* New York: W. de Gruyter.

Calvert, Randall L., Mathew D. McCubbins, and Barry R. Weingast. 1989. A theory of political control and agency discretion. *American Journal of Political Science* 33, no. 3 (August): 588–611.

Carpenter, Daniel P. 1996. Adaptive signal processing, hierarchy, and budgetary control in federal regulation. *American Political Science Review* 90, no. 2 (June): 283–302.

Chisholm, Donald. 1989. *Coordination without hierarchy: Informal structures in multiorganizational systems.* Berkeley: University of California Press.

Chubb, John E. 1985. The political economy of federalism. *American Political Science Review* 79: 994–1015.

Chubb, John E., and Terry M. Moe. 1990. *Politics, markets, and America's schools.* Washington, D.C.: Brookings Institution.

Cohen, David. 1995. Standards-based school reform: Policy, practice and performance. Unpublished manuscript, School of Education and Social Policy, University of Michigan.

Courty, Pascal, and Gerald R. Marschke. 1997. An empirical investigation of gaming responses to performance incentives. Unpublished manuscript, Department of Economics, State University of New York-Albany.

———. Forthcoming. Do incentives motivate organizations? An empirical test. In *Performance standards in a government bureaucracy,* edited by James J. Heckman. Kalamazoo, Mich.: W.E. Upjohn Institute and University of Chicago Press.

Cragg, Michael. 1997. Performance incentives in the public sector: Evidence from the Job Training Partnership Act. *Journal of Law, Economics and Organization* 13, no. 1 (April): 147–68.

Cyert, Richard M., and James G. March. 1963. *A behavioral theory of the firm.* Englewood Cliffs, N.J.: Prentice-Hall.

D'Aunno, Thomas. 1992. The effectiveness of human service organizations: A comparison of models. In *Human services as complex organizations,* edited by Yeheskel Hasenfeld. Newbury Park, Calif.: Sage Publications.

D'Aunno, Thomas, and Thomas E. Vaughn. 1992. Variations in methadone treatment practices. *Journal of the American Medical Association* 267, no. 2: 253–58.

D'Aunno, Thomas, Nancy Folz-Murphy, and Xihong Lin. 1998. Changes in methadone treatment. Unpublished manuscript, School of Social Service Administration, University of Chicago.

D'Aunno, Thomas, Robert I. Sutton, and Richard H. Price. 1991. Isomorphism and external support in conflicting institutional environments: A study of drug abuse treatment units. *Academy of Management Journal* 34, no. 3: 636–61.

Demirag, Istemi S., ed. 1998. *Corporate governance, accountability and pressures to perform.* London: JAI Press.

Denison, Daniel R. 1990. *Corporate culture and organizational effectiveness.* New York: John Wiley & Sons.

Denison, Daniel R., and Aneil K. Mishra. 1995. Toward a theory of organizational culture and effectiveness. *Organization Science* 6, no. 2 (March-April): 204–23.

Dewatripont, Mathias, Ian Jewitt, and Jean Tirole. 1999. The economics of career concerns, part II: Application to missions and accountability of government agencies. *Review of Economic Studies* 66, no. 1 (January): 199–217.

Dhonte, Pierre, and Ishan Kapur. 1996. *Towards a market economy: Structures of governance.* International Monetary Fund Working Paper.

Dickinson, Katherine P., Richard W. West, Deborah J. Kogan, David A. Drury, Marlene S. Freanks, Laura Schlichtmann, and Mary Vencil. 1988. *Evaluation of the Effects of JTPA Performance Standards on Client Services and Costs.* National Commission for Employment Policy Research Report Number 88-16, September.

DiMaggio, Paul J., and Walter W. Powell. 1983. The iron cage revisited: Institutional isomorphism and collective rationality in organizational fields. *American Sociological Review* 48, no. 2 (April): 147–60.

Diver, Colin S. 1981. Policymaking paradigms in administrative law. *Harvard Law Review* 95, no. 2: 393–434.

Dixit, Avinash K. 1996. *The making of economic policy: A transaction-cost politics perspective.* Cambridge, Mass.: MIT Press.

———. 1999. Incentives and organizations in the public sector: An interpretive review. Paper presented at National Academy of Sciences conference on Devising Incentives to Promote Human Capital, December 17–18, Irvine, Calif.

Doig, Jameson W., and Erwin C. Hargrove. 1987. *Leadership and innovation: A biographical perspective on entrepreneurs in government.* Baltimore: Johns Hopkins University Press.

Downs, Anthony. 1967. *Inside bureaucracy.* Boston: Little, Brown.

Dukes, Frank. 1993. Public conflict resolution: A transformative approach. *Negotiation Journal* 9, no. 1 (January): 45–57.

Dunleavy, Patrick. 1991. *Democracy, bureaucracy and public choice: Economic explanations in political science.* New York: Prentice Hall.

Eberts, Randall W., Christopher J. O'Leary, and Stephen A. Wandner. 1999. Targeting employment services. *W.E. Upjohn Institute for Employment Research Newsletter* 6, no. 1: 1, 3–4.

Eisner, Marc Allen, and Kenneth J. Meier. 1990. Presidential control versus bureaucratic power: Explaining the Reagan revolution in antitrust. *American Journal of Political Science* 34, no. 1 (February): 269–87.

Elmore, Richard, Charles H. Abelmann, and Susan H. Fuhrman. 1996. The new accountability in state education reform: From process to performance. In *Holding schools accountable: Performance-based reform in education*, edited by Helen F. Ladd. Washington, D.C.: Brookings Institution.

Etheridge, Rose M., S. Gail Craddock, Robert L. Hubbard, and Jennifer L. Rounds-Bryant. 1999. The relationship of counseling and self-help participation to patient outcomes in DATOS. *Drug and Alcohol Dependence* 57 (December): 99–112.

Fenno, Richard F. 1966. *The power of the purse: Appropriations politics in Congress.* Boston: Little, Brown.

Ferguson, Ronald F. 1991. Paying for public education: New evidence on how and why money matters. *Harvard Journal on Legislation* 28: 465–98.

Fesler, James W., and Donald F. Kettl. 1991. *The politics of the administrative process.* Chatham, N.J.: Chatham House.

Fiorina, Morris. 1982. Legislative choice of regulatory forms. *Public Choice* 39, no. 1: 33–66.

Fiorina, Morris P., and Roger G. Noll. 1978. Voters, bureaucrats, and legislators: A rational choice perspective on the growth of bureaucracy. *Journal of Public Economics* 9, no. 2 (April): 239–54.

Fletcher, Bennett W., Frank M. Tims, and Barry S. Brown. 1997. Drug Abuse Treatment Outcomes Study (DATOS): Treatment Evaluation Research in the United States. *Psychology of Addictive Behaviors* 11, no. 4: 216–29.

Forder, Julien. 1997. Contracts and purchaser-provider relationships in community care. *Journal of Health Economics* 16, no. 5 (October): 517–42.

Frederickson, H. George. 1997. *The spirit of public administration.* San Francisco: Jossey-Bass.

Freeman, Linton C. 1979. The multinational corporation as an interorganizational network. *Academy of Management Review* 15: 603–25.

Friedman, Jeffrey, ed. 1996. *The rational choice controversy: Economic models of politics reconsidered.* New Haven, Conn.: Yale University Press.

Friedrich, Carl Joachim. 1963. *Man and his government: An empirical theory of politics.* New York: McGraw-Hill.

General Accounting Office (GAO). 1992. *Integrating human services: Linking at-risk families with services more successful than system reform.* GAO/HRD 92-108. Washington, D.C.: U.S. General Accounting Office.

Gerstein, Dean R., and Henrick J. Harwood, eds. 1990. *Treating drug problems: A study of the evolution, effectiveness, and financing of public and private drug treatment systems.* Washington, D.C.: National Academy Press.

Ghoshal, Sumantra, and Insead P. Moran. 1996. Bad for practice: A critique of the transaction cost theory. *Academy of Management Review* 21, no. 1 (January): 13–47.

Gill, Jeffrey, and Kenneth J. Meier. 2000. Public administration research and practice: A methodological manifesto. *Journal of Public Administration Research and Theory* 10, no. 1 (January): 157–200.

Glisson, Charles. 1992. Structure and technology in human services organizations. In *Human services as complex organizations*, edited by Yeheskel Hasenfeld. Newbury Park, Calif.: Sage Publications.

Goldstein, Harvey. 1987. *Multilevel models in educational and social research*. London: Oxford University Press.

———. 1992. Statistical information and the measurement of education outcomes. *Journal of the Royal Statistical Society* 155: 313–15.

———. 1995. *Multilevel statistical models*. New York: Halsted Press.

Goodrick, Elizabeth, and Gerald R. Salancik. 1996. Organizational discretion in responding to institutional practices: Hospitals and cesarean births. *Administrative Science Quarterly* 41: 1–28.

Gore, Albert. 1995. *Common sense government: Works better and costs less*. Washington, D.C.: U.S. Government Printing Office.

Granovetter, Mark. 1985. Economic action and social structure. *American Journal of Sociology* 91, no. 3: 481–510.

Green, Donald P., and Ian Shapiro. 1994. *Pathologies of rational choice: A critique of applications in political science*. New Haven, Conn.: Yale University Press.

Gruber, Judith E. 1987. *Controlling bureaucracies: Dilemmas in democratic governance*. Berkeley: University of California Press.

Guillén, Mauro F. 1994. The age of eclecticism: Current organizational trends and the evolution of managerial models. *Sloan Management Review* 36, no. 1 (fall): 75–86.

Gulati, Ranjay, and Martin Gargiulo. 1999. Where do interorganizational networks come from? *American Journal of Sociology* 104, no. 5 (March): 1439–93.

Gulick, Luther H. 1937. Notes on the theory of organization. In *Papers on the science of administration*, edited by Luther H. Gulick and Lyndall Urwick. New York: Institute of Public Administration.

Haass, Richard N. 1999. *The bureaucratic entrepreneur: How to be effective in any unruly organization*. Washington, D.C.: Brookings Institution.

Hamilton, Gary G., and Nicole Woolsey Biggart. 1988. Market, culture, and authority: A comparative analysis of management and organization in the Far East. *American Journal of Sociology* 94 (Supp.): 52–94.

Hammond, Thomas H., and Jack H. Knott. 1996. Who controls the bureaucracy: Presidential power, Congressional dominance, legal constraints, and bureaucratic autonomy in a model of multi-institutional policy-making. *Journal of Law, Economics, and Organization* 12, no. 1 (April): 119–66.

Handler, Joel F. 1996. *Down from bureaucracy: The ambiguity of privatization and empowerment.* Princeton, N.J.: Princeton University Press.

Hannan, Michael T., and John Freeman. 1984. Structural inertia and organizational change. *American Sociological Review* 49: 149–64.

————. 1989. *Organizational ecology.* Cambridge, Mass.: Harvard University Press.

Hanushek, Eric A. 1996. School resources and student performance. In *Does money matter? The effect of school resources on student achievement and adult success,* edited by Gary Burtless. Washington, D.C.: Brookings Institution.

Hanushek, Eric A., Steven G. Rivkin, and Lori L. Taylor. 1996. Aggregation and the estimated effects of school resources. *Review of Economics and Statistics* 78, no. 4 (November): 611–27.

Hargrove, Erwin C., and John C. Glidewell. 1990. *Impossible jobs in public management.* Lawrence: University Press of Kansas.

Hart, Oliver. 1988. Incomplete contracts and the theory of the firm. *Journal of Law, Economics, and Organization* 4, no. 1 (spring): 119–39.

Hasenfeld, Yeheskel. 1983. *Human service organizations.* Englewood Cliffs, N.J.: Prentice-Hall, Inc.

————. 1992. The nature of human service organizations. In *Human Services as Complex Organizations,* edited by Yeheskel Hasenfeld. Newbury Park, Calif.: Sage Publications.

Hasenfeld, Yeheskel, and Dale Weaver. 1996. Enforcement, compliance, and disputes in welfare-to-work programs. *Social Service Review* 70, no. 2 (June): 235–56.

Heckathorn, Douglas D., and Steven M. Maser. 1987. Bargaining and the sources of transaction costs: The case of government regulation. *Journal of Law, Economics, and Organization* 3, no. 1 (spring): 69–98.

Heckman, James J., ed. Forthcoming. *Performance standards in a government bureaucracy.* Kalamazoo, Mich.: W.E. Upjohn Institute and University of Chicago Press.

Heckman, James J., and Jeffrey A. Smith. 1995. The performance of performance standards: The effects of JTPA performance standards on efficiency, equity and participant outcomes. Working paper, July.

————. 1997. The determinants of participation in a social program: Evidence from the Job Training Partnership Act. Unpublished manuscript, Department of Economics, University of Western Ontario.

Heckman, James J., Carolyn J. Heinrich, and Jeffrey A. Smith. 1997. Assessing the performance of performance standards in public bureaucracies. *American Economic Review* 87, no. 2 (May): 389–96.

———. 1999. Understanding incentives in public organizations. Paper presented at National Academy of Sciences colloquium, Devising Incentives to Promote Human Capital, December 17–18, Washington, D.C.

Heckman, James J., Robert J. LaLonde, and Jeffrey A. Smith. 1999. The economics and econometrics of active labor market programs. In *Handbook of Labor Economics*, Vol. 3A, edited by Orley C. Ashenfelter and David Card. Amsterdam: Elsevier Science.

Heckman, James J., Jeffrey A. Smith, and Christopher Taber. 1996. What do bureaucrats do? The effects of performance standards and bureaucratic preferences on acceptance into the JTPA program. In *Advances in the study of entrepreneurship, innovation, and economic growth, Vol. 7: Reinventing government and the problem of bureaucracy*, edited by Gary D. Libecap. Greenwich, Conn.: JAI Press.

Heclo, Hugh. 1979. Issue networks and the executive establishment. In *The new American political system*, edited by Anthony King. Washington, D.C.: American Enterprise Institute for Public Policy Research.

———. 1985. An executive's success can have costs. In *The Reagan presidency and the governing of America*, edited by Lester M. Salamon and Michael S. Lund. Washington, D.C.: Urban Institute.

Hedges, Larry V., and Rob Greenwald. 1996. Have times changed? The relation between school resources and student performance. In *Does money matter? The effect of school resources on student achievement and adult success*, edited by Gary Burtless. Washington, D.C.: Brookings Institution.

Heinrich, Carolyn J. 1999. Do government bureaucrats make effective use of performance management information? *Journal of Public Administration Research and Theory* 9, no. 3 (July): 363–93.

———. Forthcoming. The role of performance standards in JTPA program administration and service delivery at the local level. In *Performance standards in a government bureaucracy*, edited by James J. Heckman Kalamazoo, Mich.: W.E. Upjohn Institute and University of Chicago Press.

Heinrich, Carolyn J., and Laurence E. Lynn, Jr. 1999. Means and ends: A comparative study of empirical methods for investigating governance and performance. Northwestern University/University of Chicago Joint Center for Poverty Research Working paper 108. Prepared for Fifth National Public Management Research Conference, George

Bush School of Public Service, College Station, Texas, December 3–4.

———. 2000. Governance and performance: The influence of program structure and management on Job Training Partnership Act (JTPA) program outcomes. In *Governance and performance: New perspectives,* edited by Carolyn J. Heinrich and Laurence E. Lynn, Jr. Washington, D.C.: Georgetown University Press.

Henly, Julie. 1999. Barriers to finding and maintaining jobs: The perspectives of workers and employers in the low-wage labor market. In *Hard labor: Women and work in the post welfare era,* edited by Joel F. Handler and Lucie White. New York: M.E. Sharpe.

Hewitt de Alcantara, Cynthia. 1998. Uses and abuses of the concept of governance. *International Social Science Journal* 50, no. 1 (March): 105–13.

Hill, Jeffrey S. 1985. Why so much stability? The impact of agency determined stability. *Public Choice* 46: 275–87.

Holmstrom, Bengt. 1982. Moral hazard in teams. *Bell Journal of Economics* 13, no. 2 (autumn): 324–40.

Holmstrom, Bengt, and Paul Milgrom. 1991. Multitask principal-agent analyses: Incentive contracts, asset ownership, and job design. *Journal of Law, Economics, and Organization* 7 (special issue): 24–52.

Horn, Murray J., and Kenneth Shepsle. 1989. Commentary on administrative arrangements and the political control of agencies: administrative process and organizational form as legislative response to agency costs. *Virginia Law Review* 75: 499–508.

Hotz, V. Joseph, Robert Goerge, Julie Balzekas, and Francis Margolin. 1999. Administrative data for policy-relevant research: Assessment of current utility and recommendations for development. Report of Advisory Panel on Research Uses of Administrative Data of Northwestern University/University of Chicago Joint Center for Poverty Research.

Hoyle, Rick H., ed. 1995. *Structural equation modeling: Concepts, issues, and applications.* Thousand Oaks, Calif.: Sage Publications.

Hser, Yih-Ing, Christine E. Grella, Shih-Chao Hsieh, M. Douglas Anglin, and Barry S. Brown. 1999. Prior treatment experience related to process and outcomes in DATOS. *Drug and Alcohol Dependence* 57 (December): 137–50.

Hubbard, Robert L., S. Gail Craddock, Patrick M. Flynn, Jill Anderson, and Rose M. Etheridge. 1997. Overview of 1-year follow-up outcomes in the drug abuse treatment outcomes study (DATOS). *Psychology of Addictive Behaviors* 11, no. 4: 261–78.

Hult, Karen M., and Charles Walcott. 1989. Organizational design as public policy. *Policy Studies Journal* 17, no. 3 (spring): 469–94.

Ingraham, Patricia W., and Amy E. Donahue. 2000. Dissecting the black box revisited: Characterizing government management capacity. In *Governance and performance: New perspectives,* edited by Carolyn J. Heinrich and Laurence E. Lynn, Jr. Washington, D.C.: Georgetown University Press.

Ingram, Helen. 1990. Implementation: A review and suggested framework. In *Public administration: The state of the discipline,* edited by Naomi B. Lynn and Aaron Wildavsky. Chatham, N.J.: Chatham House.

Itoh, Hideshi. 1991. Incentives to help in multi-agent situations. *Econometrica* 59, no. 3 (May): 611–36.

———. 1992. Cooperation in hierarchical organizations: An incentive perspective. *Journal of Law, Economics and Organization* 8, no. 2 (April): 321–45.

———. 1993. Coalitions, incentives and risk sharing. *Journal of Economic Theory* 60, no. 2 (August): 410–27.

Jennings, Edward T. 1994. Building bridges in the intergovernmental arena: Coordinating employment and training programs in the American states. *Public Administration Review* 54, no. 1 (January/February): 52–60.

Jennings, Edward T. Jr., and Jo Ann G. Ewalt. 1998. Interorganizational coordination, administrative consolidation and policy performance. *Public Administration Review* 58, no. 5: 417–28.

———. 2000. Driving caseloads down: Welfare policy choices and administrative action in the states. In *Governance and performance: New perspectives,* edited by Carolyn J. Heinrich and Laurence E. Lynn, Jr. Washington, D.C.: Georgetown University Press.

Jensen, Michael C., and William H. Meckling. 1976. Theory of the firm: Managerial behavior, agency costs, and ownership structure. *Journal of Financial Economics* 3, no. 4 (October): 305–60.

Jepperson, Ronald L., and John W. Meyer. 1991. The public order and the construction of formal organizations. In *The new institutionalism in organizational analysis,* edited by Walter W. Powell and Paul J. DiMaggio. Chicago: University of Chicago Press.

Kaufman, Herbert. 1981. *The administrative behavior of federal bureau chiefs.* Washington, D.C.: Brookings Institution.

Keasey, Kevin, Steve Thompson, and Mike Wright, eds. 1997. *Corporate governance.* Oxford: Oxford University Press.

Keiser, Lael R. 1997. Controlling the child enforcement bureaucracy: Organizational characteristics and bureaucratic responses. Working paper. October.

Keiser, Lael R., and Kenneth J. Meier. 1996. Public management, policy design, and bureaucratic incentives: the case of child support enforcement. *Journal of Public Administration Research and Theory* 6, no. 3 (July): 337–64.

Kettl, Donald F. 1996. Introduction. In *The state of public management,* edited by Donald F. Kettl and H. Brinton Milward. Baltimore: Johns Hopkins University Press.

———. 2000. Public administration at the millennium. *Journal of Public Administration Research and Theory* 10, no. 1 (January): 7–34.

Kingdon, John. 1984. *Agendas, alternatives, and public policies.* Boston: Little, Brown.

Kirk, Stuart A., and Herb Kutchins. 1988. Deliberate misdiagnosis in mental health practice. *Social Service Review* 62, no. 2 (June): 225–37.

Knight, Jack. 1992. *Institutions and social conflict.* New York: Cambridge University Press.

Knoke, David. 1994. *Political networks: The structural perspective.* New York: Cambridge University Press.

Knott, Jack H. 1993. Comparing public and private management: Cooperative effort and principal-agent relationships. *Journal of Public Administration Research and Theory* 3, no. 1 (January): 93–119.

Knott, Jack H., and Thomas H. Hammond. 2000. Congressional committees and policy change: Explaining legislative outcomes in banking, trucking, airline, and telecommunications deregulation. In *Governance and performance: New perspectives,* edited by Carolyn J. Heinrich and Laurence E. Lynn, Jr. Washington, D.C.: Georgetown University Press.

Knott, Jack H., and Gary J. Miller. 1987. *Reforming bureaucracy: The politics of institutional choice.* Englewood Cliffs, N.J.: Prentice-Hall.

Koch, James V. and Richard J. Cebula. 1994. In search of excellent management. *Journal of Management Studies* 31, no. 5 (September): 681–99.

Koremenos, Barbara, and Laurence E. Lynn, Jr. 1996. Leadership of a state agency: An analysis using game theory. In *The state of public management,* edited by Donald F. Kettl and H. Brinton Milward. Baltimore and London: Johns Hopkins University Press.

Kotter, John P., and James L. Heskett. 1992. *Corporate culture and performance.* New York: Free Press.

Kramer, Ralph M. 1994. Voluntary agencies and the contract culture: Dream or nightmare? *Social Service Review* 68: 33–60.

Kreps, David M. 1990. *A course in microeconomic theory.* Princeton, N.J.: Princeton University Press.

Krull, Jennifer L., and David P. MacKinnon. 1999. Multilevel mediation modeling in group-based intervention studies. *Evaluation Review* 23, no. 4: 418–44.

Lachman, Ran, Albert Nedd, and Bob Hinings. 1994. Analyzing cross-national management and organizations: A theoretical framework. *Management Science* 40, no. 1: 40–55.

Laffont, Jean-Jacques, and Jean Tirole. 1993. *A theory of incentives in procurement and regulation.* Cambridge, Mass.: MIT Press.

Laumann, Edward O., and David Knoke. 1987. *The organizational state: Social choice in national policy domains.* Madison: University of Wisconsin Press.

Lee, Valerie E., and Anthony S. Bryk. 1989. A multilevel model of the social distribution of high school achievement. *Sociology of Education* 62: 172–92.

Lee, Valerie E., Anthony S. Bryk, and Julia B. Smith. 1993. The organization of effective secondary schools. In *Review of research in education,* edited by Linda Darling-Hammond. Washington, D.C.: American Educational Research Association.

Leiserson, Avery, and Fritz Morstein Marx. 1959. The study of public administration. In *Elements of public administration,* 2nd ed., edited by Fritz Morstein Marx. Englewood Cliffs, N.J.: Prentice-Hall.

Levine, Judith A. 1999. Policy incentives confront everyday realities: Integrating economic and sociological perspectives on the welfare-to-work transition. Working paper, School of Social Service Administration, University of Chicago.

Lincoln, James R., Michael L. Gerlach, and Christina L. Ahmadjian. 1996. *Keiretsu* networks and corporate performance in Japan. *American Sociological Review* 61: 67–88.

Linder, Stephen H., and B. Guy Peters. 1989. Instruments of government: Perceptions and contexts. *Journal of Public Policy* 9: 35–38.

Lipsky, Michael. 1980. *Street-level bureaucracy: Dilemmas of the individual in public services.* New York: Russell Sage Foundation.

Longenecker, Clinton O., and Dennis A. Gioia. 1991. SMR forum: Ten myths of managing managers. *Sloan Management Review* (fall): 81–90.

Lowery, David. 1983. Limitations on taxing and spending powers: An assessment of their effectiveness. *Social Science Quarterly* 64:2 (June): 247–63.

Lynn, Laurence E., Jr. 1981. *Managing the public's business: The job of the government executive.* New York: Basic Books.

———. 1985. The Reagan administration and the renitent bureaucracy. In *The Reagan presidency and the governing of America,* edited by

Lester M. Salamon and Michael S. Lund. Washington, D.C.: Urban Institute Press.

———. 1987. *Managing public policy.* Boston: Little, Brown.

———. 1991. The budget-maximizing bureaucrat: Is there a case? In *The budget-maximizing bureaucrat: Appraisals and evidence,* edited by Andre Blais and Stephane Dion. Pittsburgh: University of Pittsburgh Press.

———. 1996a. *Public management as art, science, and profession.* Chatham, N.J.: Chatham House.

———. 1996b. Assume a network: Reforming mental health services in Illinois. *Journal of Public Administration Research and Theory* 6, no. 2 (April): 297–314.

———. 2000a. A symposium: In government, does management matter? In *Advancing public management: New developments in theory, methods, and practice,* edited by Jeffrey L. Brudney, Laurence O'Toole, Jr., and Hal G. Rainey. Washington, D.C.: Georgetown University Press.

———. 2000b. The making and analysis of public policy: A perspective on the role of social science. Ann Arbor: University of Michigan Press.

Lynn, Laurence E., Jr., and Teresa R. Kowalczyk. 1996. Governing public schools: The role of formal authority in school improvement. *Advances in Educational Policy* 2: 31–55.

Lynn, Laurence E., Jr., and Robin L. Tepper. 1998. Governing public schools: Theory and practice. Working paper, University of Chicago.

MacCallum, Robert C. 1995. Model specification: Procedures, strategies and related issues. In *Structural equation modeling: Concepts, issues, and applications,* edited by Rick H. Hoyle. Thousand Oaks, Calif.: Sage Publications.

March, James G. 1997. Administrative practice, organizational theory, and political philosophy: Ruminations on the *Reflections* of John M. Gaus. *PS: Political Science & Politics* 30: 689–98.

March, James G., and Johan P. Olsen. 1976. *Ambiguity and choice in organizations.* Bergen, Norway: Universitetsforlaget.

March, James G., and Herbert A. Simon. 1958. *Organizations.* New York: Wiley.

Marcoulides, George A., and Ronald H. Heck. 1993. Organizational culture and performance: Proposing and testing a model. *Organization Science* 4, no. 2 (May): 209–25.

Mashaw, Jerry L. 1983. *Bureaucratic justice: Managing Social Security disability claims.* New Haven, Conn.: Yale University Press.

———. 1990. Explaining administrative process: Normative, positive, and critical stories of legal development. *Journal of Law, Economics, and Organization* 6 (special issue): 267–98.

Masten, Scott F., James W. Meehan, and Edward A. Snyder. 1991. The costs of organization. *Journal of Law, Economics and Organization* 7, no. 1 (spring): 1–25.

Mayhew, David R. 1974. *Congress: The electoral connection.* New Haven, Conn.: Yale University Press.

McCubbins, Mathew D. 1985. The legislative design of regulatory structure. *American Journal of Political Science* 29, no. 4 (November): 721–48.

McCubbins, Mathew, and Thomas Schwartz. 1984. Congressional oversight overlooked: Police patrols vs. fire alarms. *American Journal of Political Science* 28: 165–79.

McCubbins, Mathew, Roger Noll, and Barry Weingast. 1987. Administrative procedures as instruments of political control. *Journal of Law, Economics, and Organization* 3, no. 2: 243–77.

———. 1989. Structure and process, politics and policy: Administrative arrangements and the political control of agencies. *Virginia Law Review* 75: 431–83.

Mead, Lawrence M. 1997. Optimizing JOBS: Evaluation versus administration. *Public Administration Review* 57, no. 2: 113–23.

———. 1999. Performance analysis. Unpublished manuscript, New York University.

Mechanic, David. 1962. Sources of power of lower participants in complex organizations. *Administrative Science Quarterly* 7, no. 4: 340–84.

Meier, Kenneth J., and Jeffrey Gill. 2000. *What works: A new approach to program and policy analysis.* Boulder, Colo.: Westview Press.

Meyer, John W., and Brian Rowan. 1977. Institutionalized organizations: Formal structure as myth and ceremony. *American Journal of Sociology* 83, no. 2: (September): 340–63.

Meyer, John W., W. Richard Scott, and Terrence E. Deal. 1981. Institutional and technical sources of organizational structure of educational organizations. In *Organization and the human services,* edited by Herman D. Stein. Philadelphia: Temple University Press.

———. 1983. Institutional and technical sources of organizational structure: Explaining the structure of educational organizations. In *Organizational environments: Ritual and rationality,* edited by John W. Meyer and W. Richard Scott. Beverly Hills, Calif.: Sage Publications.

Meyer, Marshall W. 1979. *Change in public bureaucracies. Cambridge:* Cambridge University Press.

Meyers, Marcia K., and Nara Dillon. 1999. Institutional paradoxes: Why welfare workers cannot reform welfare. In *Public management reform and innovation: Research, theory, and application,* edited by H.

George Frederickson and Jocelyn M. Johnston. Tuscaloosa: University of Alabama Press.

Meyers, Marcia K., Bonnie Glaser, and Karin MacDonald. 1998. On the front lines of welfare delivery: Are workers implementing policy reforms? *Journal of Policy Analysis and Management* 17, no. 1 (winter): 1–22.

Michels, Robert [1915] 1949. *Political parties.* Translated by Eden and Cedar Paul. Glencoe, Ill.: Free Press.

Milgrom, Paul, and John Roberts. 1990. Bargaining costs, influence costs and the organization of economic activity. In *Perspectives on positive political economy*, edited by James E. Alt and Kenneth A. Shepsle. Political Economy of Institutions and Decisions Series. Cambridge, New York, and Melbourne: Cambridge University Press.

Miller, Gary. 1992. *Managerial dilemmas: The political economy of hierarchy.* Cambridge: Cambridge University Press.

Miller, Gary J., and Terry M. Moe. 1983. Bureaucrats, legislators, and the size of government. *American Political Science Review* 77, no. 2: 297–322.

Mills, C. Wright. 1956. *The power elite.* New York: Oxford University Press.

Milward, H. Brinton. 1994. Nonprofit contracting and the hollow state. *Public Administration Review* 54: 73–77.

Milward, H. Brinton, and Keith G. Provan. 1993. The hollow state: Private provision of public services. In *Public policy for democracy*, edited by Helen Ingram and Steven Rathgeb Smith. Washington D.C.: Brookings Institution.

———. 1998. Principles for controlling agents: The political economy of network structure. *Journal of Public Administration Research and Theory* 8, no. 2 (April): 203–21.

———. 2000. How networks are governed. In *Governance and performance: New perspectives,* edited by Carolyn J. Heinrich and Laurence E. Lynn, Jr. Washington, D.C.: Georgetown University Press.

Mintzberg, Henry. 1979. *The structure of organizations.* Englewood Cliffs, N.J.: Prentice-Hall.

Moe, Terry M. 1984. The new economics of organization. *American Journal of Political Science* 28: 739–77.

———. 1985. Control and feedback in economic regulation: The case of the NLRB. *American Political Science Review* 79, no. 4 (December): 1094–1116.

———. 1989. The politics of bureaucratic structure. In *Can the government govern?,* edited by John E.. Chubb and Paul E. Peterson. Washington, D.C.: Brookings Institution.

———. 1995. The politics of structural choice: Toward a theory of public bureaucracy. In *Organization theory: From Chester Barnard to the present and beyond,* expanded edition, edited by Oliver E. Williamson. Oxford, New York, Toronto, and Melbourne: Oxford University Press.

Mohr, Lawrence B. 1996. *The causes of human behavior: Implications for theory and method in the social sciences.* Ann Arbor: University of Michigan Press.

———. 1999. One hundred theories of organizational change: The good, the bad, and the ugly. In *Public management reform and innovation: Research, theory, and application,* edited by H. George Frederickson and Jocelyn M. Johnston. Tuscaloosa: University of Alabama Press.

Monroe, Kristen Renwick, ed. 1991. *The economic approach to politics: A critical reassessment of the theory of rational action.* New York: HarperCollins.

Mookherjee, Dilip. 1984. Optimal incentive schemes with many agents. *Review of Economic Studies* 51, no. 3 (July): 433–46.

Moore, Mark H. 1995. *Creating public value: Strategic management in government.* Cambridge, Mass.: Harvard University Press.

Nalbantian, Haig R., and Andrew Schotter. 1997. Productivity under group incentives: An experimental study. *American Economic Review* 87, no. 3 (June): 314–41.

Niskanen, William A. 1975. Bureaucrats and politicians. *Journal of Law and Economics* 18: 617–43.

Nohria, Nitin, and Ranjay Gulati. 1995. What is the optimum amount of organizational slack? A study of the relationship between slack and innovation in multinational firms. Paper presented at Fifty-fifth Annual Meeting of Academy of Management, Vancouver, British Columbia, August 6–9.

Noll, Roger G., and Barry R. Weingast. 1991. Rational actor theory, social norms, and policy implementation: Applications to administrative processes and bureaucratic culture. In *The economic approach to politics: A critical reassessment of the theory of rational action,* edited by Kristen Renwick Monroe. New York: Harper Collins.

North, Douglass C. 1990. *Institutions, institutional change, and economic performance* Cambridge: Cambridge University Press.

O'Reilly, Charles A., and Jennifer A. Chatman. 1996. Culture as social control: Corporations, cults, and commitment. In *Research in Organizational Behavior* 18. Greenwich, Conn.: JAI Press.

Orfield, Gary, and Helene Slessarev. 1986. *Job training under the new federalism.* Report to Subcommittee on Employment Opportunities Committee on Education and Labor, U.S. House of Representatives.

Orr, Larry, Burt S. Barnow, Robert I. Lerman, and Erik Beecroft. 1997. *Follow-up analyses of the national JTPA study sample.* Final report prepared for U.S. Department of Labor, July.

Orr, Larry, Howard Bloom, Stephen Bell, Winston Lin, George Cave, and Fred Doolittle. 1994. *The National JTPA Study: Impacts, Benefits, and Costs of Title IIA.* Bethesda, Md.: Abt Associates.

Ostrom, Elinor. 1986. An agenda for the study of institutions. *Public Choice* 48, no. 1: 3–25.

Ostrom, Elinor, Roy Gardner, and James Walker. 1994. *Rules, games, and common-pool resources.* Ann Arbor: University of Michigan Press.

Ostrom, Elinor, Larry Schroeder, and Susan Wynne. 1993. Analyzing the performance of alternative institutional arrangements for sustaining rural infrastructure in developing countries. *Journal of Public Administration Research and Theory* 3, no. 1 (January): 11–45.

Ostrom, Vincent. 1973. *The intellectual crisis in American public administration.* University: University of Alabama Press.

O'Toole, Laurence J. Jr., and Kenneth J. Meier. 2000. Networks, hierarchies, and public management: Modeling the nonlinearities. In *Governance and performance: New perspectives,* edited by Carolyn J. Heinrich and Laurence E. Lynn, Jr. Washington, D.C.: Georgetown University Press.

Ouchi, William G. 1979. A conceptual framework for the design of organizational control mechanisms. *Management Science* 25: 833–48.

Palmer, Timothy B., George W. Danforth, and Shawn M. Clark. 1995. Strategic responses to poor performance in the health care industry: A test of competing predictions. Paper presented at Fifty-fifth Annual Meeting of Academy of Management, Vancouver, British Columbia, Canada, August 6–9.

Parsons, Donald O. 1991. Self-screening in targeted public transfer programs. *Journal of Political Economy* 99, no. 4: 859–77.

Parsons, Talcott. 1960. *Structure and process in modern societies.* New York: Free Press of Glencoe.

Perrow, Charles. 1986. Economic theories of organization. *Theory and Society* 15: 11–45.

Perry, James L., and Kenneth L. Kraemer. 1990. Research methodology in public administration: issues and patterns. In *Public administration: The state of the discipline,* edited by Naomi B. Lynn and Aaron Wildavsky. Chatham, N.J.: Chatham House.

Perry, James L., and Theodore K. Miller. 1991. The Senior Executive Service: Is it improving managerial performance? *Public Administration Review* 51, no. 6 (November/December): 554–63.

Peteraf, Margaret A. 1992. A review of Ghemawat's *Commitment: The dynamics of strategy. Journal of Economics and Management Strategy* 1, no. 3 (fall): 575–82.

———. 1993. The cornerstones of competitive advantage: A resource-based view. *Strategic Management Journal* 14, no. 3 (March): 179–91.

Pfeffer, Jeffrey. 1997. *New directions for organization theory: Problems and prospects.* Oxford: Oxford University Press.

Pfeffer, Jeffrey, and Gerald R. Salancik. 1978. *The external control of organizations: A resource dependence perspective.* New York: Harper & Row.

Policy Studies Review. 1999. 16, no. 1 (spring).

Potoski, Matthew M. 1999. Managing uncertainty through bureaucratic design: Administrative procedures and state air pollution control agencies. *Journal of Public Administration Research and Theory* 9, no. 4: 623–40.

Powell, Walter W. 1990. Neither market nor hierarchy: Network forms of organization. In *Research in Organizational Behavior,* vol. 12, edited by B. Staw and L. Cummings. Greenwich, Conn., and London: JAI Press.

Price, Don K. 1954. *Government and science: Their dynamic relation in American democracy.* New York: New York University Press.

Provan, Keith G., and H. Brinton Milward. 1995. A preliminary theory of interorganizational network effectiveness: A comparative study of four community mental health systems. *Administrative Science Quarterly* 40, no. 1 (March): 1–33.

Provan, Keith G., and Juliann G. Sebastian. 1998. Networks within networks: Service link overlap, organizational cliques, and network effectiveness. *Academy of Management Journal* 41, no. 4 (August): 453–63.

Purkey, Stewart C., and Marshall S. Smith. 1983. Effective schools: A review. *The Elementary School Journal* 83, no. 4: 427–52.

Radin, Beryl. 2000. The Government Performance and Results Act and the tradition of federal management reform: Square pegs in round holes? *Journal of Public Administration Research and Theory* 10, no. 1 (January): 111–35.

Rainey, Hal G. 1997. *Understanding and managing public organizations.* San Francisco: Jossey-Bass.

Rampersad, Peggy Snellings. 1978. Conflict and authority in the academic organization. Ph.D. dissertation, University of Chicago.

Rapoport, R. 1960. *Community as doctor.* London: Tavistock Publications.

Redford, Emmette S. 1965. *Ideal and practice in public administration.* University, Ala.: University of Alabama Press.

———. 1969. *Democracy in the administrative state.* New York: Oxford University Press.

Riccucci, Norma M., Marcia Meyers, and Irene Lurie. 1999. Welfare reform: Implications for front-line management and practice. Paper presented at Fifth National Public Management Research Conference, George Bush School of Government and Public Service, Texas A&M University, December 3–4.

Rice, A. K. 1963. *The Enterprise and Its Environment.* London: Tavistock.

Riker, William H. and Itai Sened. 1991. A political theory of the origin of property rights: Airport slots. *American Journal of Political Science* 35, no. 4: 951–69.

Ringquist, Evan J. 1995. Political control and policy impact in EPA's Office of Water Quality. *American Journal of Political Science* 39: 336–63.

Roderick, Melissa, and Eric Camburn. 1997. Risk and recovery: Course failures in the early years of high school. Unpublished manuscript. January.

Roderick, Melissa, Anthony S. Bryk, Brian Jacob, John Q. Easton, and Elaine Allensworth. 1999. *Ending social promotion: Results from the first two years.* Chicago: Consortium on Chicago School Research.

Roderick, Melissa, Brian Jacob, and Anthony S. Bryk. 2000. Evaluating Chicago's efforts to end social promotion. In *Governance and performance: New perspectives,* edited by Carolyn J. Heinrich and Laurence E. Lynn, Jr.. Washington, D.C.: Georgetown University Press.

Romzek, Barbara S. 1998. Where the buck stops: Accountability in reformed public organizations. In *Transforming government: Lessons from the reinvention labs,* edited by Patricia W. Ingraham, James R. Thompson, and Ronald P. Sanders. San Francisco: Jossey-Bass.

Rotenberg, Julio J., and Garth Saloner. 1993. Leadership style and incentives. *Management Science* 39, no. 11 (November): 1229–1318.

Sabatier, Paul A., John Loomis, and Catherine McCarthy. 1995. Hierarchical controls, professional norms, local constituencies, and budget maximization: An analysis of U.S. Forest Service planning decisions. *American Journal of Political Science* 39, no. 1 (January): 204–42.

Sabel, Charles F. 1993. Constitutional ordering in historical context. In *Games in hierarchies and networks: Analytical and empirical approaches to the study of governance institutions,* edited by Fritz W. Scharpf. Boulder, Colo.: Westview Press.

Saffold, Guy S. III. 1988. Culture traits, strength, and organizational performance: Moving beyond "strong" culture. *Academy of Management Review* 13, no. 4: 546–58.

Salamon, Lester M. 1981. Rethinking public management: Third-party government and the changing forms of public action. *Public Policy* 29: 255–75.

Salmon, J. Warren, and David G. Whiteis. 1992. Improving public health care: Lessons on governance in five cities. *Journal of Health Care for the Poor and Underserved* 3, no. 2 (fall): 285–304.

Sandell, Steven, and Kalman Rupp. 1988. *Who is served in JTPA programs: Patterns of participation and intergroup equity.* National Commission for Employment Policy Research Report 88–03.

Sandfort, Jodi R. 2000. Examining the effect of welfare-to-work structures and services on a desired policy outcome. In *Governance and performance: New perspectives,* edited by Carolyn J. Heinrich and Laurence E. Lynn, Jr. Washington, D.C.: Georgetown University Press.

Schattschneider, E. E. 1975. *The semisovereign people: A realist's view of democracy in America.* Hinsdale, Ill.: Dryden Press.

Schein, Edgar H. 1992. *Organizational culture and leadership,* 2nd ed. San Francisco: Jossey-Bass.

Schiller, Barry. 1999. State welfare reform impacts: Content and enforcement effects. *Contemporary Economic Policy* 17, no. 2 (April): 210–22.

Schotter, Andrew. 1981. *The economic theory of social institutions.* New York: Cambridge University Press.

Schuck, Peter H. 1994. *Foundations of administrative law.* New York: Oxford University Press.

Schultze, Charles L. 1968. *The politics and economics of public spending.* Washington, D.C.: Brookings Institution.

Schwartz, Bernard. 1994. Some crucial issues in administrative law. In *Handbook of regulation and administrative law,* edited by David H. Rosenbloom and Richard D. Schwartz. New York: Marcel Dekker.

Scott, John. 1991. *Social network analysis: A handbook.* London: Sage Publications.

Scott, W. Richard. 1998. *Organizations: Rational, natural, and open systems,* 4th ed. Upper Saddle River, N.J.: Prentice Hall.

Selden, Sally Coleman. 1999. Explaining policy outputs and outcomes in the U.S. Department of Education's Rehabilitation Services Administration: A more comprehensive study. Paper presented at Fifth National Public Management Research Conference, George Bush School of Government and Public Service, Texas A&M University, December 3–4.

Shapiro, Martin. 1994. Discretion. In *Handbook of regulation and administrative law*, edited by David H. Rosenbloom and Richard D. Schwartz. New York: Marcel Dekker.

Shelanski, Howard A., and Peter G. Klein. 1995. Empirical research in transaction cost economics—a review and assessment. *Journal of Law, Economics, and Organization* 11, no. 2: 335–61.

Shepsle, Kenneth, and Barry Weingast. 1981. Structure-induced equilibrium and legislative choice. *Public Choice* 37, no. 3: 503–19.

Sherwood, Kay E., and Fred Doolittle. 1999. What's behind the impacts: Doing implementation research in the context of program impact studies. Working paper, Manpower Demonstration Research Corporation.

Simon, Herbert A. 1947. *Administrative behavior: A study of decision-making processes in administrative organization.* New York: Macmillan.

———. 1959. Theories of decision-making in economics and behavioral science. *American Economic Review* 49, no. 3 (June): 253–83.

———. 1964. On the concept of organizational goal. *Administrative Science Quarterly* 9: 1–11.

Skocpol, Theda. 1985. Bringing the state back in: Strategies of analysis in current research. In *Bringing the state back in,* edited by Peter B. Evans, Dietrich Rueschemeyer, and Theda Skocpol. Cambridge: Cambridge University Press.

Skroban, Stacy B., Denise C. Gottfredson, and Gary D. Gottfredson. 1999. A school-based social competency promotion demonstration. *Evaluation Review* 23, no. 1: 3–27.

Smith, Kevin B., and Kenneth J. Meier. 1994. Politics, bureaucrats and schools. *Public Administration Review* 54, no. 6: 551–58.

Smith, Marshall S., Brett W. Scoll, and Jeffrey Link. 1995. Research-based school reform: The Clinton Administration's agenda. In *Improving the performance of America's schools.* Washington, D.C.: National Research Council.

Smith, Peter B., Jyuji Misumi, Monir Tayeb, Mark Peterson, and Michael Bond. 1989. On the generality of leadership style measures across cultures. *Journal of Occupational Psychology* 62: 97–109.

Smith, Stephen Rathgeb, and Michael Lipsky. 1993. *Nonprofits for hire: The welfare state in the age of contracting.* Cambridge, Mass.: Harvard University Press.

Spulber, Daniel F. 1992. Economic analysis and management strategy: A survey. *Journal of Economics and Management Strategy* 1, no. 3 (fall): 535–74.

———. 1994. Economic analysis and management strategy: A survey continued. *Journal of Economics and Management Strategy* 3, no. 2 (summer): 355–406.

Stinchcombe, Arthur L. 1989. An outsider's view of Network Analysis of Power. In *Networks of power: Organizational actors at the national, corporate, and community levels,* edited by Robert Perrucci and Harry R. Potter. New York: Aldine.

Stoker, Gerry. 1998. Governance as theory: Five propositions. *International Social Science Journal* 50, no. 1 (March): 17–28.

Stone, Clarence N. 1980. The implementation of social programs: Two perspectives. *Journal of Social Issues* 36, no. 4 (fall): 13–34.

Summer, Charles E. 1980. *Strategic behavior in business and government.* Boston: Little, Brown.

Sundquist, James L. 1978. Research brokerage: The weak link. In *Knowledge and policy: The uncertain connection,* edited by Laurence E. Lynn, Jr. Washington, D.C.: National Academy of Sciences.

Sunstein, Cass R. 1990. Political economy, administrative law: A comment. *Journal of Law, Economics, and Organization* 6: 299–306.

Thompson, Fred. 1993. Matching responsibilities with tactics: Administrative controls and modern government. *Public Administration Review* 53, no. 4 (July/August): 303–18.

Thompson, James D. 1967. *Organizations in action: Social science bases and administrative theory.* New York: McGraw-Hill.

Tirole, Jean. 1988. *The theory of industrial organization.* Cambridge, Mass.: MIT Press.

———. 1994. The internal organization of government. *Oxford Economic Papers* 46, no. 1: 1–29.

Uzzi, Brian. 1996. The sources and consequences of embeddedness for the economic performance of organizations: The network effect. *American Sociological Review* 61, no. 4 (August): 674–98.

———. 1997. Social structure and competition in interfirm networks: The paradox of embeddedness. *Administrative Science Quarterly* 42: 35–67.

Vickers, Sir Geoffrey. 1983. *The art of judgment: A study of policy making.* London: Harper & Row.

Von Benda-Beckmann, Franz. 1994. Good governance, law and social reality: Problematic relationships. *Knowledge and Policy* 7, no. 3 (fall): 55–67.

Wamsley, Gary L. 1990. Introduction. In *Refounding public administration,* edited by Gary L. Wamsley and James F. Wolf. Newbury Park, Calif.: Sage Publications.

Weber, Max, trans. 1946. *From Max Weber: Essays in sociology.* Edited by Hans H. Gerth and C. Wright Mills. First published 1906–24. New York: Oxford University Press.

Weimer, David L. 1995. Institutional design: An overview. In *Institutional design,* edited by David L. Weimer. Boston: Klewer Academic Publishers.

Weingast, Barry R. 1984. The Congressional-bureaucratic system: A principal-agent perspective (with application to the SEC). *Public Choice* 44, no. 1: 147–91.

Weingast, Barry, and Moran, M. 1983. Bureaucratic discretion or Congressional control? Regulatory policy-making by the Federal Trade Commission. *Journal of Political Economy* 91, no. 5: 765–800.

Wildavsky, Aaron. 1988. *The new politics of the budgetary process.* Boston: Little, Brown.

Williamson, Oliver E. 1975. *Markets and hierarchies: Analysis and antitrust implications.* New York: Free Press.

———. 1981. The economics of organization: The transaction cost approach. *American Journal of Sociology* 87, no. 3: 548–77.

———. 1985. *The economic institutions of capitalism.* New York: Free Press.

———. 1995. Transaction cost economics and organization theory. In *Organization theory: From Chester Barnard to the present and beyond,* exp. ed., edited by Oliver E. Williamson. New York: Oxford University Press.

———. 1996. *The mechanisms of governance.* New York: Oxford University Press.

———. 1997. Transaction cost economics and public administration. In *Public priority setting: Rules and costs,* edited by Peter B. Boorsma, Kees Aarts, and Albert E. Steenge. Boston: Kluwer Academic Publishers.

———. 1998. The institutions of governance. *American Economic Review* 88, no. 2: 75–79.

Wilson, James Q. 1989. *Bureaucracy: What government agencies do and why they do it.* New York: Basic Books.

Wood, B. Dan. 1988. Principals, bureaucrats, and responsiveness in Clean Air Act enforcements. *American Political Science Review* 82: 213–34.

Wood, B. Dan, and Richard W. Waterman. 1991. The dynamics of political control of the bureaucracy. *American Political Science Review* 85, no. 3: 801–28.

———. 1993. The dynamics of political-bureaucratic adaptation. *American Journal of Political Science* 37 (May): 497–528.

Wright, Bradley E., Tamika R. Black, and Lepora J. Flournory. 1999. Research measurement in the public administration literature: An evaluation of journal publications. Paper presented at Fifth National Public Management Research Conference, George Bush School of Government and Public Service, Texas A&M University, December 3–4.

Zammuto, Raymond F. 1984. A comparison of multiple constituency models of organizational effectiveness. *Academy of Management Review* 9: 606–16.

Zey, Mary. 1998. *Rational choice theory and organizational theory: A critique.* Thousand Oaks, Calif.: Sage Publications.

Names Index

204

Subject Index

accountability
  demonstrating, 2
  under JTPA, 122
  studies of educational, 131–32
  under WIA, 171
administrative agencies
  analysis of NLRB (1948–79), 149–51
  competition and incentives within, 62–64
  decentralized operations of, 2–3
  evaluating performance of, 2
  model of behavior under uncertainty, 139–41
  primary work in public, 74–75
  studies of network structures, 141–43
  See also discretion, administrative; human services organizations; public management
administrative law
  composition of, 42
  mechanisms for exercise of, 44
  under New Deal, 42–43
Administrative Procedures Act (1946), APA, 43
adverse selection (principal-agent theory), 61–62
authority
  circumstances for nullification of, 50
  distribution of, 50
  formal institutional, 41
  governance encompasses formal and informal, 9–10, 50
  as means of governance, 176

Bay Area Rapid Transit (BART) system, San Francisco, 174
bureaucracies
  bureaucrats reducing political uncertainty, 73
  bureau-shaping behavior, 73–74
  control of, 49–50
  different types of public, 159–60
  discretion of, 48–49
  incentives in public, 62–64
  institutional and instrumental, 41
  politics of control of, 45–46
  See also discretion, administrative

career centers, local one-stop, 170, 175
Chevron U.S.A. v. Natural Resources Defense Council (1984), 43
coalitions
  conflict within enacting, 58–59
  function of legislative, 30–31
  legislators in an enacting, 45–49, 74–75
  See also interest groups; legislators
collective action (principal-agent theory), 65
common pool resources (CPRs), 174–75
concepts
  definition of, 101
constitutional order, 41–42
contingency theory, 22, 72
contracts
  bilateral principal-agent, 63
  organizations in principal-agent theory as, 61
  transaction cost approach to, 64–65
cooperation
  induced or delegated, 63
  research on, 175
culture
  link between leadership and, 69
  link to performance, 68–69

DARP. *See* Drug Abuse Reporting Program (DARP)
data sets
  combining different sources of, 115–16
  for governance research, 18–19
  improving quality of, 114
  most useful, 177
  recognizing limits of, 80
  related to participant self-selection, 100
  using administrative data, 114–15
data sources
  combined from multiple sources, 115–16
  for DATOS research, 135, 137–39
  Drug Abuse Reporting Program (DARP), 134, 139
  for governance research, 113–17
  national JTPA study, 123–125

208